# FOCUS ON THE FAMILY®

*Inspiring*

*stories to*

*encourage*

*your marriage*

# *Always*

## Betsy Holt & Mike Yorkey
### Commentary by
### Gary Smalley

Tyndale House Publishers, Inc.
Wheaton, Illinois

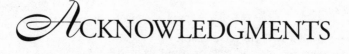

# $\mathcal{A}$CKNOWLEDGMENTS

Thanks to the couples whose stories appear in this book, for candidly sharing their flaws as well as their victories. May God use their honesty to strengthen the unions of many husbands and wives.

Thanks also to the couples who generously agreed to be interviewed for this book, but whose stories we were unable to include. May their marriages continue to inspire all who see God at work in their lives.

Thanks to Helen Laurie Tucker, who lent special assistance with the writing of her story. Her book *Then the Sun Came Up* (Star Books, 1986), which chronicled her battle with breast cancer, was an indispensable resource.

Thanks to Dr. Greg Smalley and Michael Smalley, who helped their father prepare insightful post-story comments.

And thanks to God, by whose grace the marriages in this book have endured.

ALWAYS

Copyright © 1999 by Focus on the Family
All rights reserved. International copyright secured.

**Library of Congress Cataloging-in-Publication Data**

Holt, Betsy.
    Always: inspiring stories to encourage your marriage / by Betsy Holt and
Mike Yorkey.
        p.    cm.
    ISBN 1-56179-780-4
        1. Family.   2. Family—Psychological aspects.   3. Married couples.
    4. Marriage—Religious aspects—Christianity. I. Yorkey, Mike. II. Title.
HQ518.H65 1999
306.85—dc21                                                                99-31506
                                                                                CIP


A Focus on the Family book published by Tyndale House Publishers,
Wheaton, Illinois.

Cover Design: Bradley L. Lind
Cover Photo: PhotoDisc

Printed in the United States of America

99 00 01 02 03 04 05/10 9 8 7 6 5 4 3 2

# CONTENTS

# PREFACE

A SPECIAL MESSAGE FROM FOCUS ON THE FAMILY

## *Marriage Is for Always*

Once upon a time, God created marriage.

What a glorious day that must have been. Adam in the Garden of Eden. No evil in the world. The promise of exploration and adventure. But the man was lonely, and he needed a "suitable helper." So in a stroke of creative genius, God put Adam to sleep, removed one of his ribs, and fashioned a woman. Judging by Adam's reaction, she must have been a welcome sight!

When God introduced the first man and first woman, he also ordained the institution of marriage.

> For this reason a man will leave his father and mother
> and be united to his wife, and they will become one
> flesh. (Genesis 2:24)

Those last two words, "one flesh," clearly state God's intention, that marriage was meant to last. Divorce was never part of God's plan. It was meant to last as long as both the man and woman were alive. For always!

Yet things changed after the fall. Even God, who hates divorce, permitted it in His law. Jesus acknowledged that divorce may be allowed in cases of adultery, though He did not encourage it. God clearly intended for marriage to be a picture of His love, a permanent connection between God and one man and one woman.

Today, our culture easily discards marriage. The harder the trial, the greater the chance of divorce. A diagnosis of cancer for one spouse all too often spurs the other to abandon him or her. The divorce rate for couples who have suffered the death of a baby is about 80 percent. And adultery is usually fatal to a relationship.

But it doesn't have to be. Focus on the Family has as one of its pillars:

*We believe* that the institution of marriage was intended by God to be a permanent, life-long relationship between a man and a woman, regardless of trials, sickness, financial reverses or emotional stresses that may ensue.

*Regardless . . .*

The premise of this book is simple. There are no trials you as a couple may endure that must result in the end of your marriage. None! The stories in this book show it. One couple suffered through years of financial hardship. Another couple went through the pain of the death of a child. Yet another couple endured the indignity of an affair. But all of these couples weathered the storms, with the result that their marriages lasted.

The eight marriages in this book are evidence that your marriage can go the distance. Your situation may not match exactly any of these stories. But the truth undergirding their testimonies will serve you well. That's why we asked marriage expert Gary Smalley to serve as a coach—to point out what these couples did right and did wrong, so you can learn from them.

Focus on the Family has created this book because we are committed not just to the institution of marriage, but to *your* marriage. We pray that these stories will inspire and encourage you. And we hope that if you need help in your marriage, you will contact us. We have staff ready to help—to provide resources, and to point you towards seminars and counselors who can help with your specific problems. If you're struggling in your marriage, don't suffer alone. We're here to make sure you get help.

Kurt Bruner            Al Janssen
Vice President        Senior Director

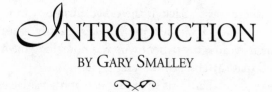

# $\mathcal{I}$NTRODUCTION

### BY GARY SMALLEY

Crisis is a part of married life, no matter how much we might wish it weren't. And when a husband and wife have been together more than 20 years, like all the couples featured in *Always*, it's inevitable that they've had their share of tough times. Such crises—for example, health problems, financial trials, struggles with a child—can eat away at the foundation of any marriage. Sadly, more and more these days the result is a couple just going through the motions of married life, or even divorce.

It doesn't have to be that way, however. While crises are unavoidable, marital collapse is not. By pulling together and continuing to honor each other—and especially by leaning on God for wisdom, comfort, strength, and provision—trials can be endured with the relationship intact. In fact, the marriage can do more than just survive; it can come out of the experience even more solid, secure, and fulfilling than it was before.

An example comes to mind of a crisis that my wife, Norma, and I experienced. We had two children at the time, with the third one on the way. But like a lot of people—men, especially—I was wrapped up in my career. It was ironic because my work involved counseling and speaking on family matters, yet I routinely neglected my own family's relational needs so I could pour more time and energy into my ministry.

I was helping a lot of people, which was good. I was also meeting my wife and children's financial needs, which was fine. And if you had asked me to identify my highest priority (after the desire to serve God), I would have said it was to be a good husband and father. But the entries in my daily planner told a different story.

My neglect of my family and the extra burden it placed on Norma were bad enough then. They grew into a can't-be-ignored crisis, however, after the birth of our third child, Michael. Caring for a healthy newborn plus two older kids is plenty of challenge. But Michael was born with severe, even life-threatening, medical problems.

Meeting his needs and being anxious about him quickly exhausted Norma, which was to be expected. And there were still the two other children

1

to parent. So where was I? Back at the office, absorbed in my job, feeling good about how much I was helping families, mostly ignoring the huge needs of my own because my patient wife was not telling me how much she needed me and that my absence was killing her.

I would like to say that I was smart enough and sensitive enough to recognize the problem at some point and begin to take corrective action on my own, cutting back on my workload and tenderly stepping in to relieve some of the enormous burden on Norma's shoulders. I'd like to say that, but it wouldn't be true.

Now, some women in Norma's place would have chosen to endure silently with gritted teeth, all the while growing more and more resentful and angry, eventually coming to hate me. Others would have gone to the opposite extreme and "blown up" at me, yelling and accusing and calling into question everything from my manhood to my integrity to my love for our family.

Either of those approaches could have greatly weakened our marriage.

Fortunately, Norma was mature and wise enough to take a third approach to the problem. After a number of weeks of trying to carry this impossible burden, and after much prayer about how best to deal with the situation, she quietly took me aside one day and confronted me. Respectfully and with honor, she reviewed the details of what was happening with me and with our family and made it clear that things couldn't continue as they were.

Everything she said rang painfully true. But this was her statement that really hit me between the eyes: "Either you start helping me or I'm going to have a complete nervous breakdown."

In my line of work, that would not have been good for business!

Thanks to God's grace working in me and the gracious way Norma presented the problem, I was able to recognize the truth. I began to back away from my work to make more time and energy for my wife and children. And in the process, I found myself getting to know them and love them better than ever before. It was such a life-changing experience that even now, I'll occasionally tell Michael (a healthy adult these days, with his own children), "You brought me back to our family."

That's just one instance of a marriage surviving and even thriving as a result of a trial. The world is full of such stories, because God is still alive and active in the lives of men and women, and He's still committed to the institution of marriage that He created. If we're part of His family through personal faith in Jesus Christ, He has promised us, "Never will I leave you; never will I forsake you" (Hebrews 13:5).

The book you hold in your hands, *Always,* is also full of such stories. They tell of couples who went through crises of various kinds, including severe substance abuse, depression, infidelity, and the death of a child. In all of them, and as you consider all of them together, this message should come through loud and clear: No matter what challenges your relationship may encounter, you and the Lord can get through them together.

*A marriage built on a foundation of faith and trust in God and honoring each other can survive any storm and thrive for a lifetime.*

Some of the couples whose stories are told here are well known, while others aren't. The principles for enduring as a husband and wife in crisis are the same in either case. And at the end of each story, I'll offer a brief commentary that I hope will help you to apply those principles and deal with crisis in your own marriage.

God bless you and your spouse as you read this book and as you go through life, including its trying times, hand in hand.

# WHEN ALL YOU'VE GOT ARE FAITH AND LOVE

## Ken and Margaret Taylor

MARRIED IN 1940

"So . . . what did you think about my letter?" Margaret West nervously asked her fiancé, Ken Taylor, one summer evening in 1940.

"What letter?" puzzled Ken. He had just arrived at Margaret's home near Portland, Oregon, after working all summer at an Inter-Varsity Christian Fellowship camp in Canada. If Margaret had written him with big news, he certainly hadn't known about it.

Margaret raised her eyebrows. "You mean you never got it?"

"No," Ken said. He studied her more closely. Her big blue eyes sparkled, and her lips were curving into a smile—not at all the face of a girl whose sweetheart was going away in 10 days to attend Dallas Theological Seminary. "What did it say?"

"I heard from Dr. Lincoln," she told him, "and he's going to give me a half-time job at the seminary in Dallas that pays $50 a month." Margaret paused and leaned in closer toward Ken. "That means we can get married next week, before you leave for school!" *No wonder he didn't mention anything about our future,* she realized.

Ken blinked, not sure how to respond. *Married? Next week?* he thought. For the year and a half they'd been engaged, the couple had agreed that once they had a sufficient income, they could get married. Ken knew that Margaret had vacationed in Dallas that summer, looking for a job, but thought nothing would come of it. Standing on the West family's porch with sweat on his brow, he did the math. With his weekend job with Inter-Varsity in Dallas, they would now have a combined income of $100 a month—and if they were prudent, they could live on that.

Ken forced a smile and pulled his fiancée close. "You're right!" he agreed. Inside, however, he was apprehensive. He loved Margaret dearly, but he had expected to marry her in three or four years, after he was finished with seminary—not a week from now!

Margaret sighed and gazed dreamily at Ken. "Isn't it wonderful?"

He nodded in silence, thinking, *I just hope we're ready.*

❧

They had known one another since their freshman year of high school and had conducted a long-distance relationship while Ken attended Wheaton College, just west of Chicago, and Margaret went to Oregon State College in Corvallis. Friends had urged them to get married after graduation, quoting the old bromide, "Two can live as cheaply as one." But Ken, cautious by nature, had vacillated. Privately, he feared this marriage. Margaret was from a well-to-do family, and he often worried, *Will I be able to provide for her and our future children?*

Whenever well-meaning friends teased them about "getting hitched," Ken was thankful he could honestly say, "We can't afford it." But now, with Margaret's job offer, that was no longer the case.

They began to make arrangements and were delighted when two friends getting married the next week, Elaine McMinn and Don Mortimer, invited them to share in all their preparations in a double wedding! In a whirlwind, Margaret found a wedding dress. Then she and Ken purchased wedding rings, telephoned relatives to invite them to the ceremony, picked up their marriage license, and ordered 200 wedding announcements to be sent out after the nuptials.

Before they knew it, the young couple was standing before their pastor, Dr. Jack Mitchell, reciting their vows. Minutes later, Dr. Mitchell pronounced Ken and Margaret husband and wife. The Taylors walked out of the church in a daze, smiling awkwardly at the guests and bidding their families good-bye. They hadn't the luxury of a reception; Ken and Margaret needed to be on the train to Dallas an hour and a half after the ceremony!

Dressed in his only suit, Ken felt his heart pound as he helped his radiant bride into the car that would take them to the train station. He knew he'd taken a momentous step, promising to love and cherish Margaret forever—and he intended to keep his word. What Ken didn't know, however, was that the financial problems he'd feared and hoped to avoid would be the biggest trial that lay in their wedded future.

⮷⳹⮶

That night, the newlyweds left Portland on the 9:30 train. They spent two days in San Francisco, touring the World's Fair, and arrived in Dallas a few days later. There they found a furnished apartment on the second floor of a large house that had been divided into several living areas. Their apartment had a tiny kitchen and access to a bathroom they shared with two other tenants. Rent was $20 a month.

On the train they had outlined a tentative budget based on their combined monthly income of $100. Ken and Margaret made an ironclad decision to tithe 10 percent off the top, no matter how bleak their financial circumstances. Fortunately for the Taylors, Dallas Theological Seminary didn't charge tuition at the time; but after deducting rent, food, utilities, and books, they rarely would have money left over for clothes or entertainment.

But Margaret didn't mind their stringent budget. Though she came from a prosperous family, her parents had grown up poor and continued to live simply, teaching their children by example to do the same. Budgeting came naturally to her. Besides, she reasoned that their situation was temporary. Once Ken graduated from seminary and landed a full-time job, things would get easier.

Since their apartment was furnished, including dishes and cookware, the young couple decided to save their wedding-gift money. Ken and Margaret knew they would need a small amount of savings for added expenses.

And a year and a half after their wedding, one came along.

One spring afternoon in 1942, the Taylors went for a walk. Margaret, feeling fatigued, stopped several times to rest, while Ken continued walking. Finally, Margaret called out, "Don't walk so fast! We can't keep up with you."

Ken whirled around and stared at his wife, who was standing, winded, a few feet away. "Did you say, 'We can't keep up with you'?"

Margaret smiled and nodded.

"Does that mean . . .?" he began, his eyes widening.

"Yes," she announced, "I'm pregnant!"

Ken wrapped his arms around his beaming wife. He knew that Margaret, who was from a large family, wanted at least six children. Ken had always assumed they would have children, but privately he was still worried: *We're hardly able to make ends meet as it is—and now Margaret will have to quit her job. Lord,* he prayed, *how will we feed another mouth, and on my income alone?*

The Taylors moved to Portland that summer to stay with Margaret's parents while Ken worked at a shipyard. When they returned to Dallas in the fall, Ken left Inter-Varsity and was offered the job as manager of the seminary dining hall. His new position didn't pay well, but it gave him and Margaret free room and board, which would help to compensate them financially when the baby was born.

On December 5, 1942, after 24 hours of difficult labor, Margaret gave birth to their first daughter, Rebecca. The money Ken had made over the summer paid for hospital and doctor costs, while they dipped into their wedding money to buy a crib, playpen, and baby buggy. Margaret also bought a used washing machine. Up until then she had done all their laundry by hand.

Ken breathed a sigh of relief after he realized all their expenses would be covered. *Lord, why do I even worry?* he prayed silently. *You have always met our needs, and I believe You always will.*

&#x2766;

*M*argaret's eyes narrowed as she surveyed the dingy apartment, and she shifted her daughter—now nine months old—onto her hip. She and Becky had just moved from Dallas to join Ken in Chicago, where he planned to finish up his master's degree in theology at Northern Baptist Theological Seminary and work as the editor of *HIS* magazine, an Inter-Varsity publication. Several days earlier, Ken had traveled ahead of the family to secure housing—and this was what he'd found.

Margaret looked over at Ken. He was leaning against the doorjamb, waiting for a response. But Margaret couldn't say anything; she thought if she tried to speak, she'd burst into tears. Instead, she tightened her grip on Becky. Unlike the place they'd rented in Dallas, this apartment had three rooms and a bath—but its walls were covered with soot since all of Chicago's chimneys, residential and commercial, belched coal smoke. The concave double mattress rested on very rusty springs, and faded linoleum was curling up in the corners. Her lower lip quivered. *This is my new home?* she thought.

Finally, Ken broke the silence. "So, what do you think?"

Margaret's face crumpled, and before she could help herself, she cried out, "It's terrible!"

Ken's eyes widened in surprise—his wife didn't usually complain. "But I thought you'd be happy here," he said. With World War II raging, housing was difficult to find. Raw materials were being used for the war effort and houses weren't being built to meet the regular ongoing need. He had been grateful to come across the apartment. It was located only a block from the seminary and had quick access to the El train, which stopped near the Inter-Varsity office. It was also on the first floor, which was convenient for Margaret, who was pregnant again. Besides, although Ken's salary had been raised to $3,000 a year, it was all they could afford.

"You won't have to be cooped up here all day, like I will," protested Margaret, staring through her tears at the dirty windows and curtains.

Ken's face softened. He walked toward his wife and smoothed her blond hair from her face. "I'm sorry, honey," he said, looking around the apartment with new eyes. She was right—the place *was* awful, and she would have to spend more time in it than he would.

Embarrassed by her outburst, Margaret straightened her shoulders. "It's okay." *He did the best he could,* she chided herself. *Stop feeling sorry for yourself and be thankful for God's faithfulness.* "We'll be fine here," she promised him quietly.

While Margaret was busy caring for Becky, Ken quickly settled into his job at the magazine. Their second child, John, was born in December of that year, just three days after Becky's first birthday.

One evening shortly after John's birth, Margaret's parents, who were in town on a business trip, came over for dinner. Margaret showed them around the tiny apartment. Then she invited them to sit at the table while she finished some last-minute dinner preparations. Her father took a seat next to Ken, looking uncomfortable and out of place in his expensive suit. Margaret's mother, however, waved the suggestion aside.

"Let me help you get dinner on the table," she said, joining her daughter a few feet away in the makeshift kitchen. She walked briskly to the stove, then stopped short. "My goodness," Mrs. West sputtered, "don't you have a kitchen sink?"

Margaret bit her lip and said quietly, "No—we have to use the wash basin in the hall by the bathroom." Her cheeks burned. "But we're not going to stay here forever," she added.

Ken twisted his dinner napkin. "I sure hope not," he agreed, hoping to lighten the situation. "Remember how we had to scrub the soot from the walls when we first moved in? I don't want to ever go through that again." He shifted uneasily in his chair. Why did Margaret's mother have to state the obvious? It just made him feel he wasn't providing for her daughter.

Margaret placed the casserole on the crowded kitchen table and picked up baby John, who was crying. *This place is certainly a long way from my childhood home in Portland,* she admitted to herself, *but we're making it. And besides, complaining isn't going to do me any good.* She glanced over at her mother. Mrs. West had her lips pursed together, saying nothing.

The Taylors stayed there until Ken's graduation from Northern Baptist Seminary in the spring, when he received his Th.M. Then Stacey Woods, general secretary of Inter-Varsity, offered to rent them his home in Wheaton for the summer. Ken would have to ride the commuter train into Chicago each day—a 50-minute trip—but that was a small price to pay in exchange for green lawns and spacious skies, so foreign to the urban grittiness of the Windy City.

Ken and Margaret were eager to make the change. They could enjoy living in a clean, big house and would have several months to find more permanent lodging.

Once the Taylors moved, they immediately began to look for a place to stay in the fall. But the wartime scarcity of housing was so acute that houses for rent never appeared in the newspaper; news of rentals spread by word of mouth. Fortunately, just days before the Woods family returned, the Taylors' pastor told them about a furnished home located directly across the street from the Wheaton College campus. They could live in the whole house or reduce their rent by subletting extra bedrooms to students. So Ken and Margaret rented three of the four bedrooms to five college girls, and they all shared the one bathroom.

The Taylors' third child, Martha, was born a few months after they moved in. To help with the birth, Ken's mother came from Portland on the train to stay with Becky and John while Margaret was in the hospital. After Margaret recovered and Ken's mother went home, though, the Taylors found they still had plenty of help with the children. Living with five college girls meant they always had a baby-sitter available, which allowed them to attend more church events and concerts at the college.

But finances were even tighter now that they had an additional mouth to feed. At Inter-Varsity, Ken was paid once a month. After Margaret cashed his paycheck and paid the tithe, rent, utilities, and commuter ticket, she divided the balance and placed it into four envelopes—one for each week—to pay for food, clothes, and extras. Still without a car, Margaret pushed the baby buggy downtown once a week to buy groceries. She walked everywhere—even in winter—with their three children, running various errands, including trips to the utility companies to pay their gas, water, and electric bills in cash. This way, she saved the cost of three-cent stamps.

Margaret rarely spoke with Ken about the measures she took to save money. In that era, wives simply "made do" with what they had, without complaint or question. Margaret reasoned that her husband worked hard, and he didn't need the additional stress of hearing about her difficulties. Besides, she felt it was her job to see that the finances were managed properly, that dinner was on the table, and that the children were warmly clothed. Ken's attention needed to be focused on his job in Christian ministry.

Once in a while when Ken arrived home from work just in time for dinner, he realized how small Margaret's world really was—most of the time within the four walls of the house. He knew that if only they could get a car, she would have a little more freedom. *Lord, I know You want me to work for a ministry,* he prayed, *but sometimes I wish I could provide more for my family.* He studied Margaret. She was bustling around their tiny kitchen, getting dinner ready, as always resourceful and frugal. Ken sighed gratefully. Regardless of their financial situation, at least he had a wonderful, supportive wife and a solid marriage.

Their strong marital foundation was indeed a blessing—and as Ken and Margaret were about to discover, a necessity.

∽❍∼

*A*fter working for three years at *HIS* magazine, Ken made a job change, accepting a position with the Moody Bible Institute to be the director of the Moody Literature Mission. He was elated with the direction God was taking his career—he had always been passionate about missions work but never had the opportunity to pursue it. Now in his current job, he would be traveling overseas and assisting in the distribution of gospel literature.

Meanwhile, though, the Taylors' housing was up in the air again. The situation was further complicated by the fact that Margaret had recently given birth to their fourth child, Peter, and had another baby on the way. The owner of the home they were subletting was moving back to Wheaton, and they needed to find a place in the city again or in an area served by the commuter train. For weeks Ken and Margaret searched for housing but found nothing.

*Are we going to end up homeless?* Ken worried. Finally, just a week before they had to move out, he reluctantly suggested their last option. He looked across the kitchen table at his wife and wearily rubbed his temples.

"Maybe you and the children should move back to Oregon and live with your parents," he said, his throat tight. "Just until we find something else." It was the last thing he wanted to suggest—moving the family into his in-laws' house would be like admitting defeat—but Ken saw no other option.

Margaret's jaw dropped in disbelief. "I . . . d-don't want to do that," she gasped. "It would break up the family!"

"I don't want to either," Ken told her hoarsely. "But we don't have any other options." He stared at his hands. *Will we ever be able to settle down?* he wondered. *Have I failed Margaret, giving her only a life of rootlessness and uncertainty?*

Margaret was quiet for several minutes. *Lord,* she prayed, *please provide a place for us to live. I want our family to be together.* The prayer calmed her a little, and she finally whispered, "We need to trust God. He'll take care of us." She didn't know how or when that would happen, but she had to hold on to her faith.

Ken nodded in silence, thankful for his wife's tenacity. She was often the stronger one in dark and difficult times.

A few days later, an "opportunity" of sorts presented itself. An acquaintance had purchased the Garfield Hotel and offered to let the Taylors live in a jerry-rigged apartment at the end of the second floor. The price was right—$65 a month.

Unfortunately, the hotel was located in Winona Lake, Indiana, 120 miles southeast of Chicago. And it was a summer hotel, with no heating or insulation. The Taylors were told they could use rental money to buy a coal stove to warm themselves—though heat from the stove wouldn't reach the far end of the hall where the bathroom was. Also, Margaret would have to cook on a hot plate, which was disheartening because she loved to bake and usually supplemented the family's meals with sweets.

Very reluctantly, the Taylors packed their few belongings and moved to the Garfield Hotel. Despite its many drawbacks, Ken and Margaret felt the hotel was an answer to their prayers, even if it wasn't the answer they'd wanted. It certainly was better than having Margaret and the children move to Portland.

But since the hotel was located so far from Chicago, Ken was separated from his family much of the time anyway. Every Monday he hopped aboard the 5:00 A.M. New York Central train and stayed in Chicago for the week, returning to Winona Lake on Friday night. He slept in a sleeping bag on a couch in his office for the first month; later he rented a room from friends.

The nine months at the Garfield Hotel were the Taylors' most difficult ever. Margaret, pregnant and alone, was the sole caretaker of their four children, and she felt imprisoned in what she considered a firetrap. With the portable kerosene heater blazing in the kitchen and the hot coal stove in the living room, there wasn't much space for the children to play. During the day, Margaret had to keep Peter, their youngest, confined in a playpen. But she didn't feel comfortable leaving the kerosene heater on while they slept and couldn't always manage to keep the fire going all night in the coal stove. In the evenings, she and the children were often bitterly cold.

Her greatest challenge, however, was the loneliness during the workweek.

Margaret missed adult companionship, and the nights felt empty without her husband there. The hotel had a phone, but the Taylors couldn't afford long-distance calls. So they wrote letters.

"I miss you so much that sometimes I wonder why we're doing this," Margaret wrote in one note to Ken, "But I know living here is our best option. Moving home to Mom and Dad's would have been unbearable—the children and I would never see you then. So we'll just have to be thankful for what we have. God will meet our needs."

When Ken read the letter, his eyes misted over. He gazed longingly at a framed picture of Margaret that he'd placed on the dresser in his rented room, wishing he could call her. *Lord,* he prayed silently, *please watch over my wife and children. Please keep them safe in that awful firetrap.* Ken hoped his absences wouldn't affect the children too much, but there was nothing he could do except pray and wait for a better housing opportunity.

The weekends were bittersweet. It was hard to connect when Ken arrived home late Friday nights, starved and exhausted after carrying his suitcase with his week's laundry for two miles from the train station. And it was hard to tell Margaret about his challenging work when she was so tired, worrying about who would take care of the four children when she went to the hospital to give birth. Even so, the weekend always flew by, and Margaret cried every Monday morning when she crawled back into bed after Ken left at 4:00 A.M.

The Taylors weren't able to solve their housing problems, but they saw God take care of them in other ways. A few months after moving to the hotel, they heard a nearby farmer was selling a 1928 Dodge that had been driven only 28,000 miles. The price for this 20-year-old car was $200. With Margaret eight months pregnant and Ken working so far away during the week, the Taylors felt they couldn't pass up the chance. So they used up most of their savings, scraped together the money, and purchased the ancient Dodge. After seven years of marriage, they finally had their own transportation! They decided Ken would drive the Dodge to work during the week the baby was due. That way, he'd be able to drive home as soon as Margaret went into labor.

Once they bought the car, Margaret felt less trapped, but she still found it difficult to manage alone during the workweek. When she was in her ninth month of pregnancy, a rusty pipe that had been frozen broke at the far end of the hotel, and water cascaded into the lobby. *If I wait for a plumber,* Margaret thought, *all that water will do a lot of damage!* She uttered a quick prayer and crept for 50 feet in the crawl space underneath the hotel to find the shut-off valve.

When the plumber later arrived to repair the damage and saw that Margaret was due to go to the hospital any day, he lectured, "Don't ever let me catch you going under this old hotel again!" He pointed to the young Taylor kids, who were watching the scene wide-eyed. "Think of the children. What if something happened to you? Next time, just let the place float away!"

Margaret sighed wearily, not sure how to respond. These days she was simply trying to survive—to hold the family together. She rested her hands on her huge belly. When the fifth baby came, their situation would become even more difficult.

*Lord, please help us,* she prayed uneasily. *I'm afraid this place is going to fall apart.*

❧

"I'm here for the return of my down payment!" Ken said, charging through the door of a Chicago developer's office several months later on a breezy day in May. He glared at the sales representative, who was at his desk, hunched over a mound of paperwork.

The man jerked his head up and frowned. "I can't give it back. You signed a contract."

Ken pressed his eyebrows together in frustration. Margaret's parents, after hearing about their plight living in the Garfield Hotel, had given them $1,000 for a down payment on a new home in Northlake, a subdivision west of Chicago. To save money, the Taylors had decided to have a developer frame the house, and Ken would finish the inside. The home was supposed to be framed by May. As the weeks passed, he and Margaret had been assured the project was on schedule.

It wasn't.

"I just visited the lot, expecting to see my house framed," Ken fumed, "and I realized you haven't even started! Were you ever planning to break ground?"

Expressionless, the salesman gazed at Ken through his spectacles. "Oh, we will," he said. "We just haven't gotten around to it. There's a building crunch, you know. A lot of people need homes."

"Well, you broke your word." Ken folded his arms. "I want out of my contract, and I want my money returned *today!*"

For several minutes the man bartered with Ken. Finally, he conceded, "Okay, here's what I'll do. If you come back to my office next Tuesday afternoon at 4:30, I'll have a check waiting for you."

"Promise?" asked Ken, eyeing him warily.

The salesman nodded. "I'll be here."

The following Tuesday, Ken left work early and took a bus to the office, but he got lost and ended up on the other side of town. He arrived breathless at 5:00, only to see a "Closed" sign hanging in the door. Staring in disbelief and panic, he wondered, *What am I going to do?* He slumped against the door. *That was the only money we had. How will I tell Margaret that it's gone?*

Slowly, staring at the pavement, Ken walked back to the bus stop. *I'm a failure,* he berated himself. *I can't provide for my family, and now I can't even get our money back.* His eyes smarted as a bleak thought ran through his head: Maybe Margaret and the children would be better off without him—maybe they *should* move back to Oregon, where at least they'd have a decent roof over their heads.

Ken returned to his rented room and phoned Margaret with the news. "Honey," he said, "the money's gone. I didn't get to the office on time." He held his breath, waiting for his wife's response.

Margaret was silent for a moment. Then she said in a cheerful voice, "Don't worry, the Lord will see us through this. Call the man tomorrow. Maybe the check was waiting for you."

Ken sighed in relief. She was right—maybe the money was still there. The following morning, he phoned the office and learned a refund check had been waiting for him. He continued to feel like a failure, though. *Will we always have to accept handouts from friends and family members?* he wondered. *Will we ever have a permanent place to live?*

෴

In June the Taylors were able to move out of the hotel and rent the professor's home in Wheaton for the second summer. Ken and Margaret—and their five children—were thankful to be together once again, enjoying the comfort of the spacious home.

That summer the Taylors met up with Doug and Virginia Muir, who had gone to college with Ken. They, too, desperately needed affordable housing. The Muirs were living with their two young children in a small trailer outside Wheaton. After living through one bitterly cold winter in the poorly insulated trailer, the couple was eager to find warmer lodging before the freezing weather arrived. As the Muirs and Taylors discussed their mutual problem, they agreed to buy a property together that could be divided into a duplex.

They searched for several weeks, finally selecting some property located on the northeast outskirts of Wheaton. But instead of one large home, the lot held *two* houses—an old, two-story farmhouse and a smaller, newer home built from scrap lumber left over from the 1933 Chicago World's Fair. The asking price was $15,000. Excited at the prospect of each family having their own freestanding residence, the couples pooled their money for the down payment. After a long, exhausting escrow, a few days before the Thanksgiving of 1948, the property closed. The Muirs took the smaller home, and the Taylors moved into the farmhouse.

Ken and Margaret's living conditions were still rugged. Instead of a furnace, the house had a pot-bellied stove; the kitchen lacked cupboards and counters; there were only three bedrooms. But after so many unsettling moves, they were happy to be homeowners.

Margaret smiled widely as she stepped into their home. "Can you believe it?" she exclaimed. "We finally have a place of our own, where we can stretch out—"

"The kids will still have to share rooms," Ken cut in.

Margaret shrugged. "I know," she said, taking in the backyard view from the window. "But we'll never have to worry about finding a rental again."

Ken nodded and said, "I'm so glad you and the kids aren't in that deathtrap in Winona Lake." He reached over and squeezed his wife's hand as they entered the kitchen. *Thank You, God,* Ken prayed, *for providing this home for us.*

"Ken," said Margaret, suddenly interrupting his thoughts, "did you notice that the kitchen floor isn't level?"

Ken stepped back and eyeballed the floor. It sloped slightly downward in one corner. He paused, thinking. "Don't worry about it," he finally said. "Since the house is on cement blocks, we can probably adjust the level by jacking up the corner a little."

Not everyone shared their optimism. When Margaret's sister Harriet came from Detroit for a visit, she looked around and then planted her hands on her hips. "What you ought to do is tear this house down and start over!" she declared.

Ken and Margaret laughed. They knew the place would require a lot of fixing up. But although the farmhouse at 1515 East Forest Avenue wasn't perfect by any stretch, it was still home. And for the immediate future, that was the only thing that mattered.

∽⤬∾

*T*he Taylors' purchase was timely. Over the next six years, from 1950 through 1956, Ken and Margaret had five more children: Mark, Cynthia, Gretchen, Mary Lee, and Alison. Because the girls soon outnumbered the boys and needed both upstairs bedrooms, Ken converted the enclosed front porch into a room—into which the outside door opened—for John, Peter, and Mark. He also turned the back porch into a dining area.

As the family grew, many weekends and vacations were spent fixing and enlarging various parts of the old farmhouse. The remodeling seemed endless, and it was expensive. With Ken's minimum salary and more mouths to feed, Margaret found handling their finances to be more and more difficult.

Their family food budget consisted of $30 a week—less, the Taylors learned, than welfare families received from the state. But Margaret was resourceful. She could afford to serve meat dinners twice a week, so she used ground beef in spaghetti sauce or cooked a can of corned beef with *lots* of potatoes. Another specialty was creamed tuna on toasted day-old bread; she also served French toast for dinner. And if there wasn't any money left in the grocery envelope at the end of the week, the family could count on potato soup for supper.

Whenever she could save a nickel or dime, Margaret did. She bought most of the family's clothes at church rummage sales and was thankful when neighbors dropped off boxes of hand-me-downs.

The holidays were particularly difficult as far as finances were concerned. When Christmas rolled around, the Taylors had little money left over to buy presents. One year, in 1954, things were even tighter than usual, making it impossible for Ken and Margaret to purchase anything for the children—including a Christmas tree.

The Taylors discussed their dilemma and decided to tell the kids one evening a few weeks before Christmas, after family devotions. Margaret closed her eyes briefly, her lashes laced with tears. *It's going to be so hard to tell them,* she thought. Of course presents weren't the real reason for Christmas—but it was still disheartening to think of the children racing downstairs on Christmas morning and not having any gifts to open.

That night Ken closed the Bible story book and leaned forward, looking into the faces of his eight children. "Kids, before we pray, there's something Mommy and I feel you should know," he said quietly. "This month, we had some bills that were bigger than usual. So there's no way we can expect to have money for Christmas presents."

He paused for this to sink in. *This is awful,* Ken thought as he watched the older children look down, trying to hide the tears in their eyes.

"We can pray about it, though," continued Ken. "If God wants to, He could send us a surprise. If He doesn't, He can still help us be thankful for Christmas. Maybe we would better appreciate God's greatest gift to us." He broke off and looked at Peter, who was still staring at the carpet. "What was that gift, Peter?" Ken asked his son.

Peter lifted his chin and mumbled, "Jesus." But there wasn't any enthusiasm in his voice. For months, he'd been hoping for a bicycle.

Margaret sighed as she gazed at her son. The fall rummage sales were over, so now she wouldn't even be able to find any cheap, used trinkets for the kids. *Why didn't I go to the toy section instead of heading for children's clothing?* she chided herself.

Her thoughts wandered as, one by one, the Taylor children petitioned God. Last year, Margaret's sister Ruth and brother-in-law Bill had sent a generous check to help the Taylors buy toys for the children. Margaret hadn't explained to the kids why they'd had so many gifts the previous year, and now she wondered if her silence had been a mistake. *Maybe if I had been honest about how we purchased last year's presents, the children wouldn't be expecting gifts now,* she thought.

She willed herself to focus on praying. That was the best thing she could do now anyway. *Lord,* Margaret prayed silently, *please allow us to give our children a nice Christmas. They're so disappointed.*

A few days later, Ken received an unexpected $25 dollar check from *Reader's Digest* for a clipping he had sent in. That was enough to buy each child a small toy and put a turkey on the table, and the Taylors were grateful. Then, several days after that, just two weeks before Christmas—a crumpled envelope arrived in the mailbox. Scribbled on the back was a note:

*Ken and Margaret—*
*I just found this in my jacket pocket. Sorry it's late.*
*Merry Christmas,*
*Bill*

Apparently Margaret's brother-in-law had been carrying the letter around for three weeks before noticing he hadn't mailed it. With eager fingers, Margaret opened the envelope. Inside was a check for $150.

A smile spread across her face, and she ran inside the house. Her sister and brother-in-law had been so generous the year before that Margaret had never expected them to send another big check.

"Kids!" she called out excitedly, "look how the Lord has answered our prayers!" Margaret waved the check in front of their noses, laughing as the children happily hopped around the family room.

She hugged each one of them, her eyes misty. *Lord, why did I doubt You?* she prayed. *You've always provided for us, financially and otherwise. Thank You for sending us this check.*

⌒∕⌒

*K*en leaned back in his chair and began reading, "Verily, verily, I say unto you—"

"Daddy?" eight-year-old Janet cut in. "What does *barily* mean?"

Ken set the Bible on his knee. "It's another word for *truly*. Jesus says that when He's about to tell us something really important."

Janet's face was screwed up in confusion. "But if that's what it means, why doesn't it say so?"

"Good question," said Ken, smiling over at Margaret. "The reason it's confusing is that the old translators translated the Bible word for word instead of thought for thought. Also, they translated it 450 years ago. The English language has changed a lot since then."

"Oh." Janet nodded, but her brow was still wrinkled in confusion.

Ken picked up the Bible and continued reading, pausing after every verse to answer the children's questions. Reading in the evenings from the King James Version—as slow-going as it was—was the custom in the Taylor household. Yet as Ken and Margaret tried to make God's Word become a part of their children's lives, they struggled to explain the language to their kids. *How can I share the Bible in words that my children can easily understand?* Ken often wondered.

After pondering the issue for a month, Ken realized the best approach would be to translate the thought in each verse into ordinary words the children could understand. Excited about the idea, he sat at his desk one Saturday afternoon in 1955 and reached for a Bible and a yellow legal pad. Ken opened the Bible at random, and his finger landed on 2 Timothy, chapter four. On one side of the notepad, he wrote the King James rendition of verse three: "For the time will come when they will not endure sound doctrine; but after their own lusts shall they heap to themselves teachers, having itching ears."

He studied the verse, analyzing each word and phrase for several minutes. Then Ken began writing and rewriting until he was satisfied with the result. "For there is going to come a time," he penned, "when people won't listen to the truth, but will go around looking for teachers who will tell them just what they want to hear."

Once he finished that verse, he paraphrased the rest of the chapter verse by verse to make each part understandable. Ken's fingers eagerly gripped the paper. *I can't wait to see if this helps,* he thought.

That evening, when Margaret had gathered the children for devotions, Ken read his own version rather than from the King James.

"Better?" he asked. The kids nodded in affirmation, so Ken said to the older ones, "Okay, let's talk about what the apostle Paul said and how it applies to our lives at school and at home."

The discussion was better than usual—they had understood!

Elated by his family's positive response, Ken began reworking a few verses for devotions each evening. As he prayed for God's direction, he began to believe that the Lord wanted him to paraphrase all of the New Testament letters into words that anyone could understand. *But when will I find the time?* he wondered.

The answer was on the commuter train, during his 50-minute rides into and out of Chicago. As the swaying passenger car bumped over the tracks, Ken sat with a Bible on one knee and a legal pad on the other.

The process was hard on the whole family, though. On Saturdays and every night after dinner and devotions, Ken disappeared to his study in the bedroom to work on the manuscript. Margaret, already exhausted from caring for their growing clan, had to keep the children from bothering their father. *But who am I to question what God is doing in my husband's life?* Margaret often reminded herself.

Progress was painfully slow, and the handwritten manuscript—which Ken dubbed *Living Letters*—went through a half dozen revisions before he thought it was publishable. By the time he was ready to submit it to a publisher, Ken had devoted six years to writing and rewriting *Living Letters*.

He eagerly submitted it to several publishers, only to receive rejections. But a Chicago printer, Paul Benson, was excited about it and agreed to print

2,000 copies of *Living Letters*. He would let Ken and Margaret pay him back as books were sold.

In July 1962, a truck from the printer filled the living room with boxes and boxes of books—and the Taylors were in the book publishing business. They named their fledgling company Tyndale House Publishers after William Tyndale, who had risked death to translate the Bible into English more than 400 years earlier. Their headquarters were in the Taylors' living room.

As the business manager, Margaret put her ability to pinch pennies to good use. When she saw that pads of postage labels cost two cents less at Woolworth's, the five-and-dime store earned her business. Instead of ordering printed stationery or address labels, she used a rubber stamp. It was a family affair—Becky and Martha had typed the manuscript on the Taylors' ancient secondhand typewriter, and now the younger children helped by packing boxes of books. Meanwhile, Ken continued working as director of Moody Press.

*Living Letters* attracted modest interest at first. Then a friend of Ken's, Doug Judson, enthusiastically recommended the book to his boss, Billy Graham. After reading it over, the Billy Graham Evangelistic Association asked to use the book as a premium for donors. The Taylors offered the books at cost to the Graham organization, but Dr. Graham insisted that the Taylors earn something, so they agreed on a five-cent royalty per book.

Six months later, the Taylors received a letter from the Graham association. Margaret tore open the envelope, still standing at the mailbox. She blinked in disbelief. Inside was a check for $30,000—after numerous printings, six hundred thousand copies of *Living Letters* had been given away by the Graham organization!

Her eyes wide, she raced back into the house. Ken would be arriving home from work at any time. *Just wait until he sees this!* Margaret thought.

When at last she heard her husband walk through the back door, Margaret raced to meet him. "Ken, look at this check!" she exclaimed, holding the paper inches from his face. "I've never seen so many zeros in my life."

Ken's jaw fell open, and he stared at the check. *This is incredible,* he realized. He shook his head as if to clear his thoughts, and for several minutes he was silent. "Margaret," Ken began slowly, "I've thought a great deal about what we should do if the book is successful, and I concluded that the money isn't ours. God gave me the ability to write *Living Letters*—and because the Bible is God's Word, I believe He should get all the royalties."

Without hesitation, Margaret nodded and said, "It's the right thing to do."

Ken smiled at his wife, his eyes soft. "Somehow, with 10 children and a small salary," he said quietly, "God has always met our needs. We've never gone hungry—or without a place to live. The Lord has given us so much."

Margaret set the check on the dining room table and turned her gaze out the window, where several of their children were playing happily in the backyard. God had blessed the Taylors with a large, loving family; an ability to communicate His Word to others; and most of all, a solid marriage. Those were worth more than any amount of money.

∽◌∼

*In 1963, the Taylors created the Tyndale House Foundation, an organization that sends money to Christian ministries worldwide. All the royalties from* Living Letters *and other Scripture-related products, such as* The Living Bible, *are funneled into the foundation. The success of* Living Letters *prompted Ken to leave Moody Press in October 1963. He takes a salary from Tyndale House Publishers, and it has become one of the larger Christian publishers in the U.S.*

*Four years after founding Tyndale House, Ken and Margaret were able to tear down the farmhouse, where they had lived in such cramped quarters for 18 years, and build a new home on the same lot. The children are grown with families of their own, but the Taylors are still thankful for the extra room. Each Christmas, the house on 1515 East Forest Avenue serves as a gathering place for most of the family. And to date, the Taylor clan—children, grandchildren, great-grandchildren, and spouses—number 64!*

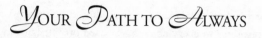

# Your Path to Always

Ken and Margaret Taylor's story offers some interesting contrasts. For example, they had a commendable attitude of contentment with very few material possessions as long as their marriage and family were strong. But many couples today seem to think they have to own a nice house, fully furnished with all the extras, along with two new vehicles and the other trappings of an affluent lifestyle. And they're willing to go deeply into debt to do it, which can put tremendous strain on their relationship as they both work long and hard to pay off that debt.

Another contrast can be seen in the incredible faith the Taylors exhibited as they teetered for years on the brink of poverty. Whatever needs they were facing, they took them to the Lord in prayer and trusted Him to provide—and He did, time after time! His answers weren't always what they'd had in mind, but their faith was always rewarded.

I'm reminded of a time in our marriage when Norma and I were in similar financial straits. We had two young children, we were all crammed into an 800-square-foot house, and the basement was always damp, which made a great breeding ground for insects. We would often wake up in the middle of the night to find cock-roaches crawling on our faces!

We tried everything we could on our meager budget to solve the problem, like those aerosol bug bombs, but nothing worked. Norma was frantic. I cried out to God for help because we simply couldn't afford the real solution, a professional exterminator. And God answered that prayer. He somehow got word of our plight to a man in our church, and that dear Christian brother secretly called Orkin and paid for them to treat our house.

All too often today, however, couples try to go it alone. Prayer is a last resort, if they think to do it even then. Or they believe God is only interested in big, spiritual issues. So, practically speaking, they live and try to solve their everyday problems as if God doesn't exist.

But as the Taylors demonstrate, prayer should be our first and our constant response to every challenge, based on our faith in a loving, caring, and powerful heavenly Father.

The Taylors also offer a contrast in the way they handled their financial trials within their marriage relationship. Growing up in a generation that experienced the Great Depression and the sacrifices required by World War II, as well as in a time of more-traditional marriage, they mostly endured in silence. Their commitment to Ken's ministry and their faith in God's provision were enough to sustain them.

In most marriages today, though, financial struggles are discussed much more openly. And a mom with young children to care for is likely to be far more vocal about her concerns. If she *doesn't* speak up, the danger is that she'll grow bitter and angry, which over time can kill her feelings of affection for her husband. On the other hand, if she does express her anxieties, the danger is that she'll do it in a harsh, critical way that will antagonize and alienate her mate—and that's often exactly what happens.

I would encourage all married couples to talk candidly and regularly about the state of their finances. But the key is to do it with respect and honor. We must always remember that our mate is our partner, not the problem. The problem, if there is one, is the lack of resources, the size of the debt, or whatever. So we discipline ourselves to speak softly and lovingly with each other about what we can do *together*, with God's help, to address the challenge.

—Gary Smalley

# A THIRST FOR MEANING

*Larry and Sue Wright*

MARRIED IN 1955

"That's disgusting!" exclaimed Sue Dombey. She stared at the two college students stumbling into the darkness. "Frank and Joyce are completely drunk!"

Larry Wright, her blind date for the evening, merely shrugged. "I guess they do get a little crazy sometimes," he conceded.

That was an understatement, Sue thought. She'd watched uncomfortably as Frank and Joyce, loud and obnoxious, had slurred their way through the entire dinner.

Sue was tired of dealing with other people's drinking problems. It was the main reason she had transferred to Oklahoma State University from Arizona State, where drunken parties had seemed to overrun the school. Now a junior, she made it her policy to let every prospective suitor know where she stood on the issue of alcohol.

Sue turned to Larry, studying his face in the orange glow of the student center lights. "I don't approve of drinking alcohol," she said. "It's disgusting." She narrowed her eyes. "I hope *you* don't drink, Larry."

Larry's eyebrows shot up. "Me? Are you kidding? Why would I want to drink?"

"I don't know why anyone would," admitted Sue. "But I definitely don't want to be around someone who does."

"Well, you'll be safe with me," Larry assured her. "I hate alcohol as much as you do."

Sue relaxed, grateful to hear those words. No one in her family had a drinking problem, but her biggest fear had always been that she might marry an alcoholic. Coping with an inebriated roommate at Arizona State had only fed her anxiety.

There would be no such trouble with Larry, of course. It was only their first date, but Sue already knew she liked Larry a lot. A senior, he was student body president—and involved in everything from the Greek system to ROTC. He even worked at the college radio station every afternoon as a disk jockey. Sue thought he was funny, handsome, and charming, too.

Now, as they walked toward her sorority house, she felt Larry take her hand. "I had a wonderful time tonight," she said shyly when they reached the door.

Larry nodded. "So did I. I'll give you a call." He squeezed her fingers, then let go as she disappeared into the building.

He waited until she was out of sight, then slumped against the doorway in relief, his palms sweaty. *I can't believe she didn't know,* Larry thought. He'd already been half drunk when he'd picked her up that evening, having stopped at a bar on the way. *Good thing grain alcohol doesn't smell.* He walked back to his fraternity house, trying not to stagger.

Larry liked Sue. But he wasn't about to give up those crazy nights at the bar with his fraternity brothers or his riotous, alcohol-fueled behavior as head of a dance band. It was too much fun.

*I just won't drink around her,* Larry decided. *Sue doesn't ever have to know.*

꩜

*J*ust three months after they'd started dating, Larry proposed. They planned to have the wedding a month later, right after Larry's graduation. Excited, Sue announced her engagement to Beth, one of her sorority sisters who had dated Larry twice.

To Sue's surprise, Beth looked horrified. "You're not going to marry Larry Wright!" Beth said.

"Why not?"

"Don't you know he's got a real drinking problem?" Beth asked. "He got unbelievably drunk both of the times we went out."

Sue's cheeks flushed. She'd never seen Larry pick up a glass of alcohol, and he'd never appeared inebriated to her. *He told me he doesn't drink,* she thought. *Besides, I would know if he had a problem.* They'd been together every day for three months. Beth couldn't possibly be telling the truth.

"I don't believe you!" Sue exclaimed. Turning, she stormed out of the room.

But Beth's words haunted Sue. All day she worried, *What if it's true? What if Larry has been drinking behind my back?* The thought made her ill, but she had to find out the truth. That evening she confronted Larry.

"Do you have a drinking problem?" she demanded. "I've been told that you do."

"Absolutely not!" scoffed Larry. "I don't have a problem." He conceded having a few drinks once in a while, but denied being a drunk.

Sue eyed him nervously. "You're not lying to me, are you?"

"No." Larry took her hand. "Okay, I admit I lied to you on our first date when I said I hated alcohol as much as you do. But right now I'm telling the truth—it's no big deal." *I can get through the day without a drink,* he thought. *I just like to have my "yah-hah" time.* He tousled Sue's brown hair and pulled her close. "Don't worry about it."

Sue sighed. Maybe Larry had fooled her before, but he seemed sincere now. And she didn't want to believe her sorority sister's words over Larry's. Sue was going to marry him; she needed to trust him, didn't she?

"Well . . . all right," Sue said reluctantly. She rested her head on Larry's shoulder. *He's right—I should stop worrying. Why shouldn't he have a couple of beers every now and then with his friends?*

But the gnawing fear in her stomach wouldn't go away.

⚶

"*G*ood morning, Phoenix!" Larry's voice boomed over the radio. "This is Lucky Lawrence at KRUX, here to wake you up to the hottest rock 'n' roll music and to keep you going through the workday! We've got a new song from Elvis coming up, so stayed tuned to the only station where the hits just keep on comin'!"

Larry punched a button and took off his headphones, tapping his foot to the music. He loved his job, working as a disk jockey during the prime morning drive-time shift.

He'd had the position for two years now, after serving a short stint in the army. He and Sue had gotten married in June 1955 and now had two daughters—Linda and Luanne.

Working for the media was fast-paced, exhilarating. A local celebrity, Larry was invited to parties and benefits where the hosts kept the food plentiful and the alcohol flowing. His radio station also hosted cocktail parties and media events; as the number-one disk jockey at KRUX, Larry was required to make an appearance. Not that he minded; he liked being in the limelight and jumped at the opportunity for free booze.

Sue didn't like the flashy media parties. But she always went with her husband, nervously counting his drinks. "Larry," she would often say, pulling him aside, "you should stop. You're drinking too much!"

"We're at a party!" Larry would reply. "I'm just being social." He would eye Sue's can of cola and think, *I can't believe I married such a square.* Unlike his wife, Larry was determined to have fun—and after a few mixed drinks, he turned into a stand-up comedian. He loved the attention and the laughs he got.

He also loved working from only 6:00 A.M. to 9:00 A.M.—and making great money. He was certain that when he became the number one disk jockey in Phoenix, life would be even better.

❦

*T*hree years later, "Lucky Lawrence" had become one of the highest-rated radio personalities in the city. He and Sue had purchased a comfortable home—and had another daughter, Laurie.

But despite having a beautiful family, a nice home, new cars, expensive clothes, influence, and recognition, Larry wasn't happy. For one thing, the pressure of keeping up his ratings had become intense. And the success he'd worked so hard to attain seemed hollow once he achieved it. Now that he was on top, Larry felt he had nothing else to strive for.

He went from one party to the next until they became a blur. *What else is there?* he often wondered. *Is that what life's about? Just eat, drink, and be merry, for tomorrow you die?*

Soon alcohol became a way to forget the pressure and emptiness. Each morning after his air shift was over at 9:00, Larry planted himself in Kim's Lounge, just down the street from the radio station. The bartender would have four fingers of vodka waiting in front of Lucky Lawrence's stool.

All Larry had to do was arrive at the bar with an armful of the latest records and he'd be able to drink all day, free. He spent hours there telling jokes and stories, keeping other customers entertained.

At the end of the day, on his way home, Larry would stop at a Circle K to buy an onion. He'd bite into it, then swish the juice around in his mouth, hoping it would take the alcohol smell away. Larry knew his wife was aware of his drinking habit, but he wanted to mask how many drinks he'd consumed.

Sue wasn't fooled. She could spot his bloodshot eyes and wobbly gait the second Larry walked through the door. Exhausted from taking care of their three daughters all day, Sue was usually irate to see her husband in a drunken stupor.

*He's never home,* she thought, *and when he is, he's drunk! Larry obviously doesn't care about my needs, or the kids'. He doesn't give me any support.* Larry had made it clear that his job was to bring home the money and hers was to keep their home and family intact. He attended the girls' soccer games and dance recitals, but when it came to raising them, Sue was on her own.

And she never passed up an opportunity to remind Larry of that fact.

"You've been drinking again, haven't you?" Sue demanded one day, shifting Laurie from one hip to the other.

Larry ignored her, brushing past and stumbling into the living room.

Sue followed. Linda and Luanne peeked around the corner, watching their parents with wide-eyed fear. "You don't take care of your responsibilities around here!" Sue told Larry. "And look at the example you're giving your girls! What kind of father are you?" Sue leaned toward him and sniffed. "How many drinks have you had? I want to know."

Larry bristled, tired of Sue's lectures. "I've only had a few!" he bellowed. "It was a stressful day, and I just wanted to relax!" He glanced at an Alcoholics Anonymous pamphlet, placed strategically by his wife on the coffee table, and threw down his keys in anger. She was always trying to reform him. "Leave me alone—I'm tired!" With that he fell onto the couch.

Sue stared through tears at her husband. *Maybe I am being too hard on him*, she suddenly thought. *Maybe he didn't really have that much alcohol.* She set down Laurie, then faced her husband. "I'm sorry," she said, her voice softening. "I didn't know you'd had a bad day. I just thought you'd had more to drink than—"

"Well, I didn't," Larry cut in. "And you *ought* to be sorry." He turned on his side and faced the back of the couch, suppressing a smirk of victory. Sure, he was drunk. But no matter how inebriated he was, Larry usually could argue Sue under the table. *I may be wrong, but I'm always Wright,* he mused before drifting off to sleep.

Sue stood over her husband for a minute, trying not to cry. Then she tiptoed down the hall to their bedroom, hoping the girls would stay occupied until she could control her emotions. It seemed she and Larry had the same fight every day, and the only way they communicated was through arguing. Often she would back down as she had today, wanting to believe her husband—but deep down she knew the truth.

She sank onto the bed. Grabbing a tissue, she blotted her tears. The very thing she'd feared most had happened: She had married an alcoholic.

❧

*O*ne night more than a year later, Sue sat wrapped in a blanket on their bed, trying to read. She glanced at the clock. It was 3:00 in the morning, and Larry still wasn't home. *Where is he?* She heard a siren in the distance. *Maybe he's been in an accident. Should I call the hospital?*

Their fighting had escalated over the past several months. Every night her husband had arrived home drunk, and every night Sue would hurl insults at him. "Look at you!" she'd declare, pointing to his disheveled appearance. "It's your fault our family's such a mess!" The kids' grades were slipping in school, and she was constantly screaming at them. Sue felt horrible about yelling at the girls, but didn't feel bad about screaming at her husband. *If he would help me out once in a while, then maybe parenting would be easier. When he shows me he loves me and he does what he's supposed to do, then I'll love him back.*

That strategy hadn't worked, though. Larry would either argue with Sue or ignore her. Lately it had been more of the latter. Tired of being grilled about his habits, Larry was coming home later and later. It wasn't unusual for him to show up around 9:00 or 10:00 P.M. But this was the latest he'd ever stayed away.

Sue angrily drummed her fingers against the cover of her book. Right now she didn't care if he *ever* came back. *Obviously he doesn't love me or the family since he's never home,* she thought. And what about their seventh anniversary last week? Larry had forgotten the occasion. It wasn't the first important date he'd missed. Why couldn't Larry be more like her father, who had showered her mother with gifts? *I can't believe he's so selfish that he'd forget our anniversary, and then a week later stay out all night,* she told herself.

Soon Sue dozed off. Several minutes later she was awakened by the squeak of the front door. Sitting up and folding her arms, she waited.

"Where were you?" Sue demanded the second Larry entered their bedroom. She glared at her husband. His eyes were red, his hair mussed. She leaned in closer.

"Quit tryin' to smell my breath," Larry muttered. "I was out." He sat on the edge of the bed and began taking off his shoes.

Sue let out a cry of frustration. All their fights, his lies, and the late nights of waiting came to a head; suddenly she couldn't take it anymore.

"You have a choice, Larry," she said in a surprisingly calm voice.

Larry looked up at her.

"You need to decide whether you want to be with me and the kids or if you want to continue drinking," she said. "You're an alcoholic and a no-good husband and father, and I am not going to put up with this any longer!" Shaking, Sue waited for his answer.

Larry said nothing. He grabbed the shoe he'd just taken off and put it back on his foot, retying the laces.

He stared at the floor—trying to hide his relief. The idea of moving out had appealed to him, but he'd been determined to keep his word by providing for Sue and staying with the family as he'd promised on their wedding day. Now, though, Sue had given him an excuse to bail out. *I didn't leave,* he'd be able to say. *She kicked me out.*

He walked to the closet. "Fine!" he said. "I'm gone!" Larry grabbed his bowling ball, tennis racket, and a couple of fresh shirts. Then he sauntered out of the room.

A few seconds later, the front door slammed.

Still in bed, Sue buried her face in her hands. She'd hoped that an ultimatum would change his attitude—not convince him to leave. Now he would have fun while she raised their three children.

During the next few days, Larry found "freedom" exciting. He moved into a hotel room and ate in restaurants. If he stayed out late, no one interrogated him.

But after three days, he began to grow weary of bachelorhood. His laundry was dirty; bowling with the guys had gotten old. He was tired of ordering from a menu, eating every meal alone. He missed Sue's dinners and the coziness of home. Feelings of obligation had begun to eat at him, too. He knew he had a responsibility to Sue and the girls.

So on the fourth day Larry showed up on their doorstep, his head lowered. "Sue," he said as she opened the door, "let me come home. I'm so sorry."

Sue leaned against the doorframe in silence, frowning. If he was truly repentant, she wanted to see it.

"I've really messed up," Larry admitted. "I promise I'll change. Things will be different this time. You'll see." He held his breath, waiting.

Sue hesitated. The girls *had* been asking for their father during the past few days, and she felt bad keeping Larry from the family. Maybe he *had* learned his lesson. Maybe things *would* be different.

She sighed. "All right. You can come home."

For a week or two, Larry tried to reform himself. He came home earlier after two or three drinks at the bar. But when work pressures began to overwhelm him again, he and Sue resumed fighting. Kim's Lounge became more appealing than home. Soon he lapsed into his routine of going there after his morning shift and staying all day.

After months of this, Sue knew that her husband probably would never change. She pushed away thoughts of leaving him; she had never believed that divorce was an answer. Besides, Larry was the father of her children— no matter how negligent he was. For now, that was enough reason for her to stay with him.

⌒⋈⌒

One day, several years later, Sue cradled the telephone receiver in her hand. She stared blankly at it. The conversation with her sister had ended almost 10 minutes before, but she couldn't bring herself to hang up.

Her sister had related the news: Their mother had been found dead that morning, having overdosed on sleeping pills.

Sue closed her eyes. *I should have seen it coming. Why didn't I check up on her?* Her mother had threatened suicide numerous times, but someone in the family had always been able to talk her out of it. *Now it's too late.*

"What's wrong?" Larry's voice cut into her thoughts.

Sue gave him the news, then dropped into a chair by the phone.

Larry approached awkwardly and put his hand on her shoulder. "I'm sorry," he mumbled. He hovered there for a minute or two; then, unsure what else to say, he walked away.

Several days later, Sue's mother's viewing service was held. Larry refused to attend, not knowing how to handle his wife's grief. *It's better if I just leave her alone,* he told himself, escaping to the radio station and the bars.

Sue was hurt, but not surprised. These days the tension was so thick between the Wrights that they weren't communicating at all.

Now that her mom was gone, Sue's main sources of support were vanishing. During the past few years she'd dealt with her marital crises by talking with her mother, father, or siblings. But the Dombey family was falling apart; Sue's father would soon marry another woman, and Sue and her siblings were left to pick up the pieces.

Sue fell into a deep depression. She thought about her mom, a model parent who had come to believe that her life had no meaning after her children were raised and had families of their own; that notion had driven her to suicide. Now, at age 31, Sue wondered if she shouldn't do the same. She was married to an alcoholic husband with whom all she did was fight; she saw herself as a poor mother, screaming at her kids as her own suffering escalated.

*Nobody loves me,* she thought, sinking deeper. *Larry doesn't care if I'm dead or alive. My parents aren't around anymore. And the kids—even if they do love me—would be better off if I weren't here.*

Sue began going to bed in the afternoons, when the girls were napping. She withdrew from friends and stayed home. Emptiness and despair plagued her, and all she wanted to do was hide.

Larry still avoided her, but felt guilty. *Something's wrong,* he thought. *I ought to do something for Sue.* He decided to restore a 1957 classic T-Bird convertible for his wife. Several months and thousands of dollars later, he was finished. He drove it into the carport one afternoon and hurried into the house to find Sue taking a nap.

"Get up!" he said excitedly, pulling open the curtains in their bedroom. "I want to show you something."

Sue squinted at the sunlight. "Why?"

"Just come outside." He led her to the carport and stood next to her, smiling. Then he pointed to the shiny black convertible. "This is for you."

Sue frowned. "What did you do *that* for?" She shook her head in disbelief. *Do you think buying me a car is going to make up for everything? Are you hoping that now I'll get over my problems?* "You don't know me at all," she said, brushing past her husband and walking back into the house. The door shut with a bang.

Larry's ears turned red. He stared, incredulous, at the closed door. *What an ungrateful wretch!* he thought. *I try to do something nice for her, and she throws it in my face!* He folded his arms. *Well, forget it! I'd rather be in the bars anyway.*

〰✕〰

"I'm goin' to bed," announced Larry, his words slurred. He and Sue had returned home from another party for the radio station. He tossed his sport coat on the floor and staggered up the stairs.

Sue smiled awkwardly at Mrs. Ballantine, their daughters' regular babysitter, who sat on the couch. "He needs to get up early for his morning shift," Sue told the tiny, gray-haired woman.

Mrs. Ballantine nodded, but Sue knew the lady wasn't fooled. In the months she'd been watching the Wrights' children, Mrs. Ballantine had seen Larry come home drunk countless times; no doubt she had noticed the couple's emotional distance, too. The two women had spent many evenings talking; after her mother's suicide a few months earlier, Sue had told the older woman all about her depression and marital problems.

Mrs. Ballantine moved the Bible she was reading off her lap and patted the cushion next to her. "Come sit with me," she said. "Let's chat for a while if you're not too tired."

The tightness on Sue's face relaxed, and she agreed.

"How are you doing?" Mrs. Ballantine inquired, her eyes full of concern.

Sue sank onto the couch. "Not too well," she admitted. Tears welled in her eyes as she told the older woman how bad things had become.

Mrs. Ballantine listened and offered words of encouragement. Then her eyes lit up. "Well, Jesus is coming again!" she announced. For several minutes she told Sue how wonderful things would be when the kingdom of God arrived on earth. "None of your problems will matter then," she added.

Sue stared at the older woman with wide, skeptical eyes. Sue had gone to church as a child, and she and Larry had attended sporadically so their girls could have some religious exposure. But Sue had never heard anyone go on like this about God. Mrs. Ballantine was talking like a woman in love. It sounded crazy.

Mrs. Ballantine leaned forward, her wrinkled hands folded, and asked Sue, "When were you saved?"

Sue's forehead furrowed. "What do you mean?"

"When did you become a Christian?"

"Oh, a long time ago!" said Sue. "I've been in church all my life." *Why would she even ask such a question?* she wondered.

Mrs. Ballantine didn't say anything. She simply shook her head.

*Now, why did she do that?* Sue thought.

After Mrs. Ballantine left, the question remained. Sue had always assumed she was a Christian. To her, being a Christian was almost like being born an American; it was part of her heritage. But it bothered her that the older woman didn't seem to agree.

The next day, Sue related the incident to Larry. "Do you think I'm a Christian?" she asked.

Larry shrugged. "Don't worry about it." He patted her on the shoulder. "You've lived a good, moral life. You'll make it one of these days."

Sue wasn't so sure. The issue continued to weigh on her during the days that followed. If going to church didn't make her a Christian, she thought, did that mean she wasn't going to heaven?

The next time Mrs. Ballantine baby-sat for the Wrights, Sue brought up the subject of church. The older woman encouraged Sue to visit a particular church which, she affirmed, was "Bible believing." The girls, she added, would love it.

That convinced Sue to try it out. The following Sunday she dragged a tired, hung-over Larry and their three girls to church. Feeling guilty about his carousing the night before, Larry had agreed to go because he knew it would placate his wife. Like Sue, he had attended church as a child—but unlike her, he had no interest in religion. Trailing his wife into the sanctuary, he thought, *Well, this will be a little bone I'll throw her once a week.*

Besides, he thought, it wasn't such a big sacrifice. After a wild Saturday night of drinking with the boys, the soft cushions on the church pews would make the perfect place to snooze.

Larry slept through most of the service, but Sue listened intently. She liked the church so much that she insisted the family attend again the next Sunday.

"God loves you personally," the pastor told the congregation that Sunday. Leaning forward on the podium, he seemed to speak right to Sue. "In fact, He loves you so much that even if you were the only person in the world, He still would have died for you. That's how great His love is."

Even from where she was sitting in the back, Sue could see the minister's eyes glisten with emotion. His message gave her a glimmer of hope. *I didn't think anyone loved me. But the God of the universe does? No matter what?*

"Even though we're all sinful, the Lord yearns to have a relationship with us," the preacher said. "If you don't know Jesus Christ, the God who takes away our sins, you can—today."

*I want to know Jesus,* thought Sue.

"I'd like to invite those of you who want a relationship with Jesus to come down to the front, by the altar. I'll lead you in a prayer asking for forgiveness of your sins and for Him to be the Master of your life."

Her pulse racing, Sue looked over at Larry. He was staring at the walls, his eyes glazed from fatigue and the aftereffects of alcohol. He probably would think she was crazy if she got up—but she didn't care. Standing, she shuffled past her husband and made her way down the aisle of the 3,000-member church.

Larry watched his wife with mild interest. Recalling his Southern Baptist roots, he knew she was going forward to make a profession of faith. He'd done it as a young boy and had seen other people do the same. But he had no intention of following his wife. He didn't want to be some Christian "do bee," always trying to do the right thing and look good. As far as Larry was concerned, that took all the fun out of life. *But if it's going to make her happy, then fine,* he thought. He was content to stay where he was.

Sue stood at the altar, tears coursing down her cheeks. Her head bowed and eyes closed, she prayed, *God, thank You for loving me. Forgive me for all the things I've done. Take my life and do with me what You please.*

When she finished praying, a powerful peace enveloped her. She smiled, her first expression of joy since her mother had passed away. Suddenly it didn't frighten her so much that she had an alcoholic husband and a marriage that was falling apart.

God loved her, and He would help her through it.

~∂∕∘~

Sue began attending church more than once a week, reading her Bible, and praying. Six months after her commitment to Christ, she joined a women's Bible study, where the weekly fellowship strengthened her faith. She learned from the example and teaching of the leaders—one of whom was also the wife of an alcoholic—who taught the younger wives how to love their husbands and children.

Soon after Sue joined, the group began studying a subject close to her heart: How to love an unlovable person. *Boy, I'm certainly married to one,* Sue thought. It was easy for her to see that Larry was a hard-to-love sinner.

But before long, the Bible study and time spent with God made her realize some unpleasant things about herself, too. Throughout their marriage, Sue had placed all the blame for their problems on Larry. She'd believed that if only he would straighten out his life, things would improve. But God began to teach her that she had contributed to their marital problems, too.

For one thing, the verbal assaults that came out of her mouth were just as bad as the liquor that poured into Larry's.

Sue came to see that the little love she gave her husband was based on his behavior. But God wanted her to love Larry *unconditionally*, whether or not he changed—just as the Lord loved her.

She knew it wouldn't be easy. Larry was making it more difficult for her to love him. He mocked her faith and dismissed her relationship with God as a phase.

*God,* she often prayed, *I don't love Larry at all. I have no feelings for this man. If I'm going to be able to do this, I need You to give me Your love for him. I'm giving this marriage and my husband over to You. I can't change him, but You can.* Sue held on to hope, reciting to herself scriptures which spoke of God's love and power. One of her favorites was Psalm 37:4: "Delight yourself in the Lord and he will give you the desires of your heart." Her desire—and belief—was that God would work a miracle in their marriage.

Though Sue didn't feel any affection toward Larry, she was determined to demonstrate love. She stopped leaving Alcoholics Anonymous pamphlets around the house and grilling her husband on his whereabouts.

When a liquored-up Larry arrived home one evening, she simply said, "Hi. How was your day?"

"Aren't you going to ask me how many drinks I've had?" Larry countered with a sneer.

Instead of arguing, Sue held her tongue. "No, I'm not," she told him, and left the room to start dinner.

"Oh, I get it," Larry persisted, following his wife into the kitchen. "Now you're going to start with your 'holier than thou' act."

Sue didn't respond.

Larry waited for a rebuttal, eager to fight. Usually he could play Sue like a yo-yo, bringing her to tears or smiles; he enjoyed the feeling of power it brought. But as he watched her pull vegetables out of the refrigerator, calmly ignoring him, he realized she wasn't going to play that game.

Grunting, he walked into the family room and turned on the TV. Sue's serene attitude bothered him. Since going forward to pray in church, she'd been consistently sweet to him. He couldn't remember the last time she'd asked him how many drinks he'd had.

Larry threw himself down on the couch, staring blankly at the TV screen. *Those ladies from church probably told her if she's nice enough, I'll shape up and be nice back,* he thought irritably. *Well, it's not going to work that way!* He decided to do everything he could to scuttle his wife's newfound kindness.

One evening, several months after Sue began attending her Bible study, she came home excited to tell Larry and the girls—the oldest now in junior high—what she'd learned that afternoon.

"Did you know what the Bible says about God's forgiveness?" she asked when the family was seated around the dinner table. "It doesn't matter what we've done! The Lord can forgive us." She quoted 2 Corinthians 5:17 (KJV): "Therefore if any man be in Christ, he is a new creature: old things are passed away; behold, all things are become new." The verse had been good news to Sue, and she thought it might help her family as well.

But her comment was met with silence. Then Larry snickered, helping himself to a piece of fried chicken. "Oh, boy," he said to the girls, "here she goes again, preaching. I'm gettin' tired of hearing it every Thursday night." Larry looked at Sue. "Don't you and the ladies have anything more exciting to talk about? I mean, the Bible's full of errors—those scribes made a ton of mistakes." As he rolled his eyes, the girls giggled in agreement.

"That's not true," whispered Sue. "The Bible is God's Word. There aren't any errors in it." Her eyes burning, she finished her dinner quickly and silently. Then, without looking at her husband or children, she put the dishes in the sink and hurried down the hall to their bedroom.

She buried her face in a pillow, weeping. Not only had she been rejected by her husband, but her kids had mocked her faith as well. *Why are they hurting me, Lord?* she prayed. *Why is this so hard?* For several minutes she lay face down on the bed, sobbing.

Then God seemed to speak: *Now you know a little bit of the rejection that I faced as I walked on this earth.*

Sue sat up, thinking of the beatings, verbal assaults, and horrible death Jesus had suffered. He had endured so much more pain on this earth—and He'd done it for her. She wiped her eyes, soothed by that reminder. *Thank You, God,* she prayed, *for loving me and helping me through this.*

Believing that the Lord understood her situation and had a purpose in her suffering made it more bearable. Larry might belittle her faith for years to come, but God would always be with her, giving her strength.

Sue sighed. It was difficult to picture her heavy-drinking, hardened spouse changing into a loving partner and faithful Christian. But her own life had been transformed, so why couldn't Larry's?

She needed to trust that eventually, God would reach her husband's heart as well.

❦

*G*od *was* working in Larry, though to Sue the process seemed tedious. It still hurt when Larry mocked her trust in God, but she felt a peace that stood out from the turmoil in their home. She continued praying for her husband and reminding herself that he wasn't going to be changed by her; only God's power could effect a turnaround. She focused her energy on their daughters, hoping to instill in them a love for God. At times she felt as if she were pedaling backward, but Sue continued to pray with her daughters and teach them the Bible.

On the nights Larry came home late, the girls climbed into bed with Sue; together they prayed God would bring him back safely. When Larry finally arrived home, he acted as though he didn't care what kind of torture he had put his family through. But inside, he was a mess. Often, while he drove home drunk, tears would stream down his face as remorse set in. *How in the world can you do this to your wife and girls?* he berated himself. He felt like the biggest jerk on earth.

Next day, nursing a hangover, Larry would plan to change—to become a better husband and father. Yet after the effects of the booze had worn off, he'd return to the bars, repeating the pattern.

Larry never expressed these remorseful feelings to his wife, but kept trying to balance his negative behavior with good deeds—like going to church. He slept through many of the sermons, with Sue elbowing him when she thought he needed to hear what was being said.

Larry couldn't ignore the example of Sue's life, however. For over a year he had watched her live out her faith at home. He could see that his wife's new attitude was more than just a phase or a ploy to get him to change. She continued to treat him kindly even when he was horrible to her—and he knew there was no earthly reason. Finally he realized that Sue had indeed been transformed by God's love.

Several months after Sue had joined the women's Bible study, an offshoot group was formed—for couples. Many of the women had unbelieving husbands, and wanted to design an outreach group that would immerse their spouses in God's Word and teach them the basics of the Christian faith.

At first, Larry scoffed at the idea. But he decided to go when one of the husbands, whom he admired, invited him. As he and Sue attended, Larry discovered that each person was expected to fill out part of a booklet in preparation for the week's meeting. There were Bible verses to look up and memorize and questions to answer.

Larry was already familiar with much of the material because of his Sunday school days as a kid. But he always did his homework—albeit with a drink in hand. *If I skip out on the workbook,* he reasoned, *someone will look over my shoulder and see that I haven't filled in the blanks.* He didn't want to be the only delinquent in the group; he hoped to look like a "good guy." Besides, he didn't want his wife to know more than he did about any subject, even the Bible.

Each person in the Bible study was required to lead one session. When Larry's turn came, Sue cringed. *There's no way he can lead our group,* she thought. *He'll turn it into a joke!* But to her surprise, Larry led a thoughtful, thorough lesson.

That wasn't the only thing that shocked Sue. As the weeks passed, she saw Larry open up to the group with questions and thoughts he'd never expressed to her. Larry had always given the impression that he knew everything; now he said, "What does that mean?" and "I don't understand that verse." Sue was thankful to get to know her husband, even if it was through the Bible study.

One summer evening, just hours before the group would meet, Larry sat at the desk in his study. Sipping a beer, he hurriedly prepared for the lesson. He looked up a verse and read: "Now this is eternal life: that they may know you, the only true God, and Jesus Christ, whom you have sent" (John 17:3).

Time seemed to stop as the words washed over him. Suddenly Larry was confronted with the truth. He set down the bottle and reread the verse. *That's what life's all about,* he thought. *Knowing God. If I don't know Him, then everything else is meaningless.*

Larry knew plenty about a life without meaning. For years he'd been haunted by a desperate emptiness, which he'd tried to fill with alcohol. Being drunk took away his sadness for a few hours, but the pain always came flooding back—often worse because it was coupled with guilt. Now he realized the only thing—the only Person—who could truly satisfy him was God.

With trembling hands Larry turned to the back of the booklet. He knew what he'd find: a short prayer and a fill-in-the-blank form for people who wanted to commit their lives to Jesus Christ. He'd secretly hoped he could make it through the study without dealing with this page. But now he wanted what Sue had. He whispered the prayer, then signed his name—acknowledging that he had asked forgiveness of his sins and placed his faith in Christ as the only way to heaven. As he did, peace seemed to surround him. He knew he'd made the right decision by asking God to lead his life.

Larry closed the booklet, ready to head out the door for Bible study. He felt energized, like a new person. *Now that I'm a Christian,* he decided, *I'm going to stop getting drunk.*

Giving up alcohol completely, however, was another matter.

❧

*L*arry didn't tell Sue about his decision to follow Jesus. He found it difficult to talk about his feelings. Eventually, he figured, she'd find out.

Several weeks later, Sue spied Larry's booklet sitting on his nightstand. Peeking in the back, she saw her husband's signature—and was overcome. She had prayed for him for two years, and finally, he had made the commitment! She closed the booklet, smiling. She decided not to say anything to Larry, knowing he would talk about it when he was ready.

It would take Larry years to open up about his decision—but he didn't try to hide his new life from Sue. Immediately he began spending time praying and reading the Bible. As he did, he realized that God would be the One to change him—by guiding Larry to make better choices so he could live a life that pleased God. Larry held on to verses such as John 15:4: "Remain in me, and I will remain in you. No branch can bear fruit by itself; it must remain in the vine. Neither can you bear fruit unless you remain in me."

Some of the changes in Larry were immediately apparent. He began wanting to attend church, and actually listened to the sermons. He stopped taunting Sue about her faith. The tension between them lessened—not only because Sue refused to be drawn into arguments, but also because Larry had become a new person.

The girls noticed the difference. "Mom, Dad, you don't fight anymore," said Linda one night when they were all seated around the dinner table.

Sue and Larry looked at each other, surprised. "You're right," Sue said, smiling at her husband. "We don't."

God was working to heal their marriage.

The Wrights' relationship deepened that summer as they saw each of the men in their Bible study become Christians. Soon the group was so large that it was time to form another offshoot. Larry expressed a desire to lead the new group in their home.

Sue balked at the idea. *He's not ready to teach,* she thought nervously. But Larry persisted. Their new group eventually grew to 40 people, then split three ways and moved to a bigger house in Phoenix. Attracted in part by the story of the Wrights' changed lives, many people became Christians under their leadership.

Meanwhile, Larry was still drinking.

He had never intended to quit his alcohol habit completely. From his perspective, his social drinking was harmless. *At least I'm not getting drunk like I was before,* he told himself, *or staying at the bars all day.* If he went at all, it was for only a few drinks, and then he would head home. And he never kept alcohol in the house anymore.

Sue had "let go" of worrying about the issue. *That's between him and God,* she reminded herself when she saw Larry had been drinking. *I can't do anything about it except pray.*

But Larry's conscience nagged at him. He knew his job at KRUX, with the free booze and constant parties, would make it easy for him to slip back into intoxication. Every day he fought the beckoning of the bars. Getting drunk wasn't something he approved of anymore, but the opportunity was hard to ignore.

When Larry considered quitting KRUX because of the temptations, he cringed. Being a radio personality seemed like the perfect vocation. He worked only three hours a day; as one of the most popular disk jockeys in Phoenix, he had job security; the high pay enabled him to provide a comfortable lifestyle for Sue and the girls. How could he give all that up?

Day after day Larry inwardly fought the idea of resigning. But the uneasiness over his job never left. He began to see that the stakes were high: He couldn't keep working in a place he knew he needed to leave, a place that made it too easy for him to lapse into chronic drunkenness and hurt his family more than he already had.

The battle made him miserable. Finally, after a year of wavering, he made his choice. *Okay Lord. I give up. I don't know what You want me to do next, but I know I need to do this.*

The next day, he walked into the station and gave a month's notice.

Within days Larry had several employment offers. A big gun in Phoenix radio for over 10 years, he watched as other Top 40 stations jumped at the chance to hire him. But he couldn't take any of their offers, all of which would have put him back in the middle of temptation.

He decided to take a job with a station that played easy-listening music— a job that paid much less than the others would have. It was a difficult choice for the Wrights; the small salary would force them to live off savings or pare down their expenses. But they believed God wanted Larry to leave rock 'n' roll radio—and they trusted He would provide for their family.

This step of faith drew them closer. As the months passed, they felt more certain Larry had made the right decision. No longer did he face the temptations he had at KRUX. His current station lacked the glamour associated with rock 'n' roll, and required announcers to squelch their personalities. Now, Larry could only cut into the music every half hour and give the station call letters.

But even with the job change, Larry still battled his drinking habit. Every day during his one-hour breaks, he made a beeline to the bar down the street for a drink or two.

He wasn't proud of it. Whenever he walked through the door, he prayed, *God, please protect my Christian witness. I don't want any Christians to see me in here. They won't understand. They'll think I'm a hypocrite.*

God answered his call for help—but not in the way Larry had anticipated.

❧

One afternoon several months later, Larry walked into the bar on his break. There he spotted Jason, a young man who had been attending the Wrights' Bible study for several weeks.

Larry stopped short. He'd never run into anyone in a bar who knew him from church. His first instinct was to walk out and find another place to get a drink. But without knowing why, he walked toward Jason and sat next to him.

"Remember me?" Larry said as he sank onto the stool.

Jason's jaw dropped. His face turned red. He stared at his Bible study leader for several seconds before asking, "What are you doing here?"

Larry hesitated. The last thing he wanted to be was a hypocrite. If he had a problem, he thought, he might as well admit it. "Well, I drink," he told Jason. "It's a little problem I've got. But one of these days"—Larry looked heavenward—"He'll take care of it. In the meantime, how about I buy you a beer?"

Eyebrows raised, Jason accepted the drink. He sat uncomfortably next to Larry, downing the beer as fast as he could. Then he stood up. "I've gotta go," he mumbled, then leaned in confidentially. "I promise I won't tell anyone I saw you."

"Hey," protested Larry, "I'm not trying to hide anything. Say whatever you want."

Jason looked stricken. He'd never seen a Christian—least of all a Bible study leader—try to minimize the issue of drinking. Pushing in the stool, he looked at Larry. "Don't worry," he said before he left. "I'll keep it quiet."

Depressed, Larry leaned his elbows on the counter and watched the young man exit. Jason probably fought the same problem, Larry thought. Yet the young man had seemed so embarrassed by and disappointed in his Bible teacher. Larry sighed, wondering if God also felt disappointed in him when he drank.

Larry paid for the alcohol, then left for the station. Somehow the atmosphere of the bar now felt stifling and dark.

Larry later learned that Jason went home and told his sister, a veteran of the Bible study, about the incident. Nothing else happened—except to Larry.

The next day, when break time came, Larry stayed at the station and sipped coffee. For the first time in years he had no desire to go to a bar. In fact, he didn't even want a drink!

He stroked his chin, thinking. This was much different from the feeling he'd often had when, driving home drunk, he'd vowed to stop drinking. Those plans had been the result of willpower and guilt—and he'd still wanted to drink.

Now he felt indifferent toward alcohol. God had taken away his thirst for liquor. He couldn't believe it. *Thank You, Lord,* he prayed, *for healing me.* For the first time in years, he felt free.

◌◦◌

*L*arry never again had a drink. He wasn't the only one who benefited from the change. Quitting also brought additional healing to his family. Now that alcohol no longer controlled his life, he was able to spend much more time with Sue and the girls.

The Wrights found time to work on their marriage, too. Larry's two days off were in the middle of the week; since the girls were in school, he and Sue spent that time together grocery shopping, working in the yard, running errands, and going out for lunch or breakfast. It had been years since the Wrights had any leisure time together, and they relished it.

Over the following months, they also spent more time leading Bible studies in their home and telling others what God had done for them. Soon they were asked to speak at women's retreats. Sue would share her story; then Larry would share his. Honest and open, the Wrights became such popular speakers that they began to travel several times a year to give talks across the U.S. and in Canada.

Meanwhile, Larry stayed in radio—playing easy-listening music and eventually moving to talk radio. Sue concentrated on raising their three daughters.

For almost 10 years Sue and Larry spoke at women's conferences. Then, suddenly, Larry felt compelled to resign from the talk-radio job he'd held for six years. It would be another venture into the unknown; he didn't have any prospects.

Nervous, Larry announced the decision to his Sunday school class. "Tomorrow I'm resigning," he said. "Sue and I have no idea what we're going to do next, but we need you to pray for us."

Sue nodded her agreement, quietly confident that God would take care of them. Larry had been in radio for 23 years, but she knew the Lord had bigger plans.

After class, a friend approached Larry. "Have you ever thought about teaching the Bible on a full-time basis?" he asked, excitement in his voice.

Larry shrugged. He enjoyed giving seminars and leading studies on the side, but had never considered full-time ministry. "Well, no," he admitted. "I'll think about it, though."

"If you decide you're interested," the man said, "my wife and I would love to help your ministry get started."

Larry couldn't help but consider the man's idea; over the next two weeks, three more men approached him with the same proposal! By the time the last man came to him, he had to conclude, *God must be trying to tell me something.*

Larry brought the four men together and told them what had happened. Awed, they all agreed that God must be leading Larry to start a men's ministry. Since one of the four was a member of Phoenix's most prestigious country club, they chose that as the place to hold an outreach Bible study for unchurched men.

Their ministry, "Abundant Life," grew quickly; 18 months later, the Bible study included 300 men. As Larry worked with the mostly married men, hearing of struggles they were having with their wives, he saw the need for a similar group for women. So Sue began a women's study, emphasizing the role of the wife.

Together, the Wrights had a hand in the improvement of many marriages. One couple, struggling with alcoholism as Larry and Sue had, was ready to file for divorce. After attending the Bible study groups, the couple found fresh hope in God—and went on to start a counseling ministry, primarily for spouses.

The Wrights also counseled married couples, albeit informally. Often these sessions encouraged Larry and Sue, too, as they recounted their own story.

In one such meeting, the Wrights sat on their family-room couch—the same one Larry had often passed out on—trying to help a young husband and wife work through their differences.

"God puts our spouses in our lives for a reason," Sue told the struggling wife. "Early in our marriage, when Larry and I were constantly fighting, I would wonder why I was still with him. His alcoholism was tearing the family apart." She paused and looked over at her husband. "After I became a Christian, I realized that Larry grew up never knowing what it meant to be loved. God wanted me to be the one to show my husband His love."

Larry put his arm around Sue's shoulders. "God knew exactly what He was doing when He put the two of us together," he said. He grinned and winked at the other couple. "Now Sue can thank God that I was such a piece of pond scum. Some men lead their wives to Christ—I *drove* mine."

They could laugh about it now—even though for years, Larry and Sue had grimly focused only on themselves as their marriage faltered. Now, as the Wrights looked first to God, they'd learned to view each other's needs as more important than their own.

And things had never been better.

❧

*Abundant Life Ministry, established in 1979, continues to reach out primarily to unbelievers in the Phoenix area. The ministry sponsors large Bible studies in country clubs, movie theaters, and conference centers—and hosts inquirers' seminars and discussion groups. Recently the Wrights' youngest daughter, Laurie, and her husband, Skip, joined the ministry and plan to carry it on after Larry and Sue are gone.*

*The Wrights also continue to speak at marriage retreats, telling their story to help others see that there is hope for any marriage that has God in it. They live in Glendale, Arizona, and are proud to have nine grandchildren.*

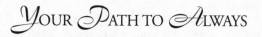

# ~Your ~Path to ~Always

Many marital conflicts are born out of false expectations and unmet
needs. Sue Wright expected Larry, her husband, to live out the ideal
she had clung to her whole life. She never wanted to be married to
someone who drank at all, let alone a person with a drinking problem.
It's as if she had a mold at the beginning of their relationship and
poured him into it.

Larry was then put in a position of having to either deceive Sue or
give up alcohol. He chose to deceive her. When she realized he truly
had a drinking problem, that left her open to feelings of anger toward
him for not being the husband she expected.

Couples and individuals need to learn what Sue came to understand after she gave her heart to Jesus Christ. Namely, *God is enough* no
matter what's going on in your life or what you might have to face.
"[The Lord] must become greater [in my life]; I must become less"
(John 3:30). When we allow Him full control of our hearts, He fills us
with a peace that carries us through life's difficulties.

Sue had always wanted Larry to change and become the man she
expected him to be. She eventually realized that her judging was just as
bad as Larry's drinking. When she released her desires and started praying for Larry to become the man *God* wanted him to be, she freed herself to trust God to work in the situation and to fill her life with lasting
joy, not some temporary relief that might come if Larry changed.

She acknowledged she couldn't control the outcome; she could
only control how she responded to Larry. Her new attitude was a turning point in their conflicts. The conflicts themselves became more
intense for a time, as Larry mocked her faith, but she truly had learned
to rely on God, coming to Him every day just like the widow in Luke
18. Now as she prayed for Larry to change, she didn't do it with any of
her own expectations. She just took responsibility for her actions and
showed love to her husband even when she didn't feel it in her heart.

When Larry finally came to God, he knew what he needed and
wanted to do, but it was still a struggle for him to do it. A turning

point came when he got a surprise dose of accountability, encountering a participant in his Bible study who apparently also had a drinking problem. When Larry was faced with justifying his actions, it left him feeling defeated, and he knew then that he would give up drinking forever.

The support and accountability we receive from others in small groups like a regular Bible study cannot be overstated. That's why I emphasize repeatedly in these commentaries the value of being in such groups. And, in turn, we can provide support and empathy to someone else facing a crisis or situation that we've been through, offering hope and the kind of wise counsel that can only be gained through experience.

If you and your spouse are not currently in a small group, check to see if your church provides such groups; more and more churches do. Or you could organize your own group with friends, neighbors, or fellow members of your church or Sunday school class who share your commitment to God and to marriage.

Once in a group, you can study together a resource like *Always* or a book of the Bible, using your discussion time to discover and reinforce helpful principles, to encourage one another, to hold one another accountable, and to help member couples work through struggles they may be having. Of course, mutual respect and confidentiality are vital to the health and success of such a group.

My wife, Norma, and I have made it a point for years to always be part of a small group, and our marriage has been much the stronger for it.

—Gary Smalley

# Then the Sun Came Up

*Irvin and Helen Laurie Tucker*

MARRIED IN 1941

"This New Year's Eve is going to be really special," Helen Tucker said to her husband, Irvin. She gazed out the car window in anticipation as the mileage markers on Interstate 95 whizzed by, pointing the travelers toward Virginia Beach.

Irvin, or "Tuck" as Helen affectionately called him, took one hand off the steering wheel and gently squeezed his wife's hand. "It *will* be special," he agreed, "because I'll be with you."

Helen was silent for a moment, then smiled over at Tuck and asked, "Do you remember our first kiss?"

Tuck chuckled. "New Year's Eve, 1940."

*I was so shy then,* Helen mused. She settled contentedly back into her seat and savored the moment. *Life is good,* she thought, enjoying the ride as she and Tuck sang, laughed at each other's jokes, and hummed with the music over the radio. Helen was beginning her 50s; Tuck was ending his. Their sons were married with families of their own, so this weekend getaway would be a time to renew their marriage and make resolutions for the new year. There would be no telephone calls, no appointments, and no distractions.

A few hours later, the Tuckers checked into their oceanfront motel, where they began unwinding from the drive that began earlier that day in their hometown of Raleigh, North Carolina. After Tuck and Helen unpacked their suitcases and settled in, Tuck eagerly plunked down in an overstuffed chair, the television remote control in hand. He flipped on the TV and managed to find a channel with a football game. Amid the sounds of a cheering crowd, the TV announcer's voice blared: *And now with our starting lineups . . .*

"Hey, Helen, just in time," Tuck said, motioning to his wife. "It's the Sugar Bowl from New Orleans."

"Great, honey," she said enthusiastically. Walking toward the bed, Helen propped up a couple of pillows to watch the opening series of downs. She had no objections to her husband's devotion to the world of sports; she liked football and enjoyed bantering with her husband about the game. "See that quarterback?" she asked. "He should have released the ball sooner."

Helen made a sweeping gesture with her right arm, as though she were passing the ball in the Superdome herself. Her upper arm swept lightly against her blouse, then froze. She felt something hard on her breast. *Oh, my goodness,* she thought, suddenly feeling sick. *Do I have a lump?*

She brought her hand to her breast and probed. It was a lump, all right—a solid, unyielding mass beneath her fingers that she could feel, even through her clothes.

Feeling lightheaded, Helen took a deep breath, then turned to her husband. "Tuck, I think I have a lump in my breast," she said hoarsely.

Tuck turned abruptly from the football game, his blue eyes wide with concern. "Oh, honey," he said as he switched off the game and sprang up from his chair. As he sank onto the bed beside Helen, Tuck gently stroked her pale cheek.

Helen stared at her husband, her heart pounding. Tuck's eyes were moist, searching hers fearfully—unusual for an attorney who always kept a close rein on his emotions. *He's scared, too,* Helen realized nervously. She took his hand in hers and brought it to her breast.

"Can you feel it?"

Tuck flinched when he found the knot. It was the size of a silver dollar. "Yes," he agreed quietly, "it's a lump." He looked protectively at Helen. Then, gathering his wife into his arms, he began to rock her back and forth like a parent soothing a hurt child. "Lord, if we ever needed Your help, we need it now," he called out urgently, his words tumbling over one another.

Helen squeezed her eyes shut and tried to quell her rising panic. Her beloved sister, Mildred, was dying of breast cancer in a Myrtle Beach hospital. Cancer had already claimed her mother and grandmother. *Will I be the fourth in our family?* she wondered, shivering involuntarily in Tuck's arms.

He found an extra blanket in a dresser drawer and wrapped it carefully around Helen's shoulders. They huddled together in silence, like two baby birds pushed out of their safe nest.

Helen's trembling began to subside after several minutes. Tuck's arms and the warmth of the blanket brought a measure of security, and she remembered the words a missionary had spoken in the couple's Bible class 25 years earlier. "Nothing," the missionary had said, "can touch a Christian without first passing through the hand of God." Like a drowning person clinging to a log, Helen held on to the hope that God still had control of her situation. *Lord, do You mean that what's happening to me has already passed through Your hands?* she prayed. *If that's true, You must have some reason for allowing this.* God's peace washed over her, and her panic began to fade.

She spoke more calmly, "Tuck, thank you for loving me. I'm feeling better now." She paused. "At least, I think I am."

"Good," said Tuck tenderly. He sat up and turned to face his wife, attempting to look optimistic. Helen already had enough to worry about—he needed to be strong for her sake. "Since it's New Year's Eve and we're far from home," he said, changing the subject, "why don't we go out to dinner? We'll begin the new year by trusting that God will take care of us. He always has."

Tuck knew it was true—the Lord Jesus *would* guide them through this trial—but he was still deeply concerned. What if the lump was cancerous? How could he face a future without Helen? *Jesus,* he prayed as Helen changed for dinner, *don't let us down now. I don't want to lose the precious wife You gave me.*

A few minutes later, they left to have dinner at a nearby hotel. Thankful for the diversion, Tuck and Helen lingered over the candlelit table, savored the fine cuisine, and enjoyed the extravagant furnishings of the beautiful, golden ballroom. Helen's remaining worries vanished as she basked in the glow of candles, but as soon as she stepped back into their dark motel room, the gnawing fear in the pit of her stomach returned. How could they prepare their sons, who lived several hours from their home, for this development in their lives? How could she handle having the same disease that had already ravaged so many of the women in her family?

Tuck sensed his wife's apprehension and wrapped his arms around her again. As they prepared for bed, he kissed her on the cheek. "Happy 1978," he said quietly, his pale blue eyes moist. "It *will* be a good year for us, honey. Just wait and see." Tuck held Helen tight, thankful he could draw her close. But inside, he wasn't so confident about the coming year. With uncertainty he fell into uneasy sleep.

For Helen, rest did not come easily that long night. Her mind persisted in worrying about the future and reviewing the major events of her life.

༄

*A*s an infant, Helen had been struck by osteomyelitis, which left her with one leg a bit shorter than the other. As she grew, the neighborhood kids had called her a "crip," on account of her limp. Through her adolescence, no one could see the deep emotional scars and insecurities about her body left by that early teasing. Helen learned to play a fair game of tennis, became head cheerleader and football queen in high school, and was an enthusiastic participant in extracurricular activities.

She continued to live with her parents after high school. When she was almost 20 years old, the family moved from Mullins, South Carolina, to Whiteville, North Carolina. Helen and her family helped the movers carry their belongings into the charming, old two-story house. She didn't notice the young, dark-haired attorney who watched his new neighbors' arrival as he walked home for lunch.

*I'm going to have to get to know that girl,* Tuck thought, noting Helen's contagious, throaty laugh and shiny, strawberry-blond hair.

Two days later, having made inquiries about the new family on the block, he telephoned. "May I speak with Helen?" he asked formally.

"I'm Helen," she said in her deep, southern lilt. "Who is this?"

"Well, I'm Irvin Tucker, your neighbor across the street," Tuck answered confidently.

"Oh." Helen raised her eyebrows in surprise. They had not been introduced yet. "Well, why are you calling?" she asked, straightforward as always.

"I was wondering if you might be free for dinner one evening this week. I'd like to take you to the Anchorage Lodge, next to Lake Waccamaw."

*He's asking me for a date?* Helen thought, taken aback by his boldness. *We've never even met!* "I'm sorry," she said bluntly, "but I can't. Thank you for calling us. Good-bye."

Tuck, however, wasn't easily dissuaded. His powers of persuasion won him a date on the third attempt. Once Helen spent time with him, she was smitten. Tuck, who was 10 years older than she, was a mature intellectual and balanced her youthful, lighthearted personality. He was also the most eligible bachelor in town. Eight months later, after a whirlwind courtship, they were married.

Despite the short dating period, their marriage was solid. The Tuckers had two boys, born seven years apart, and in the 1950s, Tuck and Helen both became Christians—asking Jesus Christ to forgive their sins and be their Lord and Savior. Their relationship was strengthened as the couple became active in their local church. Their pastor asked the Tuckers to teach the young adults' Sunday school class, and they readily agreed. Teaching others about God's selfless love reminded Tuck and Helen that their love now had a spiritual foundation—a foundation that would prove to be vital in the years ahead.

❧

As Helen lay quietly in the Virginia Beach motel room, the first signs of dawn crept through the curtains. Quietly, she got out of bed and peeked through the blinds, watching the sun rise over the eastern horizon. The date was January 1, 1978. Helen wrapped her arms protectively around her middle. Would the lump be malignant? Would she still be alive a year from now? How many more sunrises would she see? Only God knew.

*Lord,* she prayed, *don't take me home now. There's so much I still want to accomplish. I want to write a book and get more involved with the Junior Women's Club and the Cub Scouts. I want to see my grandchildren grow up. I want to grow old with Tuck.* She sighed heavily. She wasn't ready to die.

But as Helen anxiously contemplated the future, the Holy Spirit brought scripture after scripture to her mind, comforting her. She gazed at the colorful horizon and began to whisper God's promises from the Bible. "I will never leave thee, nor forsake thee," she recited quietly. "Lo, I am with you always, even unto the end of the world" (Hebrews 13:5; Matthew 28:20).

Scriptures continued to swim through her mind on the return drive to Raleigh as Helen thought about what lay ahead. She knew she needed to see a doctor at once, so when she and Tuck arrived back home, she immediately phoned her gynecologist. He referred Helen to Woodall Rose, a young surgeon who agreed to see her the following day.

The next morning, Helen sat tensely in the waiting room, squeezing Tuck's hand, before being escorted into a tiny examining room. A nurse handed her a light-blue gown. "I know you're nervous, Mrs. Tucker," the nurse said sympathetically. "But let me reassure you that each year, thousands of women find lumps in their breasts, and 75 percent receive a clean bill of health." She smiled at Helen compassionately. "There's no reason to get overly concerned."

Helen clutched the hospital gown. "I know the statistics," she replied. "But my sister, mother, and grandmother have all had breast cancer. And I'm probably next—" Her voice broke off.

"Mrs. Tucker," the nurse encouraged, "think positively about the 75 percent who *don't* have cancer when they think they might. Besides, you haven't even been examined yet."

Helen stared at the white tile floor. She didn't need to be examined—somehow, she already knew the diagnosis would be cancer. *Lord,* she prayed, *please stay close to me. I don't know if I can handle this.*

The nurse left the room. Helen's hands trembled as she changed into the gown and climbed onto the cold, hard examining table. A few minutes later, the nurse reentered with Dr. Rose.

"Hello, Mrs. Tucker," Dr. Rose greeted her warmly. He sat in a chair across from Helen and asked her a series of questions, taking notes and nodding from time to time. After Helen had described the lump and told him her family history, Dr. Rose put down her chart. "Now," he said calmly, looking at her over the rim of his glasses, "why don't you locate the lump for me?"

The nurse stood by while Dr. Rose probed the lump, his brow furrowed. "Okay, that's all for now," he said finally. "When you're finished dressing, we'll meet in my office."

Several minutes later Helen and Tuck—who had been summoned from the waiting room—sat facing Dr. Rose. Helen glanced nervously at Tuck. His face, although calm, was pale, and he was gripping Helen's hand.

"The lump is probably malignant," Dr. Rose began. "Its hardness and large size are almost sure signs that it's cancer."

The blood drained from Helen's face, and her eyes widened in fear. *I am next in the family,* she thought weakly. It felt as though Dr. Rose had given her a death sentence—and Helen wished the chair could swallow her up.

Dr. Rose sighed, his spectacled eyes filled with compassion. "I could be wrong," he continued. "It may prove to be nothing significant at all. At any rate, I've scheduled you for a biopsy next week on January 11th."

Tuck simply tightened his grip on Helen's hand and nodded to the doctor. "We'll see you then."

As Helen left the office, her thoughts were a blur. *I have eight days to sit and stew before the biopsy?* she realized miserably. *What will I do with all that time?*

Helen tried to keep busy rather than contemplate how drastically her life was going to change. She read her Bible, confessed her sins, and talked with God, trying valiantly to keep focused on Him rather than on her upcoming surgery. But the week actually proved to be a blessing, giving Helen time to fast and pray. She wanted to be prepared for her surgery, no matter what the outcome. *God,* she prayed repeatedly, *if it's Your plan to heal me, I ask that You do so. But I want Your purpose to be fulfilled in my life, whatever it is.*

As the date drew closer, Tuck tried hard not to dwell on Helen's biopsy, hoping to retain some sort of normalcy in their lives—and prevent his wife from worrying. The night before Helen was to go to the hospital, they sat quietly at the dinner table, picking at their food. They didn't share their usual chitchat about how their day had gone—none of it seemed very important.

After the dinner table was cleared, Tuck handed her an exquisitely wrapped box of her favorite perfume. As he leaned across the table, his eyes were soft. "I know you're scared, honey," he told her, "but God will take care of you. He loves you, and He'll be with you during the surgery tomorrow."

Helen's tears fell onto the green tissue paper. "Thank you, Tuck," she whispered, more for the comfort than for the perfume. She was feeling more at peace already. It was true—God *would* help them through this.

༄

*T*he day of Helen's check-in, January 10, brought blustery winds and freezing temperatures. The mood inside the hospital matched the gloomy weather. Tuck and Helen spent the day filling out paperwork, while the doctor prepared her for the biopsy. Dr. Rose informed Helen that if the lump was malignant, as he expected, she would have to undergo an immediate mastectomy—the only option available. Helen's eyes smarted at the thought. She'd always taken great delight in her femininity and enjoyed making herself beautiful for her husband.

The next morning, Helen lay on the operating table while Tuck waited in the hall with two of their close friends. Dr. Rose worked quickly, performing the biopsy and rushing the tissue mass to the pathology department. Minutes later, he returned to the operating room with the report. Dr. Rose gently placed his hand over hers. "I'm sorry," he said. "It's malignant. We'll have to operate."

Still drowsy from the anesthetic, Helen nodded her head limply—but the reality of the situation overwhelmed her. She would have to undergo a mastectomy. She closed her eyes, trying to shut out the bad news. *I wish Tuck were here,* she thought weakly.

Minutes later, Helen felt the prick of the needle, then she felt nothing. She lay unconscious while the surgeons performed a radical mastectomy, removing many of her chest and underarm muscles. The skin was then pulled back over her chest, and the wound was closed with 137 stitches. The surgery, however, didn't guarantee that Helen would be cancer-free. She would just have to wait and see whether it was successful.

When she awakened many hours later, Helen discovered she was attached to two machines—one hooked up to each arm—that simultaneously pumped medication into, and drained blood out of, her body. The drugs numbed her mind but not her body. Even moving her fingers was agonizing. And when the nurses changed her bandages, she fainted several times from the excruciating pain.

Helen spent most of the first postoperative day lying quietly in bed, struggling to endure the pain and to think clearly. Parts of Scripture materialized in her mind, and she whispered incoherent phrases of promises from

God as outside, freezing rain and sleet fell against the hospital windowpanes. A ruddy-faced Tuck returned to her room that night, wearing a soaking overcoat that was covered with frost. Not knowing how best to comfort his wife, he sat beside her bed, singing softly to her.

*She's so pale, but she smiled at me,* he thought, his eyes burning at the sight of Helen hooked up to machines. *Lord, please heal her,* he prayed. *She means so much to me.* Struggling to hold back tears, Tuck lightly rested his forehead against her fingers for a moment and felt the softness of the blue blanket around her. Tuck looked up as he felt her fingers lightly touch his forehead. She knew and understood what he was feeling—he was sure of it.

The second night after her surgery, Helen was more alert and suggested that they recite Psalm 23 together. She needed to focus on something other than her pain and her fears about the future.

"The Lord is my shepherd; I shall not want. . . ." As they spoke the words, Helen felt God's peace wash over her, and suddenly, she wasn't worried or frightened anymore. Whatever happened, God was with her—she either had heaven to look forward to or a continuing life with her husband. She glanced over at Tuck.

His voice trembled as he recited, "Yea, though I walk through the valley of the shadow of death . . ." Tuck's face was pinched, as if he were holding back a stream of emotion. Years ago, Helen had nicknamed him Coolman Luke; but he didn't fit that name right now.

Helen stopped midsentence. "Tuck, I'm not afraid to die."

Tuck turned away, biting his lip. "You aren't? I don't see how that's possible."

"But it's true. The Lord has taken my fear."

Tuck stared at the stark white hospital wall. It seemed that each waking moment, he had to fight the terror of losing her. They had been together for decades; how could he face life without his partner? *Lord,* he prayed desperately, *please don't take her from me. I need Helen.*

But no one knew what to expect, even the doctors. Helen's condition was frail, and if she did recover from such radical surgery, it would take many months. Dr. Rose told her that during the next year, her body would feel as if it were encased in an iron vest. One entire side of her body would be immovable and rigid until it slowly healed, which would result only from disciplined, painful exercise. This would prove to be the most difficult hurdle she had to overcome.

As the reality of Helen's medical condition settled in, both she and Tuck knew their marriage—the chemistry, the physical relationship, the hope for tomorrow—had changed forever. Now, after the mastectomy, Helen felt unappealing and marred. *Dr. Rose probably sliced all the way to the bone,* she often thought, shuddering. *I must look awful underneath these bandages. Will Tuck still think I'm beautiful?*

It was a terrifying thought. Tuck had always been an attentive, loving husband—he sometimes called himself a "true-blue, one-woman man" to make her laugh—but even so, Helen couldn't help but wonder if he'd find her attractive again.

A few days after Helen's surgery, an ice storm swept through the Carolinas and left Tuck with a stubborn cold so severe that doctors thought he had first-stage pneumonia. The pressure of working full-time, visiting Helen at the hospital late at night, and worrying about his wife's health had taken its toll. Tuck walked into her room one evening, unable to contain his emotion any longer.

"I don't think I can stand much more of this!" he cried out. Tuck dabbed his feverish forehead with a handkerchief. "I'm either going to collapse from this cold, or you're going to leave me, and I can't bear the thought of either one happening!" He sank into a chair next to her bed and lay his head on the blanket near her feet, crying softly.

Helen's eyes filled with tears. She didn't know what to say. In their 35 years of marriage, she'd only seen Tuck cry once, when his father died.

"I . . . j-just . . . can't take this anymore," Tuck choked out between sobs. His shoulders were shaking inside his soaking, navy-blue pinstripe suit.

Helen lay helplessly in bed, wishing she could wrap her arms around her husband. "Oh, Tuck," she began, then hesitated, trying to find the right words.

Tuck sighed, frustrated. "I should be encouraging *you*, not the other way around," he said, clenching the handkerchief until his knuckles were white. *I'm a terrible husband—a failure,* he thought despondently.

Helen's heart swelled with love for Tuck; her unflappable husband had finally lost his cool. "You've been wonderful," she whispered, exhausted. "But there's nothing either of us can do now except trust God."

∽✕∾

After two long weeks, the doctors released Helen from the hospital. She was still extremely weak, but a flu epidemic had infiltrated the hospital, and Dr. Rose didn't want Helen exposed. Her immune system was too weak—it was safer for her to stay at home. Tuck, who had finally recovered from his terrible cold, settled his wife on the living room couch.

"I'm going to make lunch," he said cheerfully, tucking a blanket up around her chin.

Helen cringed. Tuck didn't cook; he burned everything, even toast! "I'll give you a hand," she insisted.

"No," said Tuck, "Dr. Rose gave strict orders—total bed rest for two more weeks."

"Well, okay," Helen said skeptically. From the sofa she watched him bustle about in the kitchen, a disaster in the making. The refrigerator door swung wide open, the stove burners glowed, and water cascaded from the faucet. A few minutes later, Tuck triumphantly returned to the family room bearing a brass gallery tray with the results of his culinary efforts. In a plastic bowl, unappetizing crimson lumps swam in lukewarm swirls of pink liquid.

Helen arched her eyebrows.

"Tomato soup, Campbell's finest," Tuck said in defense of the meal. Beside the bowl was what looked like a year's supply of graham crackers, along with a dill pickle and cold glass of milk.

Helen smiled ruefully as she took the tray, thinking, *Oh, well, at least he tried. Maybe I can convince him to actually stir the soup next time he makes it.*

Life at home after Helen's surgery was an adjustment for the Tuckers, in more ways than one. Later that afternoon, as another snowstorm bore down on Raleigh, Tuck rushed out of the house to purchase essential supplies at the drugstore. Helen turned on the TV, where local news anchors issued dire warnings about a record snowfall, impassable roads, and power failures. She drifted off to sleep; when she awoke, Tuck was dumping his purchases on the nearest chair.

"The power is off," he said. "We don't have any heat, and the woodpile is frozen." His hard, unemotional attorney voice had taken over. "I'm going outside to see if I can find any dry wood."

Helen watched her husband put on his overcoat and hunting boots before he left abruptly. His colleagues had nicknamed him "Unflappable Tuck." *Well, they should see him now,* she thought, hurt. Here she was, facing a major crisis, and her stoic husband had left her feeling helpless, afraid, and alone. Helen shifted uncomfortably on the couch, feeling nauseated and irritable from the pain medication. *Tuck didn't kiss me or even say hello,* she thought sadly. *He knows my throat is sore and that he should take my temperature, but he didn't even ask me how I feel.*

Minutes later the door slammed again, and Tuck walked in with an armload of wood. He sprang into action, making a fire in the hearth. Helen bit her lip, her disappointment flaring again. Suddenly, though, it seemed God was reminding her, *Helen, I chose Tuck for you because I knew he would always take good care of you. This is his way of loving you right now.*

Helen cringed, ashamed of her self-pitying thoughts. It was true. Tuck *did* care for her—and God loved her even more. *Lord, forgive me,* she prayed silently. *Thank You for making me feel wanted and needed. Thank You for showing me Your love.* She dabbed at her eyes as God's peace filled her once again.

Helen would recall those feelings of thankfulness many times in the difficult days and weeks that were to come. Bed rest was only one small step in the recovery process; there were also every-other-day doctor appointments in which the nurse had to insert a needle into her wound and drain the blood, then rebandage her. Several times she lost consciousness during the procedure due to the pain. Her wounds were so sensitive she couldn't be hugged—in fact, she could hardly be touched. Even the slightest pressure against her scarred body produced agony. As a result, she and Tuck had to sleep in separate rooms.

Both Helen and Tuck missed the intimacy of pillow talk, but found other ways to make up for it. Each evening when Tuck arrived home from work, he would sit at the foot of the couch where Helen slept and gently rub her feet for an hour. Helen knew that Tuck liked to simply relax after a long day in court, and she appreciated his sacrificial gesture of love.

Meanwhile, Tuck dealt with the emotional aspect of the crisis by burying himself in his work. He was adept at masking his feelings—an essential skill for a trial attorney. Just once, shortly after his wife's surgery, Tuck brought his anxieties about Helen to work with him; he failed a client, unable to provide the man a proper defense. After that experience, Tuck vowed he'd never let his fears take control again. He knew worrying wouldn't help her anyway.

As Helen's strength gradually returned, she felt a growing desire to put her arms around Tuck's neck and hold him close—but her physical pain and insecurity about her body kept her at a distance. An affectionate, demonstrative woman, she yearned to be held by her husband, but was afraid to initiate even a hug. She wasn't just afraid of the pain; someday Tuck would see her scars, and then what would he think? Would he want to even touch her after that?

One afternoon, a few weeks after the surgery, Helen came out of the guest room to see Tuck walking down the hall just in front of her. He was wearing the blue sweater she'd given him for Christmas. Helen stopped, her heart thudding. His chestnut hair looked almost mahogany. *I even love the shape of his head,* she thought suddenly. *It's beautiful.*

"Tuck, wait a minute," she said, her voice catching a little.

Tuck turned around, his pale blue eyes gentle. "Yes?"

"I have such a desire to touch you," said Helen.

Tuck said nothing and stood as still as a toy soldier. He had wanted to be physically affectionate with his wife, of course, but knew he needed to wait for Helen to heal—both emotionally and physically.

Helen took a deep breath, willing herself to walk slowly toward Tuck. Placing her good arm around his waist, she very gently and carefully squeezed him. Without speaking, she nestled her cheek against his shoulder, content just to be near her husband. They stood there in silence for several minutes, basking in the intimacy of that simple gesture.

In the following weeks, Helen continued to heal. The doctors gave her a positive prognosis, and each day she grew stronger as she worked to regain the use of her arm, where so many muscles had been removed. She practiced raising her arm a few inches at a time, measuring her progress on the doorpost. With time the pain lessened. Soon she and Tuck were able to sleep in the same bed again, carefully cuddling at night.

But while Helen was progressing physically, she continued to worry about her scars. Tuck still hadn't seen her without her bandages. *Will he be repulsed?* she wondered.

Finally, feeling braver and stronger, Helen resolved to find out how he felt. One evening as Tuck relaxed in the family room reading court briefs, Helen decided it was time. She walked nervously into the bedroom and, with trembling fingers, took off her blouse. As she'd begun to heal, her bandage had gotten smaller and now covered only part of her chest. There would be no mistaking her scars. *This is it,* Helen thought, her stomach in knots. *In a minute I'll know Tuck's true feelings.*

Taking a deep breath, she padded down the hallway and into the family room. There she stood before Tuck, who was stretched out on the couch, reading. His eyes widened in surprise when he saw his wife, and he quickly set down the stack of papers.

Silently, her heart pounding rapidly, Helen raised her right hand high in the air. She winced—it was still a bit painful. She had spent hours doing exercises to regain use of the arm.

She held her breath. Six weeks had passed since the operation, and now the truth was out in the open. There was no escaping the missing breast, the reddish lines from the stitches, and the discolored skin grafts. She lowered her arm, waiting for him to respond.

Startled, Tuck jumped out of his chair. He flew across the room to embrace his wife, holding her as tightly as he could without hurting her. He closed his eyes. "Thank You, Jesus," he cried out, "for this precious wife of mine. Thank You for the years You've given us, for the two sons You blessed us with, and for the ways You've enriched our lives." Tuck paused, his voice wavering. "Lord, You have worked an incredible healing in my wife. Now I pray this cancer never returns. Amen."

Helen felt Tuck's warm tears running down her neck, and she began to sob happily as well. She knew that in time the scars would fade. More importantly, Tuck accepted her the way she was! Still held tightly in his embrace, Helen tilted her head up toward her husband.

"Tuck?" she whispered.

Tuck smoothed her hair back. "Yes, Helen?"

She smiled softly. "You were right," she said, referring to the words of encouragement Tuck had spoken weeks earlier. "God will never fail us."

And this time, they both knew—without doubt—that it was true.

⚮

*Helen Tucker's cancer has never returned. Helen says she and Tuck didn't always understand where the Lord was taking them, but they always knew they could count on the love He'd provided—for each other and for Him.*

*Today, Helen is trusting in God's provision and guidance even more deeply. While this story was being written, Irvin Tucker unexpectedly passed away in his sleep. Now Helen awaits her reunion with Tuck in heaven.*

# *Your Path to Always*

I must say I'm extremely impressed with the way both Helen and Irvin Tucker handled the crisis of her breast cancer. Helen, first of all, displayed a mature, powerful faith in God that gave her great peace about her uncertain future. As she said, everything that happens to those of us who love God is first filtered through Him. Nothing happens that He doesn't know about and that He can't turn to some kind of good, which is the promise of Romans 8:28. He has that incomparable way of working through trials to make us more loving, patient, and able to help others in trouble. Helen certainly demonstrated that through her response to cancer.

By pursuing our own relationship with God through prayer, worship, and the study of His Word, we can develop the same kind of faith and enjoy the same kind of peace when trials come our way.

It's good to do what we can, of course, to avoid the trial of breast cancer. My friend Dr. Joni Scott, a surgeon and breast cancer specialist, urges women to have annual mammograms, which can now detect cancers in the earliest stages (1 to 2 millimeters). When cancers are caught at less than 10 millimeters, she says, 95 percent are "completely curable."

As for the husband's role in a breast cancer crisis, Irvin Tucker was a model; I wish every husband were like him. He comforted Helen, gave her hope, and encouraged her through scriptures like Luke 12 (starting in verse 22) that talk about how God is going to meet all our needs, no matter what happens. When she needed assurance after surgery that he still found her attractive and desirable, he let her know clearly and beautifully that she was always and forever the love of his life.

Dr. Scott recommends that husbands of women with breast cancer always take part in discussions with the physician, attend treatment sessions, take their wives hat shopping or wig shopping before the hair falls out as a result of chemotherapy, and generally give all the support they can throughout the process. She tries as well to get them involved early in support groups and in contact with others who have been down the same road and are willing to discuss their experiences.

Getting help from others is a vital part of enduring health crises. Whether it's support groups of people with common experiences or loved ones helping with practical things like shopping and house cleaning, such assistance can make a huge difference. In the Tuckers' case, Irvin was able to care for Helen's physical needs after her surgery, fixing meals and so on, and many times other family, friends, or fellow church members help out as well.

One of the best ways others can help is by their prayers. Christians have always believed in the power of prayer. But now, Dr. Scott tells me, scientific studies are proving that sick people who are prayed for do "remarkably better" than those who are not. She has seen this in her own medical practice as well. Let's be eager, then, to pray for others who are ill or otherwise struggling, and to ask for the prayers of others when we're the ones in need.

Finally, Helen Tucker's experience brings to mind 1 Peter 3:3-5, which tells wives, "Your beauty should not come from outward adornment, such as braided hair and the wearing of gold jewelry and fine clothes. Instead, it should be that of your inner self, the unfading beauty of a gentle and quiet spirit, which is of great worth in God's sight. For this is the way the holy women of the past who put their hope in God used to make themselves beautiful."

Like all women dealing with disfiguring surgery, Helen had concerns about her postoperative appearance, especially in her husband's eyes. But what she actually got as a result of the cancer was a *greater* beauty in her heart—the inner beauty spoken of in 1 Peter 3 —which Tuck could see in her eyes and on her face.

That's real beauty. Thus, the very thing Helen feared losing, she actually got more of because of her ordeal. And it will grow through any major trial if we're open to letting God work in us through His Holy Spirit in grace.

—Gary Smalley

# $\mathcal{F}$ROM THE $\mathcal{A}$SHES

*Pete and Julia Flannery**

MARRIED IN 1968

*Names have been changed.

"*N*ow, Sweetie," Pete Flannery said to his fiancée, "did you really think it was necessary to tell the Vanderbilts your father never went to high school?" He glanced into the rearview mirror and loosened the bow tie on his tuxedo, waiting for her response.

Julia Farnsworth stared down at the simple black dress she'd made to wear to the benefit that evening. *I guess I said the wrong thing—again,* she thought, shifting awkwardly in her seat. "I was just trying to make conversation," she explained quietly.

"Well, you don't need to tell them *everything* about yourself." Pete tightened his grip on the steering wheel. "I'm just trying to protect you, Julia. I don't want you to look bad."

"Sure," Julia whispered through tears. She knew that wasn't entirely true. Pete loved her, but as usual he was really trying to protect himself—which was also why he hadn't told anyone about their engagement. With most of Pete's friends and family attending the benefit, tonight would have been the perfect opportunity to make the announcement. Pete had remained silent, though. And Julia knew why.

He was stalling.

It was no secret that his wealthy and powerful social circle didn't approve of her. To them, she was only a poor, uneducated girl who had captured Pete with her beauty—someone who might be okay to date once in a while, but certainly not marriage material.

Julia twisted in the bucket seat and looked at Pete, wounded. "Do you *ever* plan on telling people we're engaged?"

"Of course," Pete said. But he swallowed hard. When he'd proposed to Julia the week before, his intentions had been honorable; now he was feeling more and more nervous about marrying her. All evening, as Pete had hobnobbed with Miami's elite, he had worried, *What will my parents and friends think when they find out Julia and I are engaged?*

He wasn't sure he wanted to know. Each time he had worked up the courage to tell his friends and family, he was haunted by images of their disapproving eyes and plastic smiles.

In the seat next to him, Julia studied her ringless finger and took a deep, quavering breath. She was determined to know where things stood. "Okay . . . then what about a ring?"

"I'm sorry," murmured Pete. His voice was hollow. "I just haven't gotten around to it."

Julia felt nauseated. As soon as Pete had proposed, she'd abruptly left a promising career as a flight attendant in Nashville to move back to Miami. *Why did I come back?* she berated herself. She had transferred to Tennessee just six months earlier to escape their tumultuous, two-and-a-half year relationship. Julia had decided that if Pete wasn't willing to be serious about her, she would move on with her life. But she had never expected him to miss her, and she certainly hadn't anticipated a proposal. So when Pete had called her in Nashville, begging her to come back and marry him, Julia believed his proposal was valid. *Maybe,* she'd hoped, *he's finally changed.*

But now it looked as though Pete hadn't truly meant to follow through. She tried to ignore the fluttering in her stomach. "Well, can we set a date?"

Pete responded vaguely: "Oh, we will." He pulled up to her apartment and stopped the car.

"When?"

Pete didn't answer for several minutes. Things were getting too complicated, he thought. He'd hoped the engagement would stretch out for a few years, but now Julia was pressing him for answers he wasn't ready to give.

Still, he had to say something. *I can't keep doing this to her,* he told himself. "Julia . . ." he began slowly, "I just can't go through with this. I wouldn't treat you fairly. It's not right." His brown eyes begged forgiveness.

Julia stared at him in the darkness, her cheeks flushed in humiliation. She had already told her family and friends the reason she'd come back: to marry Pete. "How can you do this to me?" she cried. "You're going to chicken out because of your snooty friends? Doesn't it mean anything that I left my new job—my new life—for you?"

Pete was silent.

It was the final blow. Julia felt her chest tighten, and she couldn't breathe. The inside of the car seemed to spin, so she pushed open the door and stepped into the fresh, balmy air. Eyes brimming, she glared at Pete. "I just can't believe you. This is it. We're completely over. I don't ever want to talk to you again!" She slammed the door of his red sports car and ran, stumbling, into her apartment.

Pete dropped his head on the steering wheel. He felt like a rat. Julia was the only woman he'd ever truly loved, and once again, he had pushed her away.

⚮

Julia was devastated by their broken engagement. For months she refused to take Pete's phone calls, trying to move on with her life.

Pete tried to heal, too. He casually dated other women, hoping to find someone who could help him take his mind off Julia. But nobody even came close to measuring up to her. He and Julia were well suited for one another, and Pete knew it. Her easygoing, down-to-earth personality complemented his structured approach to life. Six years older, he was also attracted to her charming naiveté—not something he'd often encountered among the Miami socialites his parents had encouraged him to pursue.

*I can't be any more miserable being married to Julia than I am when we're not together,* he reasoned. *Maybe it's time to make a commitment.* It wasn't the best reason to propose, but Pete knew he couldn't continue living as he had, lonely and desperate to be with her. He continued sending Julia flowers and notes of apology—but she did not respond.

Finally, six months after the breakup, he unexpectedly showed up at her apartment. "You've got to see me," Pete demanded through the closed door.

Julia peered through the peephole, her heart thudding. Neither of her roommates was there. *If I don't speak to him, he'll never leave me alone,* she thought. With a sigh of resignation she opened the door. "What do you want?" she asked. Then, seeing him standing there, she raised her eyebrows in surprise.

Pete looked terrible. His face was pale; dark circles shadowed his eyes. He leaned against the doorframe, running his hand nervously through his dark brown hair. "I can't take this anymore," he said. "I want for us to get married."

Julia rolled her eyes. She'd heard that line before. "I'll believe it when I see a ring," she said flatly.

"Then I'll be back with one," he promised.

That evening he returned to her apartment with a ring and a bouquet of flowers. Julia's mouth dropped open when she saw the ring box.

"Julia," he pleaded, "I can't stand living without you. I'm totally falling apart. You've got to marry me."

She blinked, unsure what to say. "Are you serious?"

Pete nodded.

"What about your family?" she asked. "You know they'd never approve."

Pete stared glumly at the floor. Finally he spoke. "My parents just want what's best for me. When they realize it's you, they'll come around."

"Well," Julia said, then paused. *After all we've been through, shouldn't there be more to it than this?* She looked at Pete. He didn't appear desperately in love; he appeared *desperate*. The magic wasn't there. But somehow, even with all her doubts about their relationship, Julia couldn't tell him no. She loved him. "Okay," she agreed uneasily. "I'll marry you."

ete and Julia were betrothed for six weeks. Their engagement was just as rocky as their courtship had been. As Julia had predicted, Pete's parents were unhappy with his decision. They were always polite to their future daughter-in-law, but there was no mistaking their disappointment. Julia could read it in their awkward, formal greetings and long silences. Throughout the engagement and until the day of the wedding, Pete's mother quietly tried to change his mind. Mrs. Flannery even pulled her son aside hours before the wedding ceremony to remind him that it wasn't too late to back out.

All of this chipped away at Pete's confidence in the relationship and at Julia's self-esteem. Throughout their first year of marriage she felt as though she were on probation, while Pete wondered if he'd made the right choice.

Three years after their wedding, however, Julia became pregnant with their first child. After number one was born, two more arrived in quick succession. Suddenly Pete transformed into a doting father and loving husband. This marriage, he finally understood, was for real. Now Julia was more than the woman he'd married out of desperation. She was also the mother of his children.

The Flannerys settled into a dream home in an exclusive neighborhood. Pete's real estate business flourished as Julia cared for their three young children. The birth of their son and two daughters not only brought them together as a family, but also cemented their spiritual commitments. Soon they began attending a growing church in their neighborhood. Pete became a deacon, and Julia regularly participated in women's Bible studies and other church activities.

Finally their life together seemed to be getting more comfortable. As the years passed, Pete's parents thawed toward Julia, and Pete no longer worried that his wife didn't fit into his privileged world. They enjoyed taking trips together, playing tennis at the club, and raising their children. It was more than Pete ever thought their marriage would be.

But their tumultuous history had left a deep imprint on Julia. Regardless of the improvements in their relationship, she still felt unappreciated, unworthy, and insecure. It seemed as though Pete were always waiting for her to "slip up."

Years later, Julia would ponder whether that was why she actually did.

⟨◦⟩

"  *I*'m going over to play a quick game of Nintendo with Rolf," Pete called over his shoulder.

Julia put her hands on her hips and frowned. She had just put Emily, Joshua, and Allie to bed and was hoping to have some quiet time alone with her husband. "Wait! We haven't had any time to talk today!" she protested.

But the front door had already shut.

Sighing, Julia walked upstairs to their bedroom. In her 10 years of marriage to Pete, she had never felt so tired and neglected. A few months before, Pete had caught hepatitis A on a trip to Mexico; the illness had left him exhausted, depressed, and grumpy. Nowadays the only time Pete seemed to have energy was when he went to work—or when he walked next door to see Rolf, their friend and neighbor. Like Pete, Rolf was a successful entrepreneur; both men saw the friendship as a business opportunity.

Julia liked Rolf and Lisa Hartman, who had moved to their community just six months before. But on nights like these, Julia saw Pete and Rolf's growing friendship as a thorn in her marriage. She punched the pillow.

Several hours later she was awakened by a tickle on her neck. It was Pete, who had just arrived home. Julia pushed his nose away and squinted at the clock. It was 11:00. "It's late," she said.

Pete tousled his wife's brown, wavy hair. "I was just trying to say hi."

"Well, I was just trying to sleep," Julia mumbled. "You should have been here two hours ago if you wanted to be intimate." She rolled over. *I just don't understand him,* she thought. *He finally feels healthy enough to get out of bed, and he goes over to see Rolf! I must be at the bottom of his priority list.*

Pete shook his head, confused. "I'm home *now,*" he muttered, but got no response. It was obvious, he thought—Julia just didn't understand why it was so important for him to spend time with Rolf.

When Pete recovered from hepatitis, the Flannerys began doing more things with the Hartmans. The couples discovered they had a lot in common. They attended the same church; their children were the same ages; they enjoyed taking trips together, playing mixed doubles matches in tennis, and going out to dinner. Rolf and Pete made some investments together, and Lisa and Julia began their own pottery business.

As Julia spent more time with their neighbors, her resentment toward Rolf began to fade. A charismatic, jovial person, he always seemed interested in her life, fascinated with her blue-collar upbringing. Rolf was impressed with the way Julia had supported herself as a young, single woman, a stark contrast to how Pete had viewed her background. Not only that, but Rolf was a good listener. Much better, Julia often noted, than Pete, whose eyes tended to glaze over after she'd talked for longer than 10 minutes. Lisa sometimes complained to Julia that her husband was overbearing, but Julia secretly wondered why her friend wasn't thankful.

As the friendship progressed, Julia realized she almost had more in common with Rolf than with Lisa or Pete. They both enjoyed working in the yard, exchanging gardening tips, and discussing home improvement techniques. They were compatible tennis partners, too. When the couples played mixed doubles, Julia and Rolf paired off against Pete and Lisa. None of them thought much of the arrangement; it made the game more competitive.

Yet it was on the tennis court that Julia noticed the first spark.

ulia stretched her racket over her head and hit the tennis ball with forceful precision. She and Rolf waited on one side of the net, watching as Lisa dove for the ball. When Lisa stumbled and hit the ball into the net, they let out cries of victory.

"We won!" Julia exclaimed, running over to high-five Rolf.

Rolf draped his arm around her shoulders as they walked to the net to shake hands with Pete and Lisa. "Nice shot!" he said warmly, squeezing Julia's arm. Then he flashed his blinding-white smile at her.

Julia inhaled sharply. Rolf usually gave her a side-hug and a compliment when they won a game, but this time his tone and actions felt different— more affectionate somehow. Quickly she pulled away to shake hands with her husband. But she could still feel the warmth of Rolf's hand on her arm after he let go.

Julia pushed her feelings aside. *He wasn't coming on to you,* she assured herself. The hug was a normal gesture, not out of place on the tennis court. She glanced at Pete, then Lisa. They were laughing while Rolf good-naturedly teased them about losing the game. Obviously they hadn't noticed anything.

Julia relaxed. It must have been her imagination.

But as the weeks passed, she began to wonder. One day after a tennis match, Rolf leaned close to Julia and whispered jokingly, "I heard Pete's going out of town next weekend on Valentine's Day. Maybe I'll stop by."

Julia tried to laugh it off. *I'm sure he's kidding*, she reasoned. *If he were serious, he wouldn't say something like that with Pete and Lisa around.*

When Valentine's Day arrived, Rolf didn't come over—but he did place a red card covered with hearts in her mailbox. It read: "I'm your secret valentine. Love, Rolf." Julia's cheeks flushed when she read the card. Nervously she hurried back into the house, stashing the valentine in the drawer of her nightstand. Pete wouldn't be back until the next day, but she wanted to be careful. *I don't want Pete to get upset over nothing*, she told herself.

*And that's all it is. Nothing.*

Even so, her heart raced whenever she thought about the card. It made her nervous, but excited, too. She found it flattering that someone as successful and handsome as Rolf might find her attractive.

But she was determined to put Rolf out of her mind. After all, she was a married woman. She and Pete were pillars of the church. This was just an innocent flirtation between two friends who enjoyed each other's company . . . wasn't it?

Julia kept the card a secret from Pete and avoided the topic with Rolf. What if—as she suspected—it had been a joke after all? If she asked Rolf about it and he'd been kidding, she would look foolish. Worse, what if he had been serious and was secretly in love with her? Then what would she do? It would be best, Julia decided, to say nothing.

Several weeks later the two couples took a weekend trip to San Diego, where the men attended a business convention while Julia and Lisa shopped. In the evening the Flannerys and Hartmans were invited to a dinner party, hosted by a business associate. The host split up the married couples to make the evening more "social," so Julia found herself at a large, round table next to Rolf. Pete and Lisa were across from them.

Not knowing many people there, Julia and Rolf ended up talking to each other during most of the dinner, oblivious to everyone around them. Late in the evening Rolf set down his dessert spoon and turned to Julia.

"After Pete turns in, what are you doin' tonight?" he asked, grinning.

Julia blushed and punched him playfully on the shoulder. "Very funny, Rolf."

Rolf smiled and shrugged across the table at Pete, who returned his grin. Then, still looking in Pete's direction, he slowly reached over and massaged Julia on the knee, letting his hand linger.

This time there was no question in Julia's mind what he wanted. She felt a surge of adrenaline. *He shouldn't be doing this!* she thought. *I should take his hand off my leg.* But somehow she couldn't get herself to do it. She felt like a teenager on her first date, with clammy hands and a jittery stomach. Julia glanced over at her husband. He and Lisa were enjoying their dessert, not even looking in their direction.

So she let Rolf's hand stay there.

 ⟨✳⟩

"*We* need to talk," Rolf's voice boomed down at Julia. She looked up and dropped her gardening shovel, her pulse racing. It had been three days since they'd returned from San Diego; she and Rolf hadn't talked since. She scrambled to her feet, wiped her hands on her old "weeding" shorts, and nodded vigorously.

"You're right," she said, flooded with both relief and disappointment. Mixed feelings had plagued her since San Diego; half of her wanted to stop the flirting before things really heated up, while the other half was drawn to Rolf, the handsome business mogul who found her so attractive. She was glad Rolf wanted to talk about what happened; she thought it meant he didn't want things to get out of hand. *I'm glad at least he's come to his senses. It makes things much easier this way.*

They decided to meet in a local park for lunch the following day. When Julia arrived, though, her green eyes grew large. Rolf was sitting on a park bench, holding a dozen red roses and a bottle of champagne. He broke into a wide, charming smile as he held the bouquet out to her.

"These, my beautiful, are for you."

Julia glanced nervously around the park. "I can't take these, Rolf!" she hissed. "I thought you wanted to put the brakes on things."

His face flickered surprise. "Are you kidding?" he said. "You have to know how attracted I am to you! I can't help myself." Rolf lightly took her hand. "I only wish I could have met you sooner, Julia. You're a beautiful, strong, intelligent woman! Pete is so lucky to be married to you."

Blushing, Julia felt another adrenaline surge. "Oh . . . well . . ." she fumbled. It was exhilarating to be complimented. She'd worked so hard to gain her husband's approval, but didn't even need to try with Rolf. He already thought she was interesting and attractive. He accepted her as she was.

During the following weeks Rolf sent her notes, asking Julia to just "meet for lunch, to talk." Every time she dismissed the idea and called him to say no—only to be won over by his flattery. Soon they were lunching in the park every Thursday.

*I'm not doing anything wrong,* Julia told herself each time she saw Rolf. *We're just a couple of good friends who like to talk. I can stop this at any time.*

But she didn't stop. And despite her rationalizing, Julia knew deep down that she was speeding toward disaster. Her relationship with Rolf was crazy and wrong. Pete had his faults, but he was a good man—and Julia was constantly lying to him about where she'd been. How could there be any good in that?

She felt horrible about what she was doing, but somehow Rolf always lured her back. For months they continued to have picnics in the park, while spending time with their spouses as couples.

One hot June day as the two of them had lunch, Rolf fanned himself with his hand and said, "Julia, we can't keep meeting outside in this heat."

It was almost 100 degrees; Julia had to admit that she felt sticky, uncomfortable. She slapped a mosquito on her leg and shifted on the blanket. "I don't know . . . " she said uneasily.

Rolf traced her chin with his finger. "Baby," he said, "I'm only trying to think of what's best for us. Look around." He motioned at the empty park. "We're the only ones crazy enough to be outside in this heat. I'll rent a nice, cool apartment for us, and we'll have our lunches there for the summer."

Julia bit her lip, her stomach doing flip-flops. As long as the affair wasn't physical, she could justify it. But she knew what would happen if they started meeting indoors. *I can't do that!* she thought. *I should stop this whole thing right now.* She glanced up at Rolf. He was gazing at her with his piercing blue eyes, waiting for her answer. Her heart pounded, and she felt another rush of exhilaration. How could she say no?

"Well . . ." Julia hesitated. Then she said, "Okay, I guess you're right. We'll meet inside next week."

The last roadblock was gone.

∽✕∾

*P*ete leaned back in the patio chair, hands clasped behind his head, and gazed at the Montana sunset. Somewhere in the pastures of the dude ranch, Emily, Joshua, and Allie were horseback riding. They'd left immediately after dinner, eager to explore. Now Pete and Julia were alone. "This is great, isn't it?" he said softly to his wife.

Julia pushed the tiramisu around on her dessert plate and sighed. "Uh-huh."

Pete looked at her and frowned. He'd hoped the family vacation would provide time for them to reconnect—but Julia had been quiet, distant. *I hope I haven't said or done anything to upset her,* Pete worried. "What's wrong, Sweetie?" he asked. "You haven't been yourself all week."

"Oh, it's nothing, really." Julia looked away. *Except that I'm a slimeball for cheating on you with your best friend,* she thought. Her emotions were frayed. Being with Pete made her feel guilty, sometimes enough to end the now-physical affair. But when she and Rolf were together, she could never gather the strength to let go. It felt too good to be with someone who openly adored her.

Pete shook his head. "I don't know what's going on," he admitted, "but whatever it is, I want to love you through it."

"If you really knew me, you wouldn't say that," Julia murmured, still staring at her uneaten dessert. Her voice was almost inaudible. "You wouldn't love me either."

Pete brushed her statement aside. "You're obviously upset," he said, leaning on his elbows. "Why don't you go to counseling if you need to work through some things? I'll even come with you."

Julia tapped her fingers on the table, thinking. Counseling was a possibility. She and Pete could work on some of their issues; if they had individual appointments as well, she might be able to run her dilemma past the counselor. "Maybe that's a good idea," she conceded.

The Flannerys began seeing a therapist as soon as they returned from their vacation. During joint sessions the counselor focused on assessing their marriage—and working on problems like emotional intimacy and Julia's insecurities from the past.

During Julia's first individual appointment, however, she told the counselor about her affair. She desperately wanted guidance; guilt had kept her from talking to God since the affair had begun, and she couldn't tell anyone else about it.

Meanwhile, life was getting more and more complicated. Lisa, Rolf's wife, had distanced herself from the Flannerys. Rolf denied that his wife was suspicious, but Julia felt certain Lisa knew. That would explain why Lisa no longer jumped at the chance to spend time with Julia, and why Lisa had found ways to back out of tennis matches and dinners with the Flannerys.

"What's with her?" Pete asked one night after Lisa had canceled plans for the third time in two weeks.

"Who knows?" said Julia.

Pete frowned. It didn't make sense. Usually Lisa was the one who wanted to spend time together as couples, and now she was avoiding them at every opportunity. She had also backed out of the pottery-making business she and Julia shared, with no explanation.

For several weeks Pete continued to wonder what was going on. Finally, about a month after he and Julia had begun counseling, part of the answer became clear.

Pete was working in his home office one evening when the doorbell rang. He clicked the computer cursor on *Save* and ambled down the hallway to answer the door. But he stopped halfway there when he heard Julia greet Rolf.

"Hi, Julia." Pete listened as his friend's deep voice echoed from the entryway. "I . . . uh . . . I just came by to return the garden rake. Thanks again."

Julia mumbled something unintelligible.

Something about the sound of their voices sent a chill through Pete. They seemed tense, their words forced. Pete peered around the corner at them, only to see Rolf staring intently at Julia.

Pete shivered. *What's this?* he wondered. He decided to barge in and greet his friend. "Thanks for stopping by, Rolf," he said. "You know, I hardly ever see you anymore."

Julia stared at the floor. Rolf shrugged, then said, "Yeah. Well, I'd better be going." He nodded to Julia, patted Pete on the back, and walked out.

After Rolf was gone, Pete leveled his gaze at Julia. "Is there something going on between the two of you?"

Julia shook her head. "No! Why would you even ask that?" She pressed her eyebrows together, trying to appear shocked.

"I saw him leering at you," said Pete. "Then as soon as I came in, you could hardly even look him—or me—in the eye." He paced the floor, the knot in his stomach growing bigger.

"That's ridiculous!" Julia protested. "You're reading something into it that's not even there. Rolf and I are friends! We're *all* friends, remember?"

"Okay, Julia. Whatever you say." Pete folded his arms. "But I still think there's some kind of attraction between you and Rolf. I can see it, and I don't like it."

Julia shrugged, her face expressionless. Inside she felt sick. *I'm a horrible person,* she thought. *Look at what I'm doing to Pete.* She glanced at her husband, her throat tight. Pete's face was drawn, worry lines creased deeply into his forehead.

*P*ete didn't buy his wife's explanations. During the days that followed he was sick with anxiety, unable to sleep or eat as he watched Julia slowly slip from him. Each day she acted more strangely. She had stopped attending her Bible study months ago and was now totally uninterested in church activities, an outlet she'd once enjoyed. Her behavior toward Pete was unpredictable. At times she was loving and affectionate; but then she would shrink from his touch without explanation, upset and preoccupied.

During his individual counseling sessions, Pete had wondered out loud about the possibility that Julia was having an affair. Their therapist couldn't breach Julia's privacy, but did confirm some of his suspicions.

Fairly certain his wife was being unfaithful, Pete wanted to hear the truth directly from Julia. He continued to ask Julia if something was going on with Rolf—and she continued to deny it, telling Pete he was crazy or imagining things.

In reality, however, the one-year affair was heating up.

Rolf had been pressuring Julia to leave Pete and marry him. He promised her he would divorce Lisa, if only Julia acted first. Julia resisted, not ready to end her marriage. She felt obligated toward Pete—even though she felt passionate toward Rolf.

The stress and confusion had left Julia feeling she might buckle under the pressure. One day, during a confrontation with Pete, she did.

"I'm going to ask you again," Pete said. "Is there or is there not something between you and Rolf?"

"Why do I have to keep telling you? No, there's not." Her insides twisted as she lied, and suddenly she felt unable to keep up the charade anymore. Pete knew, and her denying things wasn't going to buy much more time.

She took a deep breath. "Okay," she said.

Pete arched his eyebrows. "Okay, what?"

"There *was* a little bit of attraction between us. We were spending some time together. But it's over. I'm breaking it off." She tugged nervously at her wavy brown hair. It wasn't exactly what she'd planned to say, but maybe it would provide some damage control. Things were getting too crazy; if she didn't do something, she might not be able to salvage either relationship.

Pete could only stare at his wife, wounded. He'd been expecting this, but it was still harrowing to hear. *My wife . . . and my best friend?* he thought. It was beyond horrible. Lowering his head, Pete left the room.

Julia sank into a chair in the family room and buried her face in her hands. Now that she'd caved in and told Pete about it—some of it, at least—she knew she had to stop the affair.

She winced. It wasn't going to be easy. Last time she and Rolf had talked, they'd dreamed about getting married and leaving their spouses. Rolf would be completely unprepared.

The next day, Julia found Rolf working in his garage. Lisa wasn't home; it was the perfect time to tell him. Julia fidgeted with her wedding ring. "I—can't do this anymore," she managed. "We've got to end things."

Rolf's face darkened. "But I need you, Julia!"

"I have to do this," she said. She glanced next door, toward her house. "Pete knows some of what's been going on. I've got to try and put our relationship back together."

"But what about our plan to build a life together?"

Julia shook her head.

"Well, if it can't be like it was, can we at least be friends?" cajoled Rolf. His bright blue eyes bore into her. "We'll just talk and get together once in a while. You're the best thing that's ever happened to me. I can't lose you."

*Be strong, Julia,* she told herself. "N-no, I can't see you at all," she said, her voice wavering. "I've got to go."

Rolf muttered something inaudible. Then he threw a power drill against the garage door. Frightened, sad, and relieved, Julia ran down the driveway and back home.

∾⊱✕⊰∾

*T*he affair wasn't over, though. Instead, a cycle began: Julia would tell Rolf she couldn't see him and would refuse to take his phone calls for several weeks; then Rolf would find a way to lure her back. He often waited for her at the end of their street, hoping to catch her before she picked the kids up from school. He left notes on her car, asking her to "meet, just to talk." Flattered by the attention, thinking herself obliged to Rolf, and feeling too weak to stand by her decision to be faithful to Pete, Julia kept giving in.

She also kept going to marriage counseling with Pete—even while sporadically seeing Rolf. No longer leasing the apartment, he met her in hotels. Somehow Julia was able to keep the continuing affair under wraps.

Pete was still wary, though. Julia had insisted things were over, but Pete no longer trusted Rolf and distanced himself from him. Pete dissolved their business partnership and stopped initiating activities and trips with the Hartmans. The friendship that had once seemed so promising was now dead.

Meanwhile, Pete determined to win back his wife's love. Sensing he was on the brink of losing Julia had helped him realize how much he truly loved her. He began reading self-help books and talking to friends, seeking advice on how to rebuild their relationship. But more than anything else, he sought God's aid. *Lord,* he prayed often, *restore our marriage. Please bring Julia back to You, and tell me how to best love her.*

Through their marriage counseling, God showed Pete what to do. As he and Julia and their therapist discussed Julia's insecurities, it became clear that she had never let go of some things that had happened during the early years of their relationship.

"Like what?" Pete asked his wife during one session. "What's still bothering you?"

Julia tapped her foot nervously. She wasn't the complaining type, and it was hard to dredge up something that had happened long ago. "Well," she said slowly, "remember what you did with my old high school annuals?"

Pete thought for a moment, then cringed. Right after they were married, he had tossed her old yearbooks, hoping to prevent his friends from seeing where Julia had gone to high school. Emblazoned on the covers of the books was "Eastside High," a reminder of the lower-income Miami community in which she'd grown up. Julia had been livid when she'd found out what her new husband had done. But she hadn't mentioned it again, and Pete had forgotten.

Now, ashamed, he stared at the carpet. "I'm so sorry," he whispered.

Julia was silent. Pete could tell the slight deserved more than an apology. The next day he called Eastside High School and asked if there were any more annuals from Julia's years still in the archives. Amazingly, there were. Pete purchased the four annuals, wrapped them up, and presented them to Julia that night. Her mouth dropped open when she looked into the box.

"Oh, wow," was all she could say.

Pete smiled at her. "Open them," he said.

Julia paged through the yearbooks, her green eyes glassy with tears. "I can't believe you did this," she said, almost whispering. Inside the books her husband had written love notes to her, telling her how much he cared for her, admitting how wrong he'd been to throw the yearbooks away.

Julia felt like an undeserving wretch. While Pete had been penning love notes to her that afternoon, she had been with Rolf. *Pete's too good for me,* she thought. *He's trying so hard, and he's being wonderful.* She tried to smile her thanks at her husband, but couldn't help thinking, *Maybe Rolf and I deserve each other.*

She pondered that thought during the following weeks and months, half-heartedly working on her marriage while maintaining the affair. It seemed she had one foot in a hotel room with Rolf and the other in her own home.

Pete, meanwhile, gave her the attention and love she'd craved for so long. He listened to her and asked her opinions. He told her she was beautiful and that he loved her.

And Julia felt even more guilty.

After a few months of this, Pete began to wonder if he was getting anywhere. Julia was quiet, depressed, and withdrawn around him—the way she'd been when he first suspected the affair. *Is it happening again?* Pete worried. Had all his efforts to regain her love been in vain?

He had to know. Trying to find out whether Julia and Rolf were still involved, Pete hired a private investigator to trail Rolf.

*Lord,* he prayed, *please let this be the right thing to do.*

⸎

"*J*ulia, you've got to come meet me," Rolf said desperately over the phone several weeks later.

Julia leaned against the kitchen counter and closed her eyes. "You know I can't do that. I told you two weeks ago—"

"I know. But I flew back into town early from a business trip just so I could see you. So when will it be?"

Julia didn't answer for several seconds. Then she checked the clock and thought out loud. "I have a tennis game in two hours. I'd have to leave right now."

"Great. Come to the Seaside Hotel. I'll be waiting there. I'm looking forward to it, Beautiful." He hung up before Julia could respond.

Minutes later she was driving reluctantly to the hotel. She knew it was wrong, but couldn't stand to leave Rolf waiting for her.

Still, it made her nervous. She could tell Pete was getting more suspicious. These days he looked worried, thin, exhausted. What if he found out the extent of the affair? Rolf had been pressuring her to move to a new town so they could start over. Part of her imagined it would be glamorous and exciting, but the other part was terrified. Her family, friends, and roots were in Miami. She wasn't ready to leave the city—or her 13-year marriage.

Julia entered the hotel and rode the elevator up. An hour later she and Rolf left the building separately, scanning the parking lot to make sure no one had seen them. As she did each time she met Rolf, she breathed a sigh of relief when she drove away.

Julia didn't know it, but someone had spotted them. Across the street from the hotel a man was sitting in a nondescript car, taking notes. He was Pete's private investigator.

ᑲᕝᑭ

*J*ulia arrived home from her tennis game several hours later, just in time to shower and pick the kids up from school. But when she pulled their minivan into the driveway, she gasped. Another van was parked there, with the words "Call Locksmith Lou—I'll Get the Job Done Quick for You!" painted on its side. Julia raced to the front door. The locksmith was kneeling on the Flannerys' welcome mat, whistling as he fiddled with the lock.

"What's going on?" demanded Julia.

The man never took his eyes from the doorknob. "I'm just doin' what I was called over here for, ma'am—changin' your locks."

The color drained from her face. *Pete found out something. He knows.* Without a word, Julia raced back to the car. The only thing she could think of was getting to her children before Pete did. She sped to the elementary school and picked up Emily, Joshua, and Allie.

"Mommy, what's wrong?" asked Allie, the youngest, noting her mother's glassy eyes and pale face.

Julia took a deep breath. "I can't explain it right now, honey. Dad and I are just having some problems."

The kids were silent. Then Joshua said, "It's okay, Mom. We love you."

*At least somebody does,* she thought, smiling feebly at them. She decided to take the kids out for pizza; she needed time to figure out what to do. The kids ate, then played games in the arcade for an hour while Julia sat nervously in their booth, planning her next step.

She called Rolf. He tried to calm her and advised her to get an attorney. Pete would probably file for divorce, he said; if so, Julia should have a lawyer. Julia wasn't sure about that. She wanted to know first what Pete intended to do. Finally she called Thomas and Annie Milano, friends to whom Pete had been talking a lot lately; maybe they could give her some insight.

"Julia, where have you been?" Annie demanded as soon as she realized who the caller was.

Julia sighed. "I'm at Pizza City with the kids."

"Well, Pete is looking everywhere for you! Will you meet him? Will you talk? You can do it over here if you want."

"I-I don't know," Julia fumbled. Everything was spinning out of control. She wasn't sure she wanted to see Pete at all.

"Please, Julia, just come over," persisted Annie. "We can decide what to do when you get here."

Julia rubbed her forehead. The kids had already asked to see their father. She knew they could sense something big was happening between their parents. Julia didn't want to upset them further. "Okay," she told Annie.

Pete and Julia met with Thomas and Annie at a Mexican restaurant; the kids stayed at the Milanos' house with a baby-sitter. Sitting across the table from his wife, Pete was petrified. *Please God,* he prayed silently, *help us. You're our only hope.*

The private investigator's report had thrown Pete into a panic. Unable to deny any longer that the affair was physical, he'd followed the advice of friends who'd encouraged him to change the locks. Now, as he looked at his wife, he saw that she was trembling and couldn't even look him in the eye. His resolve wavered.

*I never expected Julia to react this way.* He had assumed she would beg him to take her back, ask for his forgiveness—not take the kids and disappear for hours. He twisted his dinner napkin. "Let's both calm down," he began nervously.

Julia didn't say anything.

"Just come back home. We'll work through this."

She stared at her hands. She wasn't ready to leave her husband, but she didn't feel the exhilaration with him that she did with Rolf. "I'm not sure what I want yet, Pete," Julia said slowly. "You need to know that, if I'm going to come home."

"I want this marriage to work," Pete said. "But I'm tired of competing with Rolf. If you want to stay with me, you'll have to choose. It's either me or him."

Julia nodded silently. She knew she couldn't keep seeing Rolf and stringing Pete along at the same time. She had to decide—soon.

ulia began seeing a psychiatrist four times a week, for up to two hours at a time. At Pete's request, she also met with a pastor. Both helped her to see things more clearly.

"Julia," the pastor told her, "if you decide to marry Rolf, you have to understand that God could not bless the union."

"Why wouldn't God want me to be happy, though?" she protested. "What if I feel better being with Rolf than with Pete?"

"Look," the pastor replied. "You can pray for anything that's in God's will. God wants you to love your husband. So pray for it. But don't ask Him to bless a relationship that He never intended."

Julia let the pastor's words sink in. She pondered them over the next few weeks. But praying for her marriage didn't sound possible. She hadn't prayed seriously for almost two years, since the beginning of the affair.

Meanwhile, life at home with Pete wasn't easy. They were both miserable, passing through the house like strangers, hardly speaking.

*He's probably been waiting for this to happen,* she thought. *He was always so worried about me saying and doing the wrong thing, and look—that's exactly what I did.* Julia wasn't sure she wanted to rekindle their love. Every time she was around Pete, her feelings of inadequacy resurfaced. Why should she choose him over Rolf?

That issue came to a head weeks later, after Julia had been through an especially difficult session with her psychiatrist. That evening, getting ready to go out to dinner with Pete, she thought she saw her husband give her a critical once-over. She slammed the closet door and planted her hands on her hips.

"You know, Pete," she declared, "if things are going to work out for us, I have to feel free to be myself—my blue-collar, poor, uneducated self! I have to start accepting myself and liking myself for who I am, even if I did cheat on you. And if you can't handle that . . ." Her voice trailed off.

Pete looked confused. "But I accepted you a long time ago," he said. "I thought we already covered that in counseling. That was what I was trying to show you when I gave you those yearbooks."

"You mean . . . you didn't do all those nice things to make me change or feel guilty?"

"No," said Pete. "I did them because I love you."

Julia stared at him. The tender look on his face told her he was serious. "I never knew that," she whispered. Instead of being embarrassed to be with her, Pete had been loving her unconditionally. She had been blind to it.

After that, she and Pete began talking more openly. Julia felt an enormous burden had been lifted now that she understood Pete wasn't condemning her. The decision she needed to make began to come into focus.

One evening when Pete was working late, Julia recalled something her psychiatrist, Dr. Mueller, had said several weeks earlier: "Imagine you're single and you're looking for the right man. What would you think if you met and dated Pete Flannery all over again?"

Julia had been silent at the psychiatrist's office, but now she knew what her answer was. She gazed at a family portrait on the wall. *I would think, "Wow, what a great guy!"* Julia reflected on the many ways in which Pete had tried to change for her, how open he'd been to getting help, and how he'd demonstrated his love for her repeatedly—even during the affair. Pete was a far greater man than Rolf. Julia just hadn't been ready to see it.

She uncurled herself from the couch and walked toward the phone, determined to do the right thing. She punched Rolf's private number, set up a meeting time, and hung up the receiver with a sigh of relief.

She was going to tell Rolf it was over. For good.

❧

*T*he next day Julia entered the darkened movie theater, looking for Rolf. She'd allotted only 20 minutes to break it off with him, and then she was going to meet her husband at the country club to play tennis.

"Julia!" a familiar voice whispered.

She made her way to a middle seat in the back row and faced Rolf. He was sitting with his arm draped casually around the chair next to him, smiling at her. She took a deep breath to calm her nerves. "It's over," she told him firmly. "And I really mean it this time." She rose to go, but Rolf grabbed her arm.

"Baby," he said, his eyes glittering, "you can't mean that! Don't take me out of your life completely."

Julia tried to pry his fingers off her arm. "We've had this conversation before, Rolf."

"Well, I can't help it," he said, still squeezing her arm. He pawed at her with his other hand. "You mean so much to me. I'll take anything I can get from you."

Julia stared at him for several seconds. *Of course he'll take what he can get,* she realized, disgusted. *He'll take my whole life if I let him.* Rolf was a taker. He didn't care about her; he didn't want what was best for her. He never had.

Julia peeled his hands off her. "Leave me alone!" she hissed. "I don't ever want to see you again!"

Walking out, she felt freed. *I finally did it,* she thought as she drove to the country club, *and I know it was the right thing to do. Now Pete and I can start over.* Eager to see her husband, she arrived early for their tennis match and found Pete on the phone at the reception desk in the lobby.

"This is Pete Flannery," he was saying. His back was turned, but Julia could see that his knuckles were white against the receiver.

There was a long pause.

"Yes, I see," said Pete quietly.

Another pause. Then Pete's voice was tight. "Well, thanks for calling."

He hung up the phone, closed his eyes, and gripped the desk, trying to compose himself. The caller had been his private investigator, phoning with an urgent message about Julia and Rolf. Pete turned to see his wife, who was smiling up at him. Dizzy with disappointment, he could only stare at her. *She told me she wouldn't see him while we tried to figure things out,* he thought. *She lied to me—again.*

"Let's go home," he said in a strained voice. "We need to talk."

Julia breathed in sharply. *He knows,* she thought. *Someone saw me at the movie theater with Rolf and told him.* The realization made her sick. What if Pete wouldn't hear her out? What if he'd had enough and wouldn't give her another chance? What if he didn't believe she had ended things?

It was like a modern-day version of *Romeo and Juliet,* she thought. She had finally made the right decision, hoping to work on their marriage—and now it seemed their relationship was doomed. She nodded to her husband and followed him out the door.

They left Julia's car in the parking lot and rode home together. Julia glanced over at her husband, who was staring straight ahead as he drove. "Pete," she began tentatively, "I was trying to break it off with Rolf. That's the only reason I saw him today."

"Did you know," Pete said slowly, "that I hired a private investigator to follow Rolf? Why should I believe you? I know you've been seeing him off and on for months!"

Tears in her eyes, Julia stared out the window at the palm trees whizzing past. "You have no reason to trust me," she conceded. "What I've done is terrible! I've hurt you, Pete, and I regret it—deeply. The affair is over. I understand if you don't believe me or if you need time to think through all this. In fact, I do, too. I need time to pray and make things right with God and with you. Will you hear me out? Will you give me another chance?"

"I don't know," Pete said quietly. For him, the past six months had been heart-wrenching. He'd watched his wife go back and forth for so long that he didn't know what to believe, or how much more he could take.

"You have every right to distrust me," Julia said. "So I won't talk to you about it until I can guarantee that I'll never put you through this again."

Pete didn't respond.

When they got home, she ran to the bedroom and locked the door, weeping. Now that she'd stopped the affair, the guilt that had burdened her for so long was gone—and she could finally pray.

Dropping to her knees, she lay her head on the bed. *Lord,* she cried silently, *my marriage, my children, my whole life is gone. You're all I have now. Please forgive me and strengthen me. I promise You there will be no more lies, no more deception, no more fooling around. Just please—give my marriage another chance.* She covered her face with her hands, trying to muffle her sobs.

Pete spent most of the evening caring for the kids and hiding out in the study. He felt drained, hollow. He wasn't ready to see Julia, and he didn't know how to react to her admission of guilt. Had she really broken it off, or was this just another excuse for her to buy time? Pete hadn't seen much change in her before, when she'd promised to end things with Rolf months earlier. *Why should I believe her now?* he thought miserably.

He fell into a restless sleep in the guest room. Several hours later, Julia whispered his name, awakening him. She lingered in the doorway, staring with red-rimmed eyes at her husband.

He opened his eyes and waited for her to talk.

"I want to be the wife you deserve," she told him. "I've asked for God's forgiveness, and He's given it to me. I'm working on forgiving myself now, too." Even on the brink of tears, Julia felt a peace she hadn't experienced for several years. "I don't want you to take my word for it, though," she continued. "Pray about this and ask God to reveal the truth to you. Take as much time as you need."

Pete rubbed his forehead. *I just don't know . . .* he thought. For months he had been praying for God to restore their marriage, but now all he could feel were the pangs of betrayal. He'd been wounded so many times by Julia already, he wasn't sure he could handle it anymore.

He stared at the carpet. "For right now, I want to stay together for the sake of the kids." Pete swallowed the lump in his throat. "I don't know what I want beyond that."

He needed to spend some time with God. But he also needed to see a change in his wife. *Lord,* prayed Pete, *if You've changed her heart, please show me.*

⟋⟍⟋

*T*he incident caused rapid changes, and not just with the Flannerys. Rolf and Lisa quietly put their house on the market and moved a few months later to another home in the community. Having Rolf out of the neighborhood was a relief for both Julia and Pete, but reminders of the affair were everywhere. Every time Pete passed the Hartmans' old residence, he thought of Rolf and Julia; whenever his wife ran errands, Pete wondered if she was really meeting Rolf. Pete's wounds were deep, and Julia knew it. Over the following weeks, they continued to tiptoe around each other, maintaining their emotional distance.

Meanwhile, Julia prayed that God would reveal to her husband that she was a changed woman. And she was. She had started reading her Bible again and spending time with the Lord in prayer, wanting closer relationships with both God and her husband.

Pete was curt and guarded with her; yet he remained physically attracted to Julia. *Thank You, Lord,* she often prayed, *that he still finds me beautiful.* She knew their strong physical chemistry was a gift from God, and it gave her hope for their marriage.

Pete also continued to pray, hoping to find peace. He wanted to trust Julia again, but it wasn't easy.

Early one morning several months after Julia's turnaround, Pete silently petitioned again: *Lord, please show me if she's changed.* It was something he'd prayed countless times. Pete sank into his swivel-back chair with his eyes squeezed shut, praying and listening for God's direction.

All at once it was as if God told him, *Julia has changed. She's truly repented. I've forgiven her now, and so should you.*

Pete frowned. He didn't feel ready; he was comfortable with their physical relationship, but there was still so much emotional pain that forgiving Julia seemed an impossible challenge. Yet the message had been clear.

Pete knew that even though the answer wasn't easy, it was simple. He had been holding on to his anger and hurt; he would have to trust and forgive his wife if he expected their marriage to heal. She'd repented, and now it was up to him to begin moving on.

*Okay, Lord,* he prayed anxiously, *I'll do it.*

Slipping out of the study, he found Julia in the kitchen. She was wearing her terry cloth bathrobe, sipping a cup of coffee as she often did before waking the children. Pete cleared his throat. "Julia?" he said.

She looked up at him.

"I forgive you," he told her. His voice was husky with emotion. "This morning God revealed to me that you've changed and repented. I'm ready to move on."

Julia nodded, tears threatening to spill in her coffee. *Thank You, God!* she prayed. At last there was hope that they might have a loving marriage after all.

Slowly the Flannerys began to rebuild their relationship. They decided not to tell Emily, Joshua, and Allie about the affair, believing it would only hurt and confuse their kids. Since Julia knew her husband had such difficulty trusting her, she promised to be 100 percent open and honest with him. She told Pete her agenda for the day, every day, and whenever he wanted more information, she was candid. They also began to meet for lunch several times a week. Not only did it enhance the communication in their marriage, but their lunch dates also calmed Pete, since the noon hour was when he knew Julia had seen Rolf in the past. As he worked to trust his wife and spent more time with her, Pete's feelings began to soften and he slowly let down his guard.

A few months after Pete forgave Julia, the two of them went to Santa Fe, New Mexico, for a two-day marriage retreat. There a marriage and family therapist addressed topics that helped the Flannerys understand why their marriage had been vulnerable to an affair—and where their relationship needed improvement. Pete saw not only how his past words and actions had made Julia feel inadequate, but also how his lack of affection had hurt her. She needed to be held and loved, to be given more attention. Julia saw how she could have improved her communication skills as well. Afraid of appearing too demanding, she had usually waited for Pete to recognize her needs. Now she saw how letting Pete know what she needed was essential to the health of their marriage.

The Flannerys took those principles home and began to work on them. It felt like a fresh start—so fresh, in fact, that they sold their cabin in Utah and built a second home in New Mexico. Their friends the Milanos joined in the venture, becoming co-owners. Spending time with the Milanos and others was a key in rebuilding the Flannerys' marriage.

The scars, of course, were still there.

Pete didn't talk much about the affair, but Julia knew he continued to hurt. Sometimes he would tense up when they drove past a restaurant they had frequented with the Hartmans; if someone mentioned the word *affair*, he became quiet. Julia tried to anticipate her husband's "triggers" so she could respond sensitively, but they often seemed to come out of nowhere.

One evening about two years after Julia had ended the affair, she and Pete were at a movie. On screen, a man was trying to stop his wife from flying away in a helicopter with a rich, seductive businessman. The husband watched helplessly, his face twisted in agony, as the helicopter lifted higher and higher from the ground. The woman he loved was gone, and might be forever.

Suddenly Julia heard her husband sniffling. Surprised, she glanced over at Pete and took his hand. He was shaking, sobbing.

"Are you okay?" she whispered.

Pete gritted his teeth. "I'll be fine," he said hoarsely.

Julia's heart sank. She knew she was the cause of his distress. No matter how much their marriage improved, some things would remain painful for Pete. "Do you want to leave?" she asked, squeezing his hand.

He shook his head.

They stayed through the movie, then went to a coffeehouse to talk. Julia scooted her chair closer to the table and watched as Pete stirred his hot chocolate. "Sweetie, I know the movie brought up a lot of pain from the affair," she told him softly. "But remember, that's all in the past. Let's go forward from here."

Pete sipped his drink in silence. Finally he said, "All I could think about was that it must have been so exciting for you to be with Rolf." He sighed. "It's hard to believe you're just as happy being married to me."

"But I am!" Julia assured him. "I don't want that horrible, shady life anymore. Sure, it was exciting sometimes, but I felt horrible about myself and about what I was doing to you. I'm so much happier now. Believe me, that affair couldn't begin to compare to our marriage!"

Pete's face relaxed as he listened.

"Nothing is as wonderful as living a life of integrity," she continued. "Because I'm living it with *you*, I'm so thankful you stuck by me through this."

Pete smiled and took her hand. "We're going to make it," he said.

They still had a lot to work through. But the Flannerys were certain that someday the affair would become a distant memory.

They had learned that when God's hand is in a marriage, anything is possible.

❧

*Pete and Julia Flannery appeared on the* Focus *on the Family broadcast "Marriages that Survived Infidelity." Happily married, they live in Miami, where they recently helped start a Sunday school class in their church. They are involved, doting grandparents and have remained close with their three adult children, who are all deeply committed to their Christian faith and their own spouses.*

*Wanting to protect their family, Pete and Julia have never told their children about the affair. They are thankful God has brought them to a place of healing—and are proud to say they have "an exceptional marriage."*

# YOUR PATH TO ALWAYS

Pete and Julia Flannery are the perfect illustration of two key principles I talk about whenever I teach on the subject of marriage. Sadly, in the events leading up to Julia's adulterous affair, what the Flannerys demonstrated so well is what can go *wrong* when these principles aren't followed.

The first truth is that healthy relationships must be based on honor, on considering the other person to be of great worth or value and treating him or her accordingly. When a husband and wife honor each other, they both feel good about themselves and secure in—and committed to—the marriage.

From early in the Flannerys' relationship, it seems, Pete didn't honor Julia. He made her feelings and opinions subservient to those of his parents and peers, devaluing her and making her feel insecure. That, in turn, made her vulnerable to the honoring and flattering attention of another man.

The second principle is that true and lasting fulfillment of our deepest needs can only come from God as we're in relationship with Him and depend upon Him daily. If we seek fulfillment anywhere else—in money, possessions, position, career success, or another person, for instance—we're bound to be disappointed and frustrated.

This was Julia's core problem: Rather than trying to meet her needs for love, significance, and security through daily fellowship with God, she sought to have those needs met by her husband. She was depending on the wrong person. And when he let her down—as we all let others down from time to time, to one degree or another—she became even more vulnerable to the promises of another man to give her what she desperately needed.

Restoring their marriage required a lot of forgiveness by the Flannerys. And it required the resolution of their core issues. Pete finally realized how he had always dishonored Julia and had to turn that around; she came to understand that God is the only genuine, unfailing source of love and acceptance.

If we want our marriages to stay strong over the course of a lifetime, we must choose daily to honor our mates and to show, clearly and consistently, just how much we value them. ("How can I honor you in practical ways every day?" is a great date-night discussion question.) But then, in seeking to get our own needs met for things like love, joy, and peace we must seek out the One who made us for intimate fellowship with Himself.

—Gary Smalley

# BEFORE HIS TIME

*Rick and Laurie Myatt*

MARRIED IN 1979

*itting in the hallway of the maternity ward at Scripps Memorial Hospital in San Diego, Rick Myatt felt his hands shake as he slipped a pair of green hospital booties over his sneakers. In a room just 15 feet away, his wife, Laurie, was being prepped for an emergency Cesarean-section delivery.

Rick glanced at the wall clock. It was 2:08 A.M. Two hours earlier, the Myatts had been awakened by the sensation of amniotic fluid soaking their bed sheets. Laurie, pregnant with their second child, was only beginning her seventh month. Panic-stricken, the Myatts had quickly organized friends to come to their house and watch Carissa, their 18-month-old daughter. Then they had rushed to the hospital.

Rick buried his head in his hands. *Lord,* he pleaded silently, *please take care of my wife . . . and our baby. You know—*

"Good morning, Rick," interrupted Dr. Blank, Laurie's obstetrician.

Rick jerked his head up and sprang from the chair. "Hello, Doctor," he said nervously. "How are Laurie and the baby?"

Dr. Blank stroked his gray beard. "Laurie is doing fine, but it's your baby I'm worried about," he cautioned. "I'm afraid we could run into complications. Your son's lungs won't be fully developed. We'll have to wait and see what happens."

Rick nodded wordlessly, his eyes burning. The whole pregnancy had been arduous. Laurie had started bleeding during the tenth week and rushed to her obstetrician. Immediately she underwent a sonogram, which revealed she was carrying twins. But upon closer inspection, the doctor had realized one of the baby's hearts wasn't beating. Laurie's body had reabsorbed the twin who had died.

In the weeks that followed, the miscarriage had plagued the Myatts. They worried whether their second baby would survive to term. Pregnancy was no longer the joyful, exciting experience that it had been when Laurie was carrying Carissa. This time, with all of Laurie's complications, fear threatened to overwhelm her and Rick. Each day they prayed for the baby's safe delivery.

*But now that her water has broken prematurely . . .* Rick brushed off the thought. Adjusting his mask, he anxiously followed Dr. Blank into the operating room. Laurie was sitting on the birthing table, looking cold and scared, while the anesthesiologist prepared to administer an epidural.

Rick rushed to her side and grabbed her hand. "You're going to be all right," he insisted, trying to calm his wife.

Laurie wasn't so sure—about herself *or* their baby. This first-time experience with C-section delivery unnerved her. She bit her lip, her eyes smarting as the four-inch needle shot into her spine.

The doctors worked quickly. Minutes later, Dr. Blank lifted a subdued Joel Myatt into the world. Rick, still squeezing Laurie's hand, watched anxiously as the doctor thumped their tiny son on his rear end.

Joel didn't respond.

The Myatts exchanged panicked glances, then stared at the scene in horror as Dr. Blank barked out urgent orders. Still shouting instructions, he placed the four-pound, four-ounce infant in a warmer and set a stethoscope on his ribcage. "I can't find a pulse!" he cried out to another doctor.

"Oxygen!" Dr. Wilson, Joel's pediatrician, bellowed to a nearby nurse. He raced to the warmer and inserted a tube into Joel's mouth, pushing it down his trachea to ventilate his small lungs. Then he pressed two forefingers against the baby's chest to get his heart beating. Suddenly Joel whelped, and he began coughing up mucous.

Rick let out his breath—their son was alive!

Dr. Wilson turned to the Myatts. "Now that we've got him breathing, we need to perform a few routine tests," he said, obviously relieved.

"Praise God," Rick whispered gratefully. He walked quickly to the warmer, where Dr. Wilson was working on Joel.

Laurie watched longingly from her bed, taking labored, heavy breaths as Dr. Blank sewed up her abdomen. She yearned to hold her frail son. *Joel's too quiet,* she thought uneasily. *Shouldn't he at least be crying?*

"How's he doing?" she called hoarsely over to Rick, who was standing a few feet away.

Rick's throat tightened. "Things look a little unstable," he replied, "but not too bad." *I hope . . .* he added silently.

"When can I hold him? When can I feed him?" persisted Laurie.

"Well, not right away," Rick told her. "I think they're going to take him to the nursery." He watched helplessly as the nurses wheeled Joel out of the room, then he turned to stare out the dark window. *God, please let him be okay,* he prayed. Rick gazed over at Laurie. She had dark circles under her eyes and looked lonely lying by herself on the bed. Rick took a deep breath and strode back to her side. He couldn't do anything for Joel right now. His wife needed him.

Minutes later, Dr. Wilson approached the Myatts. "Your son is in the nursery, where he's being cleaned up and given oxygen," he said quietly.

"But we'll be transporting him immediately to the neonatal intensive care unit at Children's Hospital. The medical facilities there are much better equipped to handle infants with underdeveloped lungs."

Laurie's lip quivered, and Rick slumped against the bedpost, feeling as though his knees might buckle. Only critical cases were sent to Children's Hospital, located 10 miles south. *This is really serious,* he thought.

"Your baby is experiencing respiratory distress, and the first three days will be crucial," Dr. Wilson continued. "But if he makes it through this period, his chances of survival are very good."

Wordlessly, Rick smoothed Laurie's damp, blond hair. They could only wait—and pray.

&#x221D;&#x2715;&#x221E;

The hours following Joel's birth slowly crept by. At dawn, Rick went home to check on Carissa and call the elders of Seacoast Community Church, where he had been the pastor for almost one year. The small congregation had already been praying for Joel's and Laurie's health since the miscarriage—and Rick felt more peaceful knowing he could count on their prayer support. With Laurie in the hospital and Rick still working, they'd need it. Rick's wife, daughter, and son were in different areas of the city, and all three needed his love and attention.

Immediately after the delivery, Laurie was transferred to a room in the maternity ward, which she shared with another young mother and her newborn. Watching the happy mother coo and nurse her baby made Laurie's arms ache all the more for Joel, who was fighting for his life 10 miles away. Each time the mother fed and cuddled her baby, Laurie gingerly stepped out of her bed and paced the hall. *It isn't fair,* she thought, blinking back tears. *I shouldn't have to watch that.* She felt cheated. What if she were never able to hold her son? What if he died before she had a chance to really love him?

Two days after the delivery, Laurie asked to be discharged. Nurses joked that she set the world's record for a C-section recovery, but she couldn't wait to mother her baby—and she wasn't about to stay in the maternity ward one more day alone.

After Laurie's release, she and Rick drove to Children's Hospital, where nurses instructed them to scrub their hands and arms with Betadine® soap. Then they were handed sterilized, yellow gowns and ushered into the NICU, where Joel had been assigned a private nurse for round-the-clock care.

Laurie gasped when she saw Joel. Lying in an Isolette® with sensors taped all over his tiny torso, he looked dangerously fragile. Doctors had inserted a ventilator into his mouth and throat and taped bandages over his eyes to protect him from the bright lights.

Laurie placed her arms through the access holes and carefully stroked Joel's head. *This is my son,* she thought, staring longingly at him. *He's so beautiful—I wish I could hold him just once.* Choking back a sob, she pulled her arms from the isolette and sank into a nearby chair.

Rick ruffled Joel's silky blond hair. He then wound up the stuffed lamb he had brought and placed it in the Isolette®. Listening to the tinny notes of "You Are My Sunshine," he thought, *The poor fellow. Look at him, lying in that little box. He can't even cry because the ventilator is jammed into his mouth and throat.*

He turned to the nurse on duty and said, "We've been told that the first 72 hours are critical." Rick ran his hand through his thick, light brown hair. "It's already been 48 hours. How's Joel doing?"

"Very well," the nurse assured the Myatts. "We're pleased with his progress. Things are looking good." She smiled at them. "I can't tell you how important it is for him to hear your voices and receive your touch."

Rick and Laurie both let out a sigh of relief. Joel was doing okay—at least for now.

❧

Joel's condition steadily improved throughout the first week of his life, and the Myatts were allowed to hold him for short periods of time. Laurie was surprised how light he felt in her arms—like a china doll, she thought. Meanwhile, Rick continued working. But every day, he drove with Laurie to visit Joel, praying that they would soon be able to bring him home.

After several days, however, Joel's progress stalled and the doctors began to suspect that something other than respiratory distress could be wrong. Even for a premature infant, Joel had low blood oxygen counts. The doctors ran another series of tests and discovered he had *patent ductus arteriosis,* or PDA.

"Blood circulates differently in unborn babies," Dr. Lamberti, the pediatric cardiologist, explained to the Myatts. "When a baby is inside the womb, a valve in his heart remains open so the mother's blood can circulate through him. At birth, the valve closes and blood circulates properly. Joel's valve hasn't closed, which commonly happens with premature babies."

Laurie stared numbly at the cardiologist, her heart pounding. However "common" PDA was, she still felt uneasy about Joel's situation. "Is that all you really think is wrong?" she asked. "Or is there something more you should be telling us about Joel?"

Dr. Lamberti waved away her concern. "No, really. Many premature infants have PDA. But we'll be doing an ultrasound to confirm the diagnosis."

Laurie nodded as she wrapped her hand around Rick's arm, squeezing it hard. *God,* she petitioned silently, *please help Joel. We don't know what's going on, but You do.*

While waiting for the ultrasound, the Myatts prayed fervently for a miracle, asking God for Joel's condition to improve. On March 13, one week after his birth, the infant had the test. Rick and Laurie watched nervously as the doctors spoke to one another in hushed tones, using Latin-sounding phrases. After several minutes, Rick couldn't take the suspense any longer and motioned to Dr. Lamberti.

"Doctor," he asked apprehensively, "what's going on?"

"We'll let you know when we've completed the test," the cardiologist replied shortly, then turned back to the huddle of white coats.

Half an hour later, Dr. Lamberti waved Rick and Laurie into a nearby room. He handed them the ultrasound picture. "This is Joel's heart," he said, pointing to a sac-like figure. "His aorta, as you can see right here, did not fully form. The condition is called coarctation, which just means a narrowing of the arteries from birth. Because the arteries in his aorta are so narrow, the blood circulation is being picked up by other blood vessels. We call this collateral circulation." He sighed and leaned back in his chair. "This puts a tremendous strain on the heart. I'm afraid we're starting to witness signs of failure."

"Are you saying our son is going to die?" Rick asked hoarsely, his knuckles white against the edge of the seat.

"Not necessarily," replied Dr. Lamberti. "We can employ a surgical technique in which we take the artery leading to the left arm and use it to build a new aorta. Other blood vessels will pick up the load and provide circulation to his left arm." He paused. "If all goes well, Joel should live a normal life. But before we can perform the operation, he'll need to gain some weight."

Laurie gripped the ultrasound picture, the thick paper rattling slightly in her trembling fingers. The thought of having Joel's tiny chest operated on was almost too awful for her to handle. *Could he even survive such a major trauma?* she wondered.

"I'll admit this procedure has never been done on a baby as small as Joel, but let me assure you that many surgeries of this type have been performed successfully," Dr. Lamberti said slowly, looking from Laurie to Rick. "We're confident we can correct the problem and that Joel will be just fine."

Laurie stared numbly at the picture until the whites and grays blurred together. Despite the cardiologist's optimism, she was far from relieved.

*⚬✗⚬*

For the next two weeks, the Myatts settled into a routine. Rick and Laurie spent their mornings at home; Rick worked on church tasks, and Laurie cared for Carissa. After lunch, someone stayed with their daughter while they visited Joel at the hospital. They often returned there in the evenings to say good night to their son.

The routine did nothing to relieve their stress and anxiety. Their conversations became short, tense exchanges of essential information; they were unable to focus on anything other than Joel's well-being. At night, Rick and Laurie crashed, unable to sleep well despite their exhaustion. In the morning, they got up to begin yet another long, taxing day. Since Joel's doctors had explained it might be months before they performed the surgery, Rick continued to work. He struggled, however, to function on the job and stay focused as he balanced his pastoral responsibilities with visiting his son.

He and Laurie were emotionally spent. Every day the Myatts carried with them the knowledge that Joel could die at any minute. Whenever the phone rang, their first thought was that it might be bad news from the hospital. Each time they visited their son, Rick wondered if it would be the last time. Not wanting to depress or alarm Laurie, he kept his thoughts to himself, while Laurie silently asked herself the same question. Friends who brought casseroles, baby-sat Carissa, and cleaned for the family couldn't help but notice the strain and exhaustion etched across their faces.

With each visit, it was obvious to the Myatts that Joel was fighting for his life. His healthy, pink skin had turned ashen gray, and he lay quietly in his Isolette®, hardly moving.

"Is this normal?" Laurie questioned the nurse on duty one Saturday morning. "Is it okay for him to be this color?"

"Well," replied the nurse, looking from Laurie to Rick, "obviously this is not the color we want, but Joel is stabilized." She pushed up her glasses. "I heard the doctors say they've scheduled him for surgery on Monday afternoon."

The news surprised them and gave them a moment of hope. But Rick couldn't help wondering, *Will Joel even last that long?* He paced the cream-tiled floor. Even he, someone who had no medical background, could tell Joel was barely hanging on. Something needed to be done—and soon.

The next afternoon, Joel looked even worse. His color appeared gray-er—if that were possible—and his tiny lungs labored with every breath. Rick turned intently to the nurse. "Shouldn't we be doing the surgery *today?*"

"Mr. Myatt," she said calmly, "we feel certain your son will make it until tomorrow. And besides, waiting even one more day will help his chances of surviving the operation."

Laurie cut in, "But he looks really bad." She glanced at Joel, her eyes wide with fear, then turned back to the nurse. "Are you sure?"

The nurse's expression softened. "Yes," she assured them. "We're watching him carefully. Don't worry—we won't let anything happen to him."

But the Myatts were right. Early the next morning, the hospital called. Joel's condition had slipped during the night, and he was being prepped for immediate surgery. Panicked, Rick and Laurie left Carissa with her grandmother, then sped down Interstate 5 to Children's Hospital, where they prayed, stared at the walls, and paced the hall, waiting for news of Joel's condition.

Five hours later, Dr. Lamberti wearily entered the waiting room. "Well, except for the timing, everything went as planned," he said, taking off his surgical mask.

While Laurie clamped her hand over her mouth, grateful tears running down her face, Rick jumped from his chair. "Is he really going to be okay?" he asked, lightheaded with relief.

"Well, your son will never pitch left-handed," the doctor quipped.

Rick forced a smile.

"Because he's so small," continued Dr. Lamberti, "the surgery did more damage than we anticipated to the blood vessels of his left arm. We had to take the artery to the left arm and use it to build a new aorta. But he's still going to be all right. We'll send a nurse to get you when you can see him."

"Thank you, Doctor. Thank you very much," Rick said, pumping his hand. *Thank You, Lord,* he prayed. *You saved my son.*

Twenty minutes later, a nurse escorted Rick and Laurie to Joel's room. But when they walked in, the Myatts both gasped. Joel's left arm—about the length of Rick's hand—was a swollen, purple mass from his shoulder to his fingertips, and he still appeared deathly gray. *I don't think he could look much closer to dying,* Laurie thought, mortified. *What have they done to him?*

"You're probably wondering about his arm," said the nurse. "It'll be okay. The other blood vessels should pick up the slack within 24 hours and resume circulation. As for his gray complexion, don't worry. That always happens in these cases. He'll improve quickly."

When the nurse was out of earshot, Laurie leaned in toward Rick and whispered, "I'm really worried. No baby can look that bad and still be fine."

Rick swallowed hard and pulled his wife closer. "I know, honey," he agreed. "His arm looks terrible. I think *he'll* survive, but I'm worried he's going to lose that arm."

When they arrived home and told Rick's mother the harrowing news, she called the church prayer chain. That night, several close friends came to the house to pray with Rick and Laurie, asking God to work a miracle in Joel's body and get his blood flowing. *Lord,* Rick silently petitioned, *You say in the Bible that all we need to do is ask and we'll receive—so I'm asking now for You to please heal our little boy.*

God swiftly answered those prayers. Later that evening, a nurse called to report on Joel's condition. She wanted them to know that a couple of hours earlier, his fingertips had turned pink. Within two days, blood began flowing through Joel's entire left arm, and some color returned to his cheeks. The Myatts were ecstatic—their son was finally getting better!

Joel remained in the NICU for the next two weeks, and he began to gain weight and breathe on his own. His left arm had been paralyzed because the nerves had been deprived of blood during the surgery. In preparation for his release, Laurie learned physical therapy exercises to help restore the use of Joel's arm.

Finally, on April 12th, one month after his birth, Joel was cleared to go home. The Myatt family was united at last.

❧

Laurie stood in the driveway, cradling Joel, who was swathed in three blankets. She stared at the front of their home, her eyes filling with tears. On the garage door, some friends had taped a huge banner that read, "Welcome Home, Joel!" *Thank You, God, for bringing my baby home,* she prayed gratefully.

She knew that caring for Joel wouldn't be easy, though. His health was improving, but he was still frail. The nerves were regenerating in his left arm, making him sensitive to pain—and fussy.

In the days that followed, Laurie spent most of her time walking around the house with her son, rocking him in her arms, trying to soothe him. She also carried him on morning and afternoon walks around the neighborhood while Carissa happily toddled alongside, pushing her toy stroller with her baby doll. Carissa, who had been sheltered from most of the crisis, liked helping her mom bathe Joel in the bathroom sink. She quickly developed a protective love for her baby brother, repeatedly kissing his puffy cheeks and stroking his swatch of curly, blond hair.

Rick, who had returned full-time to his work at the church, often took Joel off an exhausted Laurie's hands at the end of the day. And when Joel woke up in the middle of the night crying, Rick let his wife rest while he brought the baby into the family room, where he held and rocked his son.

In late May, Laurie took Joel to the cardiologist for a post-surgery check-up. Dr. Lamberti pronounced Joel in good health. He had put on weight, his aorta was functioning normally, and he'd regained movement in his left arm and wrist. Joel would need at least two or three more surgeries by the time he was nine or ten years old—his aorta would have to be enlarged to accommodate his growing body—but overall, his prognosis was positive. Laurie let out a sigh of relief. For the first time in three months, she felt some peace.

⸎

One evening about three weeks later, Laurie poked her head into their home office. "I finally got Carissa to go to sleep," she told Rick. "And I'm going to feed Joel and put him to bed."

Rick was going over his sermon outline, but noted her signal that they soon would have some time to themselves.

Laurie padded back to the family room, where Joel was resting in a portable crib. She walked over to him and smiled. He was dressed in his light-blue terry cloth pajamas, apparently sleeping quietly. Bending over the crib rail, she patted him softly.

Joel didn't move.

*No, this can't be happening,* Laurie thought. She whirled around and shouted, "Rick, s-something's the matter!"

Rick froze. Then, feeling numb, he jumped out of his seat and raced into the family room.

Laurie was murmuring, "I don't think Joel's breathing." As Joel lay in his mother's arms, his blue eyes were closed, and his mouth was open partway.

Laurie leaned her head next to his tiny lips. "Nothing." She shook her head.

Rick placed his fingers on Joel's neck but was unable to find a pulse. "You're right," he croaked. He grabbed the phone and dialed 911. "We have an emergency," he half-shouted into the receiver, his voice cracking. "Our baby isn't breathing!"

The dispatcher verified their address, then said, "We're sending units immediately, but you need to stay on the line until an ambulance arrives."

Rick pleaded, "Please hurry." Still gripping the phone, he looked at Laurie. She was kneeling on the floor, breathing into Joel's mouth and nose and pressing her fingers against his chest, just as she'd learned in the CPR course she'd taken through the hospital.

*One, two, three, four, five . . . breathe,* she recited silently, struggling to keep track of breathing cycles. *Please start breathing, Joel. You can make it.*

"How's he doing?" Rick cried out. "Is he breathing?"

Sobbing and breathing into Joel's lungs, Laurie couldn't answer.

Within five minutes, a fire truck, ambulance, and police car arrived and raced Joel off to the hospital. The Myatts quickly agreed that Laurie would stay with Carissa while Rick went on to the emergency room.

"I'll call as soon as I have news," said Rick as he dashed out the door.

Laurie made a few phone calls to activate the church's prayer chain, then kept the line clear, waiting and praying.

At the hospital, some friends arrived to comfort Rick, but nothing anyone said or did eased his anxiety. He tried to control his panic as he paced and prayed, *Lord, don't take my son. Please save Joel.* After several minutes, Rick slumped against the wall, burying his face in his hands and trembling. Somehow, he knew it was just a matter of time before a doctor entered the waiting room with the dreadful news.

The small group maintained their vigil for nearly an hour until the ER doctor walked into the room. "Is Mr. Myatt here?" he asked gravely.

"I'm here," Rick said, his heart pounding.

"Please come with me." The doctor led him to a treatment room and motioned Rick into a chair. He mumbled, "I'm terribly sorry to tell you this, but we couldn't revive your son." The doctor stared at the floor. "We did everything we could."

Wordlessly, Rick shook his head as if he were trying to shut out the awful news. Tears flooded his eyes, and he smothered a sob. After a long minute, he wiped his face and took a shaky breath. "Can I see him?"

The doctor avoided Rick's gaze. "I'll take you to him."

In the sterile treatment area, Joel's small, still body lay on an infant bed. *Why, Lord?* Rick asked desperately, moving to the boy's side. *Why my son?* He picked up Joel and cradled him against his chest, rocking him back and forth, sobbing.

After a few minutes, two of Rick and Laurie's friends, Howard and Jane Greiner, were allowed into the room. They both wrapped their arms around him, tears streaming down their own faces. "We're just so sorry," Jane said quietly. After 10 minutes with Joel, the Greiners drove Rick home.

Laurie sprang from the couch when she saw her husband walk through the front door. "Why didn't you call?" she asked nervously, her blue eyes searching Rick's. "What's going on?"

Rick's face twisted, and his eyes brimmed with tears. "Joel's gone," he cried out as he held out trembling arms to Laurie. "I just couldn't tell you over the phone."

Laurie's knees buckled, and she fell against Rick. "No, God, please!" she cried out. *This can't be happening. It just can't.* She sobbed with Rick for several minutes, with the Greiners watching silently. Finally, Laurie whispered, "I want to go see him. I want to say good-bye."

The Greiners drove the Myatts back to the hospital. Another couple, who'd been in the ER with Rick, stayed with Carissa. This time, when Rick saw Joel's lifeless body, he turned quickly away. *I can't handle seeing Joel like this a second time.*

Laurie moved toward her son, tears blurring her puffy eyes, and picked him up, cradling him gently. She swallowed hard. Joel's body felt stiff and cold—completely unlike the soft, cuddly baby he'd been just a day before. She looked into his face. *My son is dead,* she realized numbly. *I'll never hold him again.* Laurie handed her son back to the nurse on duty, then fled, hysterical, from the room.

∽✕∾

"*L*aurie?" a familiar voice came through the phone line several days later. "I'm coming over tomorrow to do some cleaning for you. Is there anything you need me to pick up? Anything special you and Rick want for dinner?"

Laurie rubbed her forehead. "I don't think so," she said, her voice hollow. "Thanks, Julie."

She hung up the phone, grateful for her friend's kindness. Laurie didn't know what needed to be cooked, cleaned, or washed, but Julie Johnson would—and she was just one of many friends who had helped the Myatts during their grief. Friends had baked casseroles, vacuumed, watched Carissa, and gone on errands for the family. *I don't know what we'd do right now without our friends,* Laurie thought, her hand still on the receiver. Nowadays, everything seemed to require more energy than she had. She sighed and willed herself to move. *I'd better put Carissa down for her nap.*

Though they didn't discuss it much, Laurie and Rick each felt mired in a deep bog. They survived from hour to hour, struggling to think clearly. By the time Carissa went to bed, they were too exhausted even to talk. Grief-stricken and emotionally empty, Rick and Laurie took a break from their usual church activities, including the weekly Bible study they hosted in their home. Before Joel's death, they had socialized quite a bit with people in the church, leading small groups and inviting members into their home. Now, they just didn't have the energy and joy that had been characteristic of their ministry.

What little emotional strength they had, they channeled into Carissa, who simply accepted the news that Joel was in heaven and frequently blew kisses to him up in the sky. But questions continued to haunt Rick and Laurie as the days passed.

After taking two weeks off work, Rick was scheduled to preach the following Sunday. He had been going through the Gospel of Luke. According to the schedule, he would be preaching on chapter 15, where Jesus spoke on the parables of the lost sheep, the lost coin, and the lost son. Sitting in his home office, Rick could only stare at the blank computer screen. *How am I going to preach when I can only think about Joel?* he wondered. And how could he be a spiritual leader when he had so many unanswered questions of his own? He bit his lip, his eyes burning. *God, don't You say in the Bible, "Ask and you will receive?"* he thought in confusion. *For months, we had hundreds of people praying for Joel's health. Why didn't You grant those requests? And if You were planning to do what You wanted anyhow, why did I even pray?* He wadded up a piece of paper and threw it at the wall.

While Rick was considering questions of faith, Laurie was wondering if she'd ever get over Joel's death. Every day, she had to walk past an empty baby room; every day, she found another toy or article of clothing that Joel would never wear; and every day, it seemed, she saw infants and their mothers—in church, at the store, in the neighborhood. Even her two best friends had newborn baby boys. The pain was always fresh; when would it start to heal?

Laurie's inner questions revealed her feelings of guilt. She suspected that she hadn't been a good enough mother. Had she held Joel enough? Loved him enough? Had she performed CPR correctly? What should she have done differently?

Rather than talking about her concerns—she felt too guilty to admit her inadequacies to Rick—Laurie turned to her journal. *I miss Joel so much I can hardly stand it,* she penned, tears flowing. She wiped her red-rimmed eyes. *I wish I could hold him just one more time. Lord,* she wrote furiously, *if You are truly a loving God, how could You allow Joel to be born when You knew he'd only experience pain and then die quickly?* She buried her face in her hands. It just didn't make sense.

Friends tried their best to comfort the Myatts. Most of the visits were helpful and most of the people perceptive. However, several earnestly recited Romans 8:28 over coffee and cake: "In all things God works for the good of those who love him." Rick and Laurie knew that verse well, but it wasn't a comfort to them. How could their situation possibly have a good outcome? And how could God be working for their benefit when He seemed so distant?

❧

*L*aurie and Rick ate their dinner in silence. Laurie alternated between feeding herself and spooning baby food into Carissa's mouth. Joel had died three weeks ago, and this was the first meal she had needed to cook since then. Their friends had finally moved on with their own lives again. *Everyone else is getting over it,* she thought bleakly, staring at the empty space where Joel's high chair should have been. *Except me—and it's my fault he's not here.*

Rick glumly twirled his spaghetti around his fork. In the past, he and Laurie had filled the dinner hour with long, lively conversations, but now, he couldn't think of anything to say. *It hurts too much to talk,* he decided.

"Rick," Laurie's voice suddenly cut through the quiet, "can you finish feeding Carissa? I need to wipe up this mess." She pointed to the spilled milk on the floor and got up from her chair to grab a sponge from the sink.

Rick finished chewing, then took the jar of baby food and began to spoon-feed Carissa, sighing heavily. Would the pain ever go away? Would life ever get easier?

Several days later—almost a month after the death of their son—the

Myatts received the coroner's report, which listed the cause of Joel's death as "complications of congenital heart abnormality." But the report didn't make sense to Rick and Laurie. Up until the time Joel stopped breathing, his color had been good, and his prognosis had been excellent at his three-month checkup. Wanting an answer to alleviate their pain, the Myatts contacted Joel's doctors. Dr. Lamberti and their pediatrician, Dr. Wilson, expressed reservations about the coroner's report as well. They decided that Joel had died from Sudden Infant Death Syndrome (SIDS), which strikes a relatively high percentage of premature infants.

Dr. Wilson contacted the San Diego chapter of SIDS, and the organization sent a representative to visit the Myatts. The woman listened closely as the couple recounted the events leading up to Joel's death. Then she leaned forward and looked seriously from Rick to Laurie. "When a couple loses a baby, the odds of them getting divorced become enormously high," she said.

Laurie raised her eyebrows. "How high?"

"Around 80 percent," the representative answered. She pressed her lips together, then continued. "I want you to be aware that your marriage is going to be severely tested in the coming weeks and months. This time of stress can be either a breaking or a bonding time. You're going to have to fight to keep your relationship intact."

Rick grabbed Laurie's hand, surprised. "I think we have a solid marriage," he said, convincing himself that he didn't sound a bit defensive. "We've worked hard at it and have spent a lot of time together. We know about the importance of investing in our relationship."

Laurie nodded in agreement, but her stomach was in knots. *Eighty percent?* she thought fearfully. *That's pretty high.*

"We also have a lot of support from our family and church friends," Rick finished, still squeezing Laurie's hand.

The SIDS representative smiled kindly. "What you're saying sounds good, and I agree that having a strong network of support is helpful. I just want to alert you that from my experience with couples in your place, you need to guard your marriage carefully. Be intentional in your relationship. Make sure you're connecting."

After the woman left, Laurie stayed on the sofa for almost an hour, cradling a sofa pillow, thinking and praying. The representative's parting words had pierced her. Laurie realized the woman was right; she and Rick hadn't really talked for weeks—their individual pain had eclipsed everything else. *I've been so caught up in my own hurt and guilt,* Laurie realized sadly, *that I don't know how Rick's doing. I haven't been there for him at all.*

The next day she continued to think about the stony wall of silence she and Rick had unintentionally built. Laurie knew that as time went on, it would only get more difficult for them to breach that wall and connect emotionally. *We need to talk,* she decided. So after she put Carissa to bed, she walked tentatively into the family room, where Rick was studying. She sat next to him on the couch and delicately put her hand on his shoulder.

"I was thinking about what the SIDS woman said." Laurie's face crumpled as she tried to hold back tears, but she forced herself to go on. "I feel distant from you, Rick," she told him, "and that scares me. What's going on in your head?"

Rick put down the book and gazed at his wife, his heart thudding. Despite his faith in their marriage, he, too, had been bothered by the words of the representative. He admitted, "For the last month, I've felt empty. I've just been trying to get through each day."

"I feel the same way, and I think it's affecting our marriage." Laurie hesitated and glanced at Rick. His blue eyes were also watery. Letting the words tumble out, she continued, "Actually, I feel like this whole thing is my fault. Maybe if I'd performed CPR correctly, Joel would still be here. I'm so sorry, Rick." Sobbing, Laurie pressed a tissue to her face. *There,* she thought bleakly. *I said it.*

Rick's jaw dropped. *I can't believe Laurie thinks she's responsible,* he thought. "Honey, you did everything you could," he said in shock. "You know you did."

"But if I had seen him a minute earlier or kept better count of my breaths, Joel would have lived. I just know it."

Rick wrapped his arms around his wife. "You are the best wife and mother, Laurie. Carissa and I are so lucky."

Laurie was silent for several minutes. Finally, she whispered, "Thank you." For over a month, the guilt had suffocated her. Now she could breathe.

The Myatts sat on the couch for over an hour, talking candidly. As they did, they realized they were both feeling the same way—sad, scared, and alone—and they needed to talk about it. Most of their friends had moved on and probably didn't want to hear about their pain for the twentieth time, but Rick and Laurie each needed to release their volatile emotions and talk with the only other person who truly understood.

Slowly, over the next few weeks, they intentionally developed an attitude of service toward one another. They started to once again hug one another, take the time to ask each other about how they were doing, and then really listen. They both prayed, asking God for the wisdom to know how to love each other, for His help to enable them to see beyond their own individual struggle with grief.

As their marriage mended, Rick's and Laurie's relationship with God began healing as well. Fueled by a desire to understand the pain in their lives, they studied the Book of Job independently. Laurie was comforted by the realization that, although Job was almost devastated by his circumstances, in the end, God didn't fail him. No matter how bleak things appeared, God wouldn't fail her either.

Rick studied Job's life, looking for answers to his own questions. After weeks of poring over the Scriptures, he realized that although the Lord hadn't healed their son, He had still heard their prayers. The point of prayer, Rick finally understood, wasn't necessarily to get the answers he wanted, but to connect with God. This knowledge didn't take away his pain, but it did enable him to continue praying.

Meanwhile, Rick labored to keep his ministry going. Most of his sermons were based on life experience, so he often preached on the lessons he'd gleaned from Joel's death, emphasizing that relationships—with God and with people—should be our top priority, and that our only hope is in the resurrection of Jesus. As Rick grieved, those realities had suddenly become more present in his daily life, and he repeatedly used them in his sermons. Yet overall, he was still confused and sad, unable to make sense of his feelings and circumstances. Rick struggled to believe whether God really loved them, whether He even cared.

They were still on an emotional roller coaster. For several months after Joel's death, Rick and Laurie would coast along until they saw a blond-headed infant boy or found one of Joel's baby rattles or toys. Then they would plunge back into grief. Most of the congregation understood that their grief was ongoing; most remained supportive and willing to listen when the Myatts needed to talk about their pain.

A few members of the congregation, however, couldn't grasp why Rick and Laurie couldn't simply "get over it." They grew tired of the Myatts' struggle. When this happened, Rick's questions about God's character resurfaced. *Lord, I've always believed You are a loving, good God,* he prayed silently, *but it's hard to keep trusting that when I hurt so badly. Why are You allowing this?*

God heard Rick's prayer.

✧

*I*n late August, on a particularly difficult evening, Rick had gone over to the home of his close friend Russ Johnson. Russ knew something about Rick's pain: The previous year, he and his wife had a daughter who had been stillborn.

"Russ," Rick said tightly, "how did you get through it? I mean, how did you ever find joy again? How did you learn to trust God again?"

"I was stuck in my pain for a long time," Russ admitted. "But one day, as I read through the Book of Lamentations, I realized something." He walked to a nearby bookshelf, picked up a Bible, and began flipping through the pages. Then Russ read,

> I remember my affliction and my wandering, the bitterness and the gall. I well remember them, and my soul is downcast within me. Yet this I call to mind and therefore I have hope: Because of the Lord's great love we are not consumed, for his compassions never fail. They are new every morning; great is your faithfulness (Lamentations 3:19-23).

Russ set down the Bible. "When the prophet Jeremiah wrote those words, he was suffering, just like you are right now. But he still believed in the goodness and faithfulness of God. . . . Rick, can you believe that God is good even when everything in life screams that He is not?"

Rick ran his fingers through his hair, silent for several minutes. Finally, after months of feeling overwhelmed by his grief and confusion, he understood what the true issue was. Just as many others had, he was facing a crisis of faith—struggling to believe despite the circumstances. He took a deep, quivering breath. He didn't understand why Joel had died, but he had to trust that God was still in control—and still good.

Tears blurring his eyes, Rick nodded decisively. "I have to. If I don't, what good is my faith?"

❧

*R*ick, Laurie, and Carissa sprawled out on a red-checked beach blanket. During the summer, the church organized beach cook-outs on Friday nights, giving everyone a chance to decompress at the end of the workweek. All around the Myatts, people were grilling hamburgers, eating, and talking, while others rode the waves on their boogie boards. Laurie leaned back on her hands, watching the waves contentedly. Summer was almost over, and she would miss these barbecues.

She looked up as Michele Kennedy dropped by their blanket. "Here, let me watch Carissa," their friend said, motioning toward the toddler, who had moved off the blanket and was now scooping sand with a pail. "Go take a walk if you want."

Laurie gave Rick a hopeful look, and he nodded.

Rick pulled Laurie up from the blanket, and they began walking down the beach, hand in hand. He sighed peacefully, gazing at the sky as the orange-hued sun neared the horizon, then glanced at his wife's profile. "You know, Laurie, I'm so glad we had that talk and we're working on things. I may not have shown it enough lately, but nothing is as important to me as our marriage—outside of our relationship with God." He stopped and turned to face Laurie, brushing a wisp of blond hair from her face. "I want to always protect our marriage."

Laurie smiled, blinking back happy tears. "I do, too," she said. "Rick, I love you so much—more than I ever have."

Rick pulled his wife close, his arms wrapped tightly around her waist. His throat was choked with emotion. The reality of losing Joel was still painful—and most likely, it always would be. Somehow, though, even in their suffering, even in tragedy, God had brought Rick and Laurie closer and made them stronger. No matter what their circumstances, He would be with them in the days ahead.

❧

*Eleven months after Joel's death, Toby Myatt was born. Joel's memory, however, will always be present—Rick and Laurie know that their son is with his Father in heaven, and one day, they will see him again. Rick looks on that day with hope and joy. Though he made a decision of the will to trust God shortly after Joel died, it took many years for him to feel true peace.*

*The Myatts acknowledge that the first few years after the death of their son were the hardest period of their ministry. Now, however, more than a decade later, Seacoast Community Church has grown to 750 members and is thriving. Rick and Laurie feel their marriage has blossomed as well, reflecting their strengthened enthusiasm and love for God.*

# Your Path to Always

My family and I can relate personally to the terrible loss suffered by Laurie and Rick Myatt. Just a few years ago, my daughter, Kari, lost a baby prematurely, and it was traumatic. The pain in her heart nearly broke mine; as a parent, seeing your child suffer is far worse than anything you endure yourself.

Sadly, couples who go through a serious loss like the death of a child often end up divorcing. But that doesn't have to happen. From our experience with Kari and from counseling with many couples who have suffered in the same way, I've learned some keys to surviving such loss with your emotional, spiritual, and marital health intact and even strengthened.

First, you and your spouse need a support team of family and friends to be there for you—to listen, to put an arm around your shoulder, to comfort, and to provide practical help like preparing meals. What you *don't* need, especially right after the loss, are advice, clichés, or Scripture quotations. Be proactive about seeking out these supporters and about letting them know just what you are and aren't asking them to provide.

Second, you and your mate need to allow yourselves to go through a time of grieving. Acknowledge the loss, and accept the pain as normal. Don't try to pretend that it doesn't hurt or that life will soon be back to the way it was. Feelings of loneliness, loss, heartsickness, discouragement, and maybe even depression are perfectly natural for a while. You're not less of a person or less of a Christian if you experience them. They may be there, in fact, for a long time, and that's okay.

Third, you eventually need to decide to move ahead with your lives and find out what you'll need to enjoy life in the future. Perhaps, for example, it would help to get into a small group, to become more active in your church, to learn a certain kind of prayer, or to develop a deeper relationship with God in general.

Along those lines, I've found that one of the real keys in any kind of trial is to start doing—as soon as possible—what it says in 1 Thessalonians 5:16-18 and begin rejoicing as you pray without ceasing. You return to the source of all true joy: the Lord. You don't thank Him for the loss of the loved one—be honest with Him about how much you're hurting—but you do thank Him for the pain and the heartache. You can say, "God, as bad as we feel right now, we know You're going to use this to make us more loving, more patient, and more sympathetic to the pain of others, like You are. Some day, we'll be able to look back and see many ways in which You've used this trial to benefit our family and us. In faith, we thank You for that."

Finally, you need to make a daily practice of placing your hope and your life in God's hands. I've got notes to remind myself to do this on the dashboard in my car, on my office desk, and on my computer at home. This habit helps you to keep your focus on Him. He's your source of life, joy, and purpose. Reputation, money, health, fame, possessions—none of these will satisfy the soul. But every good and lasting thing—anything that truly satisfies—is a gift from Him. So I pray, "Lord, I admit I'm weak. I need your grace for whatever circumstances I'm facing. Your wisdom is far above the things this world offers, and You know just what I need today. So lead me in Your will, help me to serve others in Your name, and thank You for making good to come out of whatever pain I may experience."

With support from others, a time of grieving, and then moving ahead with your eyes fixed on God and His goodness, you and your marriage can survive even so devastating a loss as the death of a child.

—Gary Smalley

# AFTER THE LOVE HAD GONE

Steve and Donna
Thurman

MARRIED IN 1973

"Steve, come in the kitchen!" Donna Thurman called eagerly to her husband as soon as she heard their apartment door creak open. "I have a surprise for you."

Steve stopped short, his hand on the doorknob. The apartment was strangely quiet. Usually he could hear the sounds of a sports event on TV or the radio playing. A knowing smile spread across his face. *Donna must be up to something*, he thought. Any second now, she would surely dump a bucket of ice water on his head or pop out from behind a corner to scare him.

The college newlyweds were constantly playing practical jokes on each other. Just that morning, Steve had nestled a fake spider in Donna's hairbrush, placed the brush face down, then watched in anticipation as his wife combed her long, blond hair. Spotting the plastic bug, she had screamed and flung the brush across the room.

Steve snickered at the memory. It didn't matter how many times he'd scared her with spiders in her hairbrush and snakes in her underwear drawer; Donna always flipped out.

But what revenge did she have planned for him now? He closed the door and crept around the corner, peeking into the kitchen. As he did, his hazel eyes widened. On the kitchen counter was a platter of barbecued hamburgers and a bowl of baked beans—his favorite meal. There stood Donna, lighting candles at the tiny table, which she'd covered with a white, lacy cloth. Steve watched as she blew out the match. All at once she turned to where he was hiding.

"Steve? What are you *doing?*"

Steve's shoulders relaxed, and he peeled himself from the wall. "This looks incredible," he said. Apparently Donna had forgotten about his spider prank—at least for now. He walked over to her and kissed her on the cheek. "A candlelit dinner? My favorite food? What's the occasion?"

Donna smiled. "I know how stressed you've been about graduation and finding a job." She waved him into a kitchen chair and grabbed the food from the counter. "This is my way of saying I'm here for you."

Steve's eyes blurred with tears as he stared at her. He and Donna were both seniors in their spring semester at the University of Texas, and he *had* been nervous about life after graduation. His lack of direction had worried him so much that lately he hadn't been able to sleep at night or concentrate in class.

"I believe in you, Babe," continued Donna. She dropped into the chair across from him and leaned forward. "I want to help you get to where you want to be—whatever that means."

Steve nodded, speechless. *I'm so blessed to have Donna as my wife*, he thought. He knew her support would be vital in the months ahead.

⟳❧⟲

*T*hat pleasant dinner was a sharp contrast, however, to an evening the Thurmans experienced a short time later.

It was a Monday night. Arriving home, Steve tossed his backpack on the dresser in the bedroom, ready to flop on the couch to watch football with Donna. Just then a long, white envelope on the dresser caught his eye. When he looked at the contents, his face turned red. *We owe $1,300 at Melba's Boutique? Isn't Donna supposed to be* paid *for working there, and not the other way around?* Suddenly all thoughts of Monday Night Football vanished.

"Donna!" he called. "Can you come in here for a minute?" He felt queasy. Growing up, he had always been careful with money—having learned its value while mowing lawns in the searing summer heat of Texas and California. To Steve, credit cards were an anathema; he could never bring himself to spend money he didn't have in the bank. He hoped his wife had a good explanation for the bill.

Donna popped into the bedroom. "What?" she asked quickly. "The game's almost on."

Steve pointed to the bill from Melba's Boutique. "What's this?" he asked.

Donna winced. She had meant to pay the minimum on the bill before Steve saw it, using money she'd saved. She tried to appear nonchalant. "Oh, nothing," she told him with a shrug. *I hope he doesn't make a big deal out of this,* she thought.

*"Nothing?"*

"Well," Donna admitted, "it's money I owe on some clothes. Whenever I find a piece of clothing with a flaw, I buy it at a huge discount. The way I look at it, I'm saving a lot of money on my purchases."

"Saving money? Don't you realize you're putting us into debt?" sputtered Steve. He threw his hands in the air. "How come you never told me about this?"

Donna folded her arms. "Because I didn't think it was that big a deal!"

"You didn't think it was that big a deal?" Steve repeated, the timbre of his voice rising two octaves. "Then tell me how we're going to pay for this!"

"I'll pay for it!" Donna cried. Then she frowned. "You're such a tight-wad. Why can't you loosen up and be spontaneous once in a while?"

Fuming, Steve paced the tiny bedroom. "We don't have the money to be 'spontaneous,' like you want. Listen, we can't pay for all the latest fashions, so you better not do this again!"

"Fine!" Donna said, nearly choking on the word. She stomped out of the bedroom. *He's so selfish and unsupportive!* she thought. As far as she was concerned, Steve deserved the silent treatment for being such a jerk.

Apparently he felt the same way about Donna. Days passed, and the Thurmans barely said a word to one another. They avoided eye contact whenever possible, each waiting for the other to apologize first.

Neither did. They worked to pay off the debt, but the argument was buried.

Eventually the newlyweds moved on to other things—papers, finals, and preparations for graduation. But the issue of the clothing bill sat like a land mine, ready to explode.

⚜

*A*s graduation drew near, Steve's anxiety about the future intensified. Finally he decided to pursue becoming a fighter pilot—the only career he'd ever seriously considered. His father had been an Air Force navigator, and Steve was used to the military lifestyle.

After graduation, the Thurmans moved from Austin, Texas, to Dallas; Steve enrolled in the Marine Corps Officer Training program, located in Quantico, Virginia.

But he soon found himself in a dilemma. One afternoon before he was scheduled to leave for Quantico, he visited Donna's brother-in-law, Burl, who was taking classes at Dallas Theological Seminary. Steve listened intently as Burl described seminary life and learning. Suddenly everything seemed to click in Steve's mind. He hadn't thought about seminary before, but now it sounded like the perfect fit. He wasn't even sure why, but knew it was an idea he had to pursue.

Excited, Steve went home to pray and talk things through with Donna. To his relief, she was equally enthusiastic about the idea. At Steve's request, the Marines released him to pursue graduate school.

Only two possible roadblocks remained, it appeared. The first was Steve's poor academic record. An unmotivated college student, he had found football games and social activities infinitely more appealing than studying. Steve knew that he would need to enroll immediately in a few summer classes to better his chances of getting into seminary.

The second potential snag: money. Tuition would be expensive, since Steve probably wouldn't be eligible for any loans or scholarships.

None of that worried the Thurmans, though. They had both been planning to work full-time anyhow; why not put the money toward additional schooling? And how hard could it be to take a few classes on the side? Steve was confident seminary would be a snap. Learning about God was something he knew he'd find fascinating; and since Donna had also graduated, she'd be able to help him with his papers and homework.

They would get through it, whatever "it" was.

Just a day after visiting Burl, Steve had made his decision. He would enroll in seminary. God, he believed, was directing him to be a pastor.

◇◆◇

*T*wo years later, Steve sat next to Donna in church—struggling to keep his eyes open. As usual, he'd gotten only about four hours of sleep the night before. As the pastor talked on, Steve's eyelids began to feel heavier and heavier; his head inched perilously toward the back of the wooden pew in front of him. Suddenly he felt something pinch his arm. His head snapped up, and he blinked.

Donna was staring at him. "*Steve,*" she hissed. "Wake up!"

Steve straightened in the pew, thankful that Donna had caught him before he started snoring. Nowadays it seemed he fell asleep in church every week. Life in his second year of seminary was hectic; in addition to Steve's heavy course loads, he and Donna had a daughter, Lindsey, and a son, Travis. And since Steve had no loans or scholarships, he and Donna both held two or three jobs to make ends meet.

It was a dizzying schedule of around-the-clock work. Each morning, Steve got up at 3:00 to deliver newspapers. He returned home around 6:00 or 6:30, took a shower, and headed off to seminary. After being in class all morning, he spent his lunch hour studying in the library. Arriving home by midafternoon, he had just enough time to change clothes and wolf down an early dinner—before leaving again to wait tables three or four nights a week.

While Steve was in class, Donna cared for the kids, typed her husband's papers, and earned extra cash typing specifications for an architect friend. She also collected the paper route money every two weeks, driving with the children into Dallas's most crime-infested area—fearfully clutching her Mace® for protection.

Weekends were equally busy. Every Saturday morning the Thurmans cleaned a medical building together. Then, in the afternoons, Steve drove across town to clean a church—where he was also the on-call Sunday janitor.

Neither Steve nor Donna *ever* got a break. Allotted only four or five hours of sleep daily, Steve couldn't get up in the middle of the night to help his wife feed or rock the babies. Donna was forced to carry the responsibility alone. After seven nights a week of tending to fussy children, she, too, was bleary-eyed and crabby as she tried to watch the kids and work odd jobs.

Gradually, as the semesters passed, Donna and Steve set aside the long, heartfelt conversations they'd enjoyed during their courtship and early marriage. Usually too tired to do more than recite the day's events, they simply tried to survive. Chronic sleep deprivation quickly sharpened their disagreements; they found themselves tense and guarded around each other, especially when it came to finances.

They lived on the money Steve made as a waiter. Each night after he finished his shift, he counted his tips and took out several envelopes. Into one marked "Rent," he placed a $10 bill so the family wouldn't be caught short at the end of the month. Other envelopes received a few dollars each night for seminary tuition, car insurance, and incidentals.

Trying to control their finances and keep the family out of debt, Steve paid all the bills—giving Donna the checkbook only when necessary. He cringed when he thought of the enormous debt she'd racked up at Melba's Boutique during college. To pay off Donna's closet full of "bargains," the Thurmans had been forced to give up football games, movies, and restaurant meals for an entire year. Steve was determined to never let that happen again.

*We don't have any money for "extras,"* he told himself, *and Donna can't be trusted with our finances. She'll spend us into a state of homelessness if I let her.*

Donna disliked the way he controlled their finances, though. Since Steve was home for only a few hours every afternoon, she had to spring her requests for the checkbook before he rushed off to the restaurant. She knew her husband would allocate money only for necessities like groceries, gas, and clothing for the kids—so she often made impulse buys when given the checkbook.

*He practically goes ballistic whenever I ask for money, no matter what it's for,* she thought. *If I didn't buy a few things here and there behind his back, I'd be completely deprived.*

Donna's additional purchases, however, just made Steve more wary of handing over the checkbook—even when her requests were valid. Doctors' appointments, for example, became a bone of contention. It seemed Lindsey and Travis got sick every month from allergies; Donna was constantly having to ask her husband for money to take the kids in for an exam.

"Steve?" Donna asked on one such occasion, her heart pounding. "I've got to take Lindsey to the doctor. I think she has another ear infection."

Steve looked up from his taco salad and closed his eyes for a few seconds. Every time the family spent money, he saw more hours of work in his whirlwind, exhausting future.

He sighed. "Okay." He dug into his back pocket for the checkbook. "If Lindsey's sick, then you've gotta take her in. But it's only for an appointment, right?"

"Well, I don't know. Remember what the doctor said he'd have to do if she got another ear infection?"

Steve's stomach lurched. He remembered, all right. "Yeah—she'll have to get those tubes put in her ears again," he muttered. Last time the procedure had cost $800! It seemed like a miracle that the Thurmans had received a tax refund around the same time and were able to pay off the bill. *But that was last year,* Steve thought. *How in the world could we afford to pay a bill like that again?*

Donna took the checkbook from her husband and grabbed her purse. "Well, I just thought I should prepare you in case Dr. Holloway recommends it again," she said, her eyes avoiding Steve's. She felt trapped when the kids got ill. She couldn't stand to see them sick, but doctor visits were expensive—and the family didn't have insurance.

She glanced over to see her husband wearily rubbing his temples. This harried life didn't remotely resemble the fun, fulfilling existence they'd dreamed their marriage would be. Blinking back tears of frustration, Donna hurried out of the kitchen. As always, she had someplace to be.

❧

Almost two years later, Donna walked through an antique store with Lindsey, Travis, and Zach—their newborn—in tow. She and her friend Kate, on their way to shop for kids' clothes, had stopped in the antique store to browse. *I know I shouldn't be in here,* Donna thought, *but it's so unfair that I'm not allowed to get anything for the house.*

She sighed. The Thurmans had just bought a small, older home, using up their savings. Now that they finally had a place of their own, Donna wanted to fix it up.

Steve, however, had repeatedly said, "No way." Due to graduate from seminary in a few months, he had landed a part-time associate pastor's job—but since he planned to pursue a doctorate in the fall, the high cost of tuition still loomed. And with three children, finances were tighter than ever.

It was hard for Donna to resist buying nice things—especially living in Dallas. It seemed all their friends had big, beautifully decorated houses, luxury cars, and closets full of the latest clothes. Donna fingered the price tag on an expensive pottery-vase lamp, then let the tag drop.

"Donna," her friend said, "why don't you just get it? I can tell how much you want the lamp."

Donna shook her head. "I can't, Kate. You know how tight Steve is with money. In fact, I shouldn't even be in this store. The only reason I have the checkbook is to buy Lindsey a pair of shoes. Hers are falling apart."

Kate folded her arms. "Steve's always controlling you, Donna. He won't let you buy *anything*. It's not right."

Donna stared again at the lamp. *It's true,* she thought suddenly. *I haven't bought anything nice for the house—or myself—in weeks.* She picked up the lamp and looked at her friend. "I'm going to get it," she said. "Steve will just have to understand."

But when Steve got home that afternoon and spotted the lamp on their living room end table, he was anything but sympathetic.

"Donna," he said quietly, "what is this?"

Donna swallowed. "We needed a lamp."

Steve spoke slowly, as if holding in a torrent of anger. "Do . . . you . . . realize . . . that you cannot do this? We simply do *not* have the money to purchase any extras. Why can't you understand that?"

Steve's stomach felt as if it were in knots. *I can't believe this,* he thought. *We're barely making ends meet, and she buys an expensive antique lamp?*

"I'm tired of being parented," Donna shot back. "You don't trust me to get anything!" Her lip quivered, and her eyes began to water. "You treat me like I'm five years old. Kate's right—I should be allowed to buy things once in a while!"

"Kate? I can't believe Kate talked you into this!" Steve cried. "She has a ton of money. What does she know about living on a budget?" He glared at the lamp, then addressed his wife. "When you can prove you're responsible, then maybe things will change."

"Fine," Donna said, her face turning red. "Once again, you win. You know—"

"I'm tired," Steve interrupted. "And I don't want to talk with you when you get emotional like this. Besides, I have to change the tire on the car before I go to work." He brushed past her and went outside.

Donna sank into a faded blue chair in their living room, tears flooding her eyes. She could hear Steve outside, kicking the tire on their old Volkswagen Beetle. When they fought, Steve controlled his temper around her and the children, but tended to take out his anger on inanimate objects.

She sighed, unfolded herself from the chair, and walked outside. Maybe she could calm him down. She didn't want him making a scene in front of the whole neighborhood.

Donna found him in the driveway on his hands and knees. She watched as he alternated between grunting at the flat tire and checking his watch.

"Steve," Donna began carefully, "it's not that big a deal. You'll get the tire changed."

Steve shot her a glance. "It *is* a big deal. You obviously have no idea what kind of pressure I'm under. I'm relying on this car to get me to my multiple jobs, where I'll earn a few pennies. But now I can't even take the tire off! I'm exhausted, and all I want to do is fix this and leave for work so I can pay our bills."

*And cover all your little shopping sprees,* he added silently. Steve rubbed his forehead, then turned back toward the car.

"But—" Donna began.

Steve grunted again. "I don't have time for this, okay?"

Donna marched back into the house. *I'm sick of the way he treats me. He's so stingy and uptight, and he never takes what I say seriously.* She dropped onto the couch, pulled her knees up to her chest, and sat that way for several minutes. When Steve walked back into the house, she looked in the other direction. She didn't feel like talking anymore.

Steve felt the same way. Without a word he grabbed his jacket and keys, then slammed the door behind him.

The Thurmans continued their silent war for two weeks. They conversed only when it was necessary to coordinate schedules and talk about the kids. When Steve came home from class, Donna served him dinner— then abruptly left the room. Just looking at him made her feel angry and hurt.

Steve also avoided his wife, thankful that he was too busy to be around the house much anyway. He had plenty of reasons not to confront his wife. For one, he was exhausted. He also didn't want to spend his precious few hours at home arguing. Besides, this wasn't the first time they'd gone several weeks without speaking.

*It won't go on forever,* Steve reasoned. At some point, one of them would get tired of the tension and say wryly, "Okay. I forgive you for what you've done." Then they would both start laughing. Maybe they'd stop the fighting with a practical joke, or forget what they were angry about, or break the tension with a trip to see Donna's parents or a night out with friends.

But this time the silence lingered until Sunday evening at their biweekly Bible study, almost three weeks after the fight. Steve and Donna sat next to each other with folded arms, determined to keep physical and emotional distance.

The group engaged in small talk for several minutes. Then Michael, one of the men in the group, looked straight at the Thurmans. "Hey, I can tell there's some tension between you two," he said, leaning forward on his elbows. "Let's talk about it."

In some gatherings such a statement might have seemed intrusive, but this group was unusually close. Steve's shoulders relaxed, and he looked up from the carpet. He and Donna often avoided hashing things out with one another, but they usually were willing to reveal their feelings to the Bible study. "It's been a pretty horrendous couple of weeks," he admitted.

Donna nodded. "We could use your prayers right now. Things aren't going so well. We've been really mad at each other."

"Well, then, let's pray," Michael said simply.

The rest of the couples bowed their heads as Michael asked God to help the Thurmans better love and understand one another. By the time the prayer was finished, Steve and Donna were able to smile tentatively at each other.

The Thurmans were thankful for their Bible study group. It had become a haven, meeting on one of the few nights Steve was off work. The time they spent with other open, struggling couples often infused Steve and Donna with just enough strength to endure the pressures they faced.

Yet even with the support of others, the Thurmans' cycle of fighting-followed-by-silence continued. And it wasn't only because of financial issues.

ᑐᑌᑌᑌᐤ

"Steve?"

He could hear Donna calling from behind him. Her voice sounded quiet, wounded.

"Can I talk to you for a minute?" Donna added.

Shutting the front door after saying good-bye to the last of their Bible study members, Steve yawned wearily. One year after their three-week war of silence, life had become even more hectic. Steve was a year into his doctoral program, in addition to working full-time as an associate pastor of Fellowship Bible Church in Park Cities, a suburb of Dallas. Donna recently had given birth to their fourth child, Jordan.

Every two weeks the Thurmans hosted a Bible study of nine married couples. Tonight the group had discussed meeting more frequently, splitting up the men and women every other week. *I think we came up with some good ideas tonight,* Steve thought as he locked the door. But he could see from the look on his wife's face that she felt differently.

"Babe," Donna began, cradling a pillow from the couch, "having the women meet at our house for coffee every other Thursday is fine. But I don't want to be the teacher."

*Here we go again,* Steve thought, shaking his head. "Why not?" he asked, irritated. "Everybody else thought it was a good idea, and so do I." He folded his arms as if waiting for her to dispute the obvious facts.

Donna stared at him, her eyes filled with hurt. Why couldn't he understand that she liked hosting people in their home, but teaching wasn't her gift? Teaching made her nervous, uncomfortable. She'd rather be out mowing her elderly, non-Christian neighbor's lawn or building a relationship with a hurting, single mom in hopes of leading her to God. Trying to explain, she began, "But I don't want—"

"We're in this ministry together," Steve said, cutting her off as he paced the carpet. "Where's your commitment, Donna? There's stuff I don't like to do either, but I have to because I'm a pastor. And as my wife, I think you're also under certain obligations."

Donna sank deeper into the sofa, feeling a twinge of guilt mixed with anger. When Steve talked like this, she felt she was being parented. It wasn't the first time they'd had this discussion, either. Donna knew she wasn't the "ideal" pastor's wife who played the piano, taught children's Sunday school classes, and headed up the women's ministry. In fact, she had resisted being forced into that mold.

But now, as she listened to Steve talk about commitment and ministry, her resolve melted. *Maybe he's right,* she thought, trying to swallow the lump in her throat. *Maybe I am being selfish. I'm a pastor's wife, and I should be supporting Steve's ministry.*

She looked back at Steve, who still towered over her. "Okay, I'll do it," she said.

Donna did lead the women's group every other Thursday in a Bible study. Gradually, though, the meetings became less study-oriented and more social. Donna didn't mind; she knew she wasn't a natural teacher and that it was healthy for the women to meet for coffee. But the drift toward fellow-ship frustrated some of the women, and they criticized Donna for veering from the original plan.

When that happened, she felt more guilty than ever. *You're not good enough to be in church ministry,* she berated herself. *You can't handle the hectic schedule, and now you can't even teach a women's Bible study.*

She couldn't communicate those feelings to Steve, though. He didn't understand why teaching was such an issue for her. To him, the facts were clear: Donna needed to support him by volunteering in the church, and sometimes that included teaching. So he continued to press her to fulfill roles in which she wasn't gifted, believing it was her duty to take on certain responsibilities, no matter how she felt about them.

This unexpressed conflict strained their marriage all the more, amplifying their exhaustion and financial struggles. As the tension between them mounted, the Thurmans found themselves going for longer periods of time without talking. In the past their fighting and silence had been punctuated by happy times; they'd always been able to reconnect or find something to joke about. But now it was months since they'd really laughed together or had a memorable date. It seemed they fought about something almost every day. And when they weren't arguing or avoiding one another, they were simply existing.

*Our marriage is totally lifeless,* Steve thought one day a few weeks later.

He was hurrying home from class so Donna could use the car. Pulling into the driveway, he checked his watch. He was late; Donna had to be at church to drop the kids off for Vacation Bible School in five minutes. He knew she would be mad.

And she was.

"Where were you?" Donna demanded. "Oh, forget it. I don't have time to talk about this." Carrying Jordan, she guided their three other kids out the door.

Steve stared at his wife's retreating figure. *It's amazing that we have four kids,* he thought, *since there's practically no intimacy in our marriage.* He was tired of her, tired of the bitter silence, and especially tired of their wedlock.

He stared through the kitchen window, watching as the Beetle pulled out of the driveway. *Maybe it would be better if she just never came home,* he thought suddenly. *Maybe that would be the answer.*

The idea gave him a moment's relief from the tension. If Donna wasn't around, he would be free! There would be no fighting, no hassles, and no responsibility.

All at once Steve's conscience checked him, and he was flooded with guilt. He had no business even thinking that. Having one of them leave was definitely *not* going to solve anything.

Steve sighed. He was going to have to stick things out with Donna. He'd made a commitment to God to love and honor his wife, and he needed to stand by it.

Staying in a loveless marriage seemed horribly unappealing, though. Steve poured himself a glass of milk and leaned against the kitchen counter, grimacing at the thought. *What it means,* he told himself, *is that I'm going to be miserable.*

✑

Steve tore out of the tension-filled house several weeks later, thankful to be on his morning jog. His feet pounded the Dallas pavement, echoing the angry throbbing in his head.

He and Donna had both started jogging in the early morning, taking turns so that someone would be home to watch the kids. Clenching his jaw, he pumped his legs faster. Just thinking about Donna made him seethe.

He jogged for several more minutes, running through a park, working off steam. Then he rounded a corner; just over the hill, Steve could see the outline of their house. His stomach churned at the thought of walking through the front door.

Still running, he thought about something that had happened several months before. An acquaintance had left for a business trip—and disappeared for a year, bailing out of his marriage and the responsibility to his kids. Steve let the idea flicker through his mind. Then, just as quickly, he brushed it away. Several weeks earlier, he'd promised God that, no matter how awful things got, he'd stay in the marriage. *You knew you'd be miserable,* Steve reminded himself. *It's the price you have to pay.*

He wiped the sweat from his forehead as he thought about his wife. She was a ghost of the woman with whom he'd fallen in love. Now he hardly knew Donna.

*I feel dead toward her,* he realized suddenly. The thought overwhelmed him with sadness. He'd focused on his anger and bitterness and the lifelessness of their marriage for so long; he hadn't realized that underneath it all, he felt *nothing* for his wife. Was there any hope for them?

Steve pondered that as he ran. He truly didn't know. It had been months since they'd had fun together, and he wondered if they ever would again.

Several minutes later a new thought cut through the despair: *Ask God to help you love your wife. You've got nothing to lose.*

He stopped, panting in the already hot morning air. The idea surprised him. Praying for their marriage didn't seem appealing at the moment; surely Donna, not he, should be the one to work on things. Surely he, unlike his wife, knew the kind of sacrifices that needed to be made in ministry—financially and otherwise.

Steve sighed. If he was going to stay with her, something needed to change. He couldn't keep living as he was—angry and, even worse, indifferent toward his wife. *I guess,* he reluctantly decided, *that praying is my only option.*

During the next few months, Steve prayed on his three-mile jogs—asking God to change his attitude and restore his love for Donna. As he did, the Lord began to thaw his heart, showing him that their marital problems weren't one-sided; he needed to work on some things, too. Steve saw his tendency to control. He slowly realized that he needed to be more flexible and understanding, to hear Donna's concerns. He needed to stop seeing Donna as the opposition, rather than his beloved partner.

*Lord,* he prayed desperately, *please help us.*

As Steve prayed, his attitude gradually became more tender. He started looking forward to going home and seeing his wife. He enjoyed planning their date nights. He laughed with her more often. He even resumed playing pranks—and when he did, he was reminded of Donna's joyful demeanor, which had originally drawn him to her.

Meanwhile, God was also working in Donna's heart. Steve didn't know it, but she had begun praying for their marriage during *her* morning runs.

Not that she was optimistic. She felt helpless, suffocated, impassive, resentful. How many times had Steve put her down, made her feel like a child when she tried to express her feelings? *Steve's so insensitive,* she had repeatedly told herself. *He doesn't even try to understand me. He thinks everything is my fault.* She'd lost count of how many times he'd made her cry or feel guilty over something, and she was sick of it.

But Donna was even more tired of not talking, of fighting over money, of passing her husband as if they were strangers on the street. Pondering their situation over the following weeks, she finally concluded: *This is nuts! We can't keep on going like this.*

Donna didn't want to give up. But she knew their marriage was in such a shambles that only God could fix it. So she, too, asked Him, *What can I do to change? How can I make our marriage better?*

She began to pray that God would help her be the kind of wife she needed to be, so that their marriage could be what it needed to be. She also began to see that she should quit fighting her husband about finances; God had given Steve wisdom in that area. No matter how much Donna wanted to believe she was prudent, she had to admit that she'd often been irresponsible with their money, just as Steve had said. Donna determined that the next time he told her they couldn't afford something, she simply would say, "Okay. You're right."

That opportunity came several weeks later.

❧

"I'm trying to talk to you, Steve," Donna said, "and you're not listening." She looked away from her husband, trying to hold back tears. Everything was ruined. Donna had wanted to make Steve a nice dinner and connect with him—something she knew he craved from her—rather than hit him up with her frustrations and demands. Instead, the conversation had turned to money.

*Why didn't I just keep my mouth shut?* she thought miserably. Why had she mentioned her need to buy a baby shower gift?

"No, I don't think you're hearing *me*," Steve replied. "The gift will have to wait. We cannot afford it right now."

His words set off a warning bell in Donna's head. She bit her lip. *Lord,* she prayed, *help me to be more understanding.* "Okay," she began cautiously. "I'm sorry. I know it's not in the budget. It's just—" Her voice broke off.

"What?"

Donna took a deep breath and tried to speak calmly. "I feel like a child. I don't have any freedom here. I can't be my own person. I can't even work within a budget because you're always the one in charge of it."

Steve's face lost its pinched expression. *It's true,* he realized. *This is exactly what God has been telling me.* The system he'd devised was controlling and limiting to his wife. He studied Donna; her nose was red, a sure sign that she was about to cry.

"You're right," he said finally. "This isn't working. We need a new plan."

Donna's eyes widened. Steve furrowed his brow in thought, then suddenly slapped his hand on the table in excitement. "Donna," he asked, "how much money do you think you need each month to run the family in terms of things like groceries, clothes for the family, birthday presents, makeup, and appointments?"

"I have no idea," she said, shrugging. *Where is he going with this?* she wondered.

"Well, let's sit down and figure it out."

The Thurmans set aside their dinner plates. For the next 45 minutes, they worked out a budget. When they were finished, Steve eagerly faced Donna.

"I want you to go open a second checking account," he told her. "Every month, I'm going to give you a check for $500 to deposit into your account. I'll still pay all the bills from our first account, but this money is *yours* to manage. I don't want to know how many groceries you buy or clothes you get. That's your deal now." He searched her blue eyes. "This way, we won't always be in conflict over finances, and you won't have to constantly ask me for money."

Donna frowned. "But what if it's not enough?"

"I'm giving you all we can afford," Steve reminded her. "I know you'll still be strapped for money, but at least now you'll have control over it."

Donna leaned her chin on her hand, thinking. "That's true," she said at last. Steve had finally heard one of her concerns! She smiled. "I like this plan." Steve knew he'd have to trust Donna's judgment; Donna realized she'd need to be more responsible than she had been in the past. But they both felt confident it was the best decision they'd made in years. Things finally were looking up.

❧

*T*he new budget alleviated a lot of the conflict between Steve and Donna. It didn't resolve all their problems, though—especially regarding her role in the church. Steve still didn't understand why his wife resisted leading Bible study groups and Sunday school classes.

Ironically, it was at church that Steve began to realize his mistake.

The pastoral staff at Fellowship Bible had been reading through and discussing Frank Tillapaugh's book *Unleashing the Church* during staff meetings. Much of the book focused on helping Christians understand their spiritual gifts in order to help them be more effective in ministry. By serving in the areas best suited to them, church members would complement each other's gifts, strengthening the body of Christ.

Fellowship Bible had been founded on the principle of God's grace. The staff wanted to act on that principle by applying 1 Corinthians 12, where the apostle Paul describes how the parts of the church body contribute to the whole.

As Steve read through the book and prayed for God to make him more sensitive to his wife, he began to see that those truths also applied at home—and that he hadn't been living them out. Instead of encouraging Donna, he'd been telling her to ignore her God-given strengths. She had the gift of evangelism—not teaching—and he needed to help her use it.

Gradually, Steve recognized that he'd acted insensitively toward Donna for years, often ignoring or belittling her when she tried to explain her feelings about teaching. Other people had noticed it, too. Steve cringed as he recalled how, several years earlier, a friend had commented on the subject. He and Donna had invited a couple, close friends from church, over for a barbecue. The women had gone in the kitchen, leaving Steve and Gaylon alone to grill hamburgers. Gaylon had taken the opportunity to graciously confront Steve about the insensitive way he often treated Donna. Embarrassed, Steve had pretended he didn't know what his friend was alluding to; Steve promised to "think about it." But in his heart, he'd known Gaylon was right. Now he couldn't believe how gracelessly he had treated his wife for so long.

He thought of the times he had taught on Ephesians 4:29: "Do not let any unwholesome talk come out of your mouths, but only what is helpful for building others up according to their needs. . . ." But he hadn't followed that command—and it had damaged their marriage.

Steve was determined to change his attitude; slowly, he did. The next time someone wanted Donna to teach, he spoke in her defense.

"Donna's real strength is in evangelism," he explained to the church elders when one of them asked why his wife's name wasn't on the list to help lead a ladies' Bible study. "Right now, she's investing her time in helping one of our neighbors. The lady is without family, and she doesn't know God. Donna really wants to be there for her."

The elders were silent.

Steve suspected some of them didn't agree with the way he and Donna approached ministry, but now he didn't let it bother him. He knew it was more important to focus on what *God* thought about their marriage and ministry.

As time passed, Steve continued to look for practical ways to love his wife and show her grace. But it wasn't always easy, and their conflicts didn't immediately vanish.

A few months after opening the second checking account, Donna spent too much on framed prints for the living room, putting herself $150 into credit card debt. She tried for weeks to set aside money in an attempt to pay back the debt; the last thing she wanted to do was ask Steve for a loan. But it didn't work. Money was so tight that she found it difficult to stay within the budget at all, let alone save much cash.

Steve knew his wife had spent too much on the prints. But this time, rather than reacting in anger, he prayed for God's direction.

Through prayer and Bible reading, Steve had been discovering that he needed to follow Jesus' example of servanthood. Jesus had looked for ways to serve those He was responsible to lead, and Steve knew he needed to do the same for Donna. Though at first his actions were done only out of obedience, Steve had come to enjoy serving Donna. His deeds were revitalizing his love for her.

With that in mind, he took a different approach to the debt. For Christmas, he placed an envelope on the tree for her. Inside was a check for $150 and a note that read: "I appreciate what you do to make the house a warmer, better place. Don't worry about the debt. It's erased."

When Donna opened the note on Christmas morning, she was speechless. She had expected a sermon from Steve on her need to be responsible, not a gracious offer to repay her debt.

But Steve wasn't the only one who had changed.

Donna had also been convicted by the sermons on grace she was hearing at church; she realized she needed to apply those principles to her marriage as well. How often had she stayed angry with Steve, finding it easier to ignore him than forgive? True, he'd been thoughtless at times, but she'd allowed her hurt to fester into bitterness. Her grudges had damaged the marriage as much as Steve's insensitivity had.

She felt her heart soften, and forgiveness began to come easily. She no longer wanted to hold the anger. Ready to show him grace, she had resumed doing special things for him, knowing that performing even simple gestures such as packing him a lunch or trying to connect with him would make a difference in her attitude.

And it did. As Donna started to serve Steve, her resentment melted away. Slowly, love replaced bitterness, and she wanted to spend time with her husband. She wanted to talk deeply with Steve and hear how he was doing; she looked forward to their date nights.

The Thurmans' marriage was gradually becoming more healthy. One night, about a year after they'd begun praying for each other, Steve and Donna sat across from each other at Raphael's, Donna's favorite Mexican restaurant.

"Kid," Steve said.

Donna looked up. When she saw Steve's serious expression, surprise flickered across her face. "Uh-huh?"

Steve squeezed her hand. "Over the last year," he told her quietly, "I've been praying on my morning jogs that God would change my heart and help me to better love you." He paused. "I believe He's done that."

Donna's mouth dropped open. "That's amazing!" she gasped.

"Amazing that I've been praying?" joked Steve.

"No. It's amazing because I've been doing the same thing!"

Steve leaned forward. "Really?"

"Absolutely," Donna said, nodding, "and God has changed my entire perspective. Every day, I've been learning to look at my life and ask God to change me."

She smiled, her eyes glittering. At one point, Steve and Donna had both thought there was no hope for their marriage. Now they knew God's plan was greater than their despair. Without their realizing it, God had taken two squabbling spouses and turned them into loving partners and best friends— the way He'd intended them to be.

☙❦❧

One day, not too long after that, Donna stood over the washing machine. She measured the laundry detergent and closed the cover with a *thud*.

Finally, she had a little time to catch up and do some cleaning. The kids were entertaining each other, constructing a "fort" under the kitchen table. Donna left the tiny laundry room and headed for the stairs, where she spied her tennis shoes sitting on the bottom step. Grabbing them, she made her way up to the master bedroom and opened the closet.

She bent down to put her shoes away, thinking, *Now, if the kids will stay busy for just another 20 minutes . . .*

Suddenly her heart fluttered, and she lurched back. "Ahhh!" she screamed, her arms flailing.

Nestled in the bottom of the closet was a stuffed armadillo, calmly staring up at her. Donna had always hated armadillos. Their bony-plated skin terrified her. And the only person in the world who knew that was—

"Steve!" she exclaimed, exasperated. Donna grabbed the phone and dialed the church, where her husband was working that day. The church secretary transferred her to Steve's office.

"Hello?" Steve's voice came through the line.

Donna said nothing.

"Hello?" he persisted.

Biting her lip, Donna tried not to laugh.

There was a pause on the other end. Then Steve snickered. "Did you find something in your closet, Kid?" he asked.

Silence.

"I hope you didn't scare him," said Steve lightly. "Armadillos are sensitive."

Unable to hold in her laughter any longer, Donna hung up the phone, giggling. It was all part of the game. She'd call Steve again later.

Right now, she had things to do . . . and pranks to plan.

Clearly, the love was back.

✐

*In 1986, Steve and Donna Thurman moved with their children and nine other couples to Colorado Springs to plant Fellowship Bible Church. Now with 3,000 members, Fellowship Bible has one of the largest congregations in the city. After witnessing phenomenal growth for almost 11 years, however, Steve and Donna felt God leading them to New Zealand, a country in which only five percent of the people are reported to be Christians. The Thurmans moved there in 1996 to launch Mariner's, a leadership training center which assists existing churches and helps to plant new ones. Steve and Donna agree that they—and their family—never could have handled moving so far away if it weren't for their strong relationship.*

*Now, after more than 25 years of marriage, the Thurmans have become even closer and have grown in their appreciation of and love for one another. Their playful streak is wider than ever; Steve often can be found jogging on the New Zealand coast, with Donna hiding behind a sand dune, waiting for the perfect moment to scare him.*

*Steve explains their relationship this way: "The turnaround in our marriage reflects the application of the grace of God. It also mirrors what happened in the first chapter of Genesis—out of nothing, God created something wonderful."*

Married couples have found many ways to design a loving and satis-fying relationship, but the experts have discovered that there are only four primary ways to *ruin* a marriage. I call these four destruc-tive patterns "divorce germs." It's as if couples move through their lives totally unaware of the infection setting in. And Steve and Donna Thurman were a typical American couple who became infected with *all four* germs.

First, they withdrew from conflict, sometimes for days.

Second, they then escalated into repeated, heated arguments over the same issues.

Third, they infected each other with the "biggie": belittling each other. Donna felt treated like a little kid, and that made her feel invalidated; her comments about Steve were statements of his inferiority compared to other, more sensitive and giving husbands. Any time a husband and wife start treating each other as inferiors, the infection seeps in deep.

Lastly, they both had some highly exaggerated and false beliefs about each other. Steve thought that Donna would bankrupt them and wasn't "pulling her weight." Donna believed that Steve was unreasonably tight and simply didn't care about her burden as a mother of young children.

Each of these four germs is so destructive because of the level of anger it instills in the marriage partners. When all four have infected a relationship, the results can be disastrous.

Steve and Donna each needed to make a commitment to begin honoring the other again. That commitment, as I've said before, is the foundation of any healthy relationship. When you start seeing your mate as more valuable, it's difficult to continue belittling him or her. Honoring words and actions are so powerful, in fact, that they actually—over time—reverse the damage caused by previous belittling.

Steve and Donna, by God's grace and conviction, individually came to realize how much they really meant to each other and began increasing their value for each other. Even when their feelings weren't "on board" yet, they worked at giving each other honor. And as the value of a mate increases within one's heart, so, too, does the motivation to keep loving and caring for that person. (One of the best ways to increase honor is to start making a list of all the things you appreciate or value about your mate. Turn this into a habit and watch the list grow through the years.)

When Steve and Donna turned to the Lord for strength to keep going in the relationship, He answered their prayers, because He's more concerned about how much we love one another than we are. And as He softened their hearts, they began talking more, working on their problems together and with mutual respect, and getting to really know and understand each other. In short, they were killing those divorce germs that had made their marriage so sick for so long.

The beautiful thing is that, as the end of their story makes clear, Steve and Donna have continued to grow in their love and support for each other through the years. They haven't made the mistake of taking the relationship for granted and letting those germs reinvade. And their reward is the kind of marriage that all of us want.

—Gary Smalley

# THE LAST
## OF THE
# ANGRY MAN

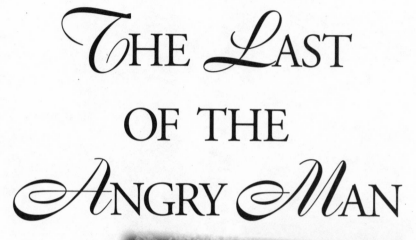

*Raul and Sharon*
*Ries*

MARRIED IN 1968

*Bang . . . bang . . . bang!*

Raul Ries pounded on the front door of the home he shared with his wife, Sharon. The house was silent. He put his ear against the door, then let out a string of profanity.

Of course Sharon wasn't home—it was Sunday night! She was in church, like always. *I'm sick of Miss Perfect Christian!* he thought with a sneer. *Why does she always have to go to church and lock me out?* Now he'd have to break in through the kitchen window.

Raul never carried a house key; he enjoyed interrupting whatever his wife was doing and making her come to the door. *All Sharon has to do is just take care of the house and the boys, anyway,* he told himself.

Straightening his shoulders, he walked around the side of the house. It was obvious, he thought angrily. Unlike his wife, he worked hard. He went to college at night; during the day, he brought home the money as the owner of a prosperous kung fu studio in Los Angeles.

Still muttering to himself, Raul shoved open the side gate and picked his way across their backyard. Then he unhooked the screen from the kitchen window and crawled into the dark house. Striding down the hallway, he fumbled for a light switch—and tripped over something.

*Suitcases!* Sharon was going to leave him! Swearing, he kicked a bulging trunk.

He couldn't believe she was actually going through with it. His wife had often talked about taking the boys and leaving him. In return, Raul had threatened her: *I'll kill you if you go.*

And he'd meant it. If Sharon divorced him, she'd most likely remarry at some point. Raul couldn't stand the thought of his high school sweetheart raising their boys with another man. He'd rather murder her.

He narrowed his dark eyes. Obviously Sharon hadn't believed his threats. If she had, she wouldn't have left their luggage in plain view. *Well, she'll learn not to mess with Raul Ries,* he vowed. He had killed in Vietnam, and he would kill again.

It wouldn't be so tough. He'd shoot her and the boys, then shoot it out with the police. He would leave this earth in a blaze of glory.

Searching the closet, Raul quickly found his .22-caliber rifle and a box of ammunition. Then he sat on the couch, loaded 18 rounds into the gun, and folded his well-muscled arms—waiting for his wife's return.

155

~⚬~

*R*aul had first met Sharon Farrel when they were juniors at Baldwin Park High School in a suburb of Los Angeles. They came from vastly different backgrounds.

Raul, whose family was abusive and alcoholic, arrived at school each day bearing the mental image of his father beating his mother. Raul had learned from an early age to stay away from his drunken dad or he'd be hit as well.

Raul found fighting to be a release for his own volatile emotions. Repeatedly getting kicked out of school and then being reenrolled on the pleas of his parents, he had earned a fierce reputation among the other boys.

Sharon lived in another world. The daughter of missionaries, she had moved to the United States during her junior high years—having grown up in Chile and Colombia, where her parents planted churches and schools. Fluent in Spanish and an excellent student, she was involved in Pep Club, Student Council, Drill Team, German Club, and her church youth group and choir.

With different classes and different circles of friends, the two students might never have met. But their lockers were close to each other. One day in the fall, Raul noticed a striking redhead shut a nearby locker door. He nudged his friend Tom, whose girlfriend shared a locker with the mysterious beauty.

"Who's that chick?" asked Raul, nodding in her direction.

Tom grinned at him. "Oh, that's Sharon Farrel."

Raul looked Sharon up and down, watching as she chatted and laughed with friends. A wide smile spread across his face. The girl was a knockout. And even from a distance, Raul could see she had a sparkling personality. *I'm gonna have to get to know her,* he decided.

From that day on, Raul smiled at Sharon whenever they crossed paths. Soon they began making small talk. She had her eyes on him, too. Because of her South American background, Sharon was drawn to people of Spanish descent. Whenever she and Raul met, she secretly admired the boy's greenish-brown eyes, brown skin, and black hair. He reminded her of a *conquistador* from Chile's colonial era.

The juniors continued to bump into each other on campus; gradually, they developed a casual friendship. After several months of flirting, Sharon saw her chance to get to know Raul better. Every year Baldwin Park High sponsored an All-Sports Dance, and each team chose a princess to "rule" over the dance. Sharon had many friends on the tennis team, and they had selected her to represent them. Now, as a princess, she needed an escort.

A week and a half before the dance, she approached Raul during lunch. Twisting a lock of long, red hair around her finger, Sharon watched him lean against the wall with his buddies, talking animatedly.

She cleared her throat. "Raul? Can I ask you something?"

Raul led her a few feet from his friends, then spread his hands in mock generosity. "Sure—ask me anything!"

"I don't know if you've heard, but I'm a princess for the All-Sports Dance, and . . . " Her voice trailed off. "Would you be my escort?"

"No kidding? I'd love to take you there!" Raul knew he'd be trading his usual Friday night carousing for a simple dance, but it would be worth it. Sharon wasn't like any girl he'd taken out. She wasn't cheap or easy; she seemed smart, fun, joyful—and interested in him.

During the following weeks, Raul and Sharon bought tickets and made plans. When the night of the dance finally arrived, Sharon stood in front of the mirror as her mother zipped her into a white organdy dress that was trimmed with yellow taffeta. Sharon had spent weeks sewing the dress, and half the afternoon arranging her hair in a cascade of curls.

"So, who's Raul?" her mother asked as she pulled up the zipper.

Sharon fastened her earrings and tried to sound nonchalant. "Oh, he's just a friend from school." *A very cute one,* she thought dreamily.

Mom cut into her thoughts: "Is he a Christian?"

The question made Sharon squirm. "I don't know, Mom!" she said. "He's just my escort tonight. I don't plan on marrying him!"

Mom said nothing.

Sharon knew what she was thinking, though. It had been drilled into her and her older sister, Shirley, since they were children: Get an education, choose a career, and don't think about boys until you're 26 years old. Mom always emphasized that God would bring the Christian man of His choice at the right time.

Sharon didn't like talking about boys with her parents, but assumed she'd follow their advice. A goal-oriented young woman, she wanted to finish college, then become a missionary to Chile before even thinking about marriage. Still, she craved a deep relationship. Connecting with someone who loved God would be great—but she hadn't found that chemistry with a Christian guy.

That made Raul all the more attractive.

After taking one last look in the mirror, she walked downstairs to introduce Mom and Dad to her latest crush. *Raul and I are only going to the All-Sports Dance—what does it matter if he isn't a Christian?* she thought. It was just one harmless date.

✿

Their date that night *was* innocent and fun. Raul put on his best behavior when he met Sharon's parents; then the two of them left for the school, where they danced, laughed, and stared unabashedly at each other.

After it was over, Raul brought Sharon home on time—and that was it. He never mentioned wanting to see her again.

The following year, the seniors flirted in the hallway. Raul always told Sharon how beautiful she looked, but he never asked her out. Then a few months before graduation, Sharon was elected homecoming princess. Again she needed an escort. Raul agreed to go with her.

Even as he sweet-talked Sharon, however, Raul was getting into fights and cavorting with his friends on the weekend. One Friday night, a week before the homecoming dance, he got into a brawl with a young man who had asked Raul's ex-girlfriend to a party. Infuriated that someone would "mess around with his chick"—even if he was no longer dating her—Raul punched and kicked the other boy, using kung fu techniques he'd been studying, until his victim lay unconscious. Finally, his buddies nervously pulled him off the boy; they bolted when they heard police sirens.

The following Monday, Raul was called into the principal's office. There two plainclothes policemen met him. They escorted him to the West Covina police station, where he was fingerprinted and booked on assault and battery charges. The student Raul had beaten up was listed in critical condition. Because of that, the school barred him from attending homecoming.

Two days before homecoming, Raul called Sharon with the bad news. "I can't take you to the dance," Raul said quietly. "I got into a little fight last weekend at a party, and now the school won't let me go to homecoming."

Sharon clenched her jaw, trying not to cry. "Just because of that?"

"Yeah, well, you know how uptight they are," said Raul.

Sharon was devastated. For weeks she'd dreamed about attending the dance with him! *It won't be homecoming if Raul's not there,* she told herself.

But on the night of homecoming, Raul sneaked in anyway. He and Sharon danced until midnight. Raul's rebellious attitude scared Sharon, but her excitement over seeing him seemed to cancel out her fear.

Raul still had to face the authorities, though. When his sentencing came the next week, he pled guilty to assault and battery, facing up to two years in jail. As Raul waited with shaky knees, the judge peered at Raul's file for what seemed like hours. Finally, the judge looked at him.

"Raul Ries," he said sternly, "if you are willing to enlist in the Marine Corps, your sentence will be suspended."

Raul couldn't believe his luck. Immediately, he opted to join the military. *You beat the system!* he congratulated himself, smirking. Now he'd be able to go back to school and graduate.

Beneath his cocky exterior, however, Raul was also relieved. Since his arrest he'd worried about what Sharon might do if she found out. A sweet, naive church girl, she probably wouldn't want anything to do with a convicted felon.

Now Sharon wouldn't have to know about his lawless side—and if he was to have any chance with her, he needed to keep it that way.

⤙✖⤚

"*Y*ou enlisted in the Marine Corps?" Sharon asked him several weeks later, shock and fear in her eyes.

The news made her feel sick. She and Raul had just started getting attached to each other, and now he was leaving for military training! Sharon was planning to take classes at a junior college in town, hoping Raul would stay close by. But it looked as though their relationship was about to come to an abrupt halt.

Even worse, the war in Vietnam was raging. It was 1966, and the U.S. was losing men by the hundreds. *What if he's sent to Vietnam and gets killed?* she thought.

Raul wasn't concerned. He simply shrugged and said, "Sharon, don't worry—I'll be fine!" He kissed her cheek. "I'll write you every day from boot camp."

Sharon was doubtful. But Raul would keep his promise, writing daily.

Soon their relationship took on a whole new dimension. They spent much of their free time together, talking about their hopes and dreams. Believing she could convert Raul, Sharon took him to church several times and talked at length about her desire to be a missionary.

When Raul walked forward to pray at the altar one Sunday, Sharon was ecstatic. *He's going to be a Christian! Things will turn out great!* she thought.

But Raul hadn't walked the aisle for spiritual reasons; he wanted to impress Sharon. He didn't want to lose her, after all. Sharon inspired him to be a better person; he felt less angry when he was around her, more peaceful and alive. He had fallen for her, and it showed in his letters—which continued after he was sent to Vietnam, four months after boot camp was over.

"Sharon, I love you," he wrote impulsively in one note. "Let's get married when I get back from the war."

Raul's plans scared and excited Sharon. She loved him, too—but she still had two years left before graduation, and wanted to return to Chile first. Besides, she wanted him to become a Christian before things got any more serious. She had already experienced a painful relationship with another unbeliever she'd tried to convert. This time, she would do it right.

With trembling hands she tried to put him off in her next letter: "I can't marry you, Raul. Not until you're a Christian."

"But I *am* a Christian!" Raul wrote back. "Didn't I go to church with you? We'll go every Sunday when I get back. Don't worry, I could never hurt you—you're the only girl I've ever loved!"

When Sharon read the note, her brow wrinkled in confusion. *Of course Raul wouldn't hurt me,* she thought. She pictured him dodging bullets to save another Marine in combat. *He's wonderful.*

But the military didn't think so.

Despite earning two Purple Hearts, Raul was wreaking havoc on the Marines—just as he had on his high school administrators. He'd seen 11 months of blood and death. The war was brutal, and Raul believed that if he was sent out one more time, he'd die. More than anything else he wanted out—and to be back in California with Sharon, physically and mentally intact.

So he started defying the system, hoping to be released. He broke every rule he could, even threatening his superiors with death if they sent him back into battle.

Raul continued his rebellion for several weeks. Finally the Marines sent him to a psychiatric hospital in Oakland, California. After giving him a battery of tests, however, a psychiatrist saw through Raul's scheme to escape and recommended a dishonorable discharge. Raul was to be sent to Camp Pendleton, about an hour south of Los Angeles, until the papers could be processed.

Not wanting Sharon and his parents to know the real reason for his homecoming, Raul told them that all the Marines who'd been in combat had to stay at a psychiatric hospital for six months afterward. "You know how they brainwash you when you go in," he explained. "Well, at the hospital, they have to make you normal again before you can reenter society."

Sharon and the Rieses accepted his excuse without question. They were simply thankful to know he was safe at Camp Pendleton.

Meanwhile, as Raul waited to have his papers processed, he continued to cause trouble for the military. *Why play by the rules? I'm getting a dishonorable discharge anyway,* he reasoned. Within days of arriving at Camp Pendleton, he was stripped of all his freedom, including weekend liberty. Still, he managed to bribe the guards and sneak out each Friday night to see Sharon.

Sharon had no idea Raul wasn't allowed to be off base every weekend, but she could tell he had changed. The boyishness in his eyes had disappeared and been replaced with a newfound seriousness—a sharp, piercing expression. It drew her to him. He was even more handsome and mature than she'd remembered.

Soon after they were reunited, Sharon decided that even if Raul wasn't a Christian, she wanted to marry him eventually. As they spent time together each weekend, their passion intensified. She found it harder to tell Raul "no" when he pressured her toward a sexual relationship.

"I can't do this, Raul," she said during one date.

"Why not, my little redhead?" Raul asked, confused. "I love you!"

Sharon sat up in the passenger seat of Raul's car and tried to explain: "Because God created sex for marriage, and I want God's blessing on our lives."

Raul kissed her forehead, undaunted. "Then we'll get married."

"I'm not ready to get married, Raul," she protested. "I need more time."

"Okay, I'll get you pregnant," he said, running his fingers through her red hair. "Then you'll have to marry me."

"Sorry, Raul," said Sharon, pushing him away playfully. "I'm determined that will never happen."

But a few weeks later, it did.

It was Easter weekend. Raul and Sharon, planning to go camping with Raul's family, went early Friday morning to stake out a good campsite. All day they waited for the Rieses to arrive—but a last-minute change of plans kept Raul's family from showing up. When night fell, Raul and Sharon realized they would be alone.

The physical temptation became intense. Around midnight, Sharon gave in. Immediately afterward, she was overcome with guilt. The next morning she sobbed all the way home from the campsite. *I broke my vow to God,* she thought.

As she cried, Raul looked over at her from the driver's seat. "What's wrong, Sharon?" he asked, confusion in his eyes. "I love you!"

Sharon slumped. "I know," she said. "But this wasn't the way our relationship was supposed to be."

*I shouldn't even be dating you,* she thought. She knew she had defied God by again pursuing a relationship that was wrong. Now she'd further complicated things by having premarital sex.

"What if I'm pregnant?" she asked, tears stinging her eyes. The thought had haunted her all morning.

Raul pulled the van over to the side of the road and stopped. He put his arms around Sharon, trying to reassure her. "Then I'll *have* to marry you!" he insisted, only half-joking.

His promise of marriage would soon be put to the test.

⟋⟍

*F*acing Raul three weeks later, Sharon choked out the words: "I'm . . . I'm pregnant."

She blinked hard, trying to stay calm. In the past month she had read the Psalms one by one in search of comfort. When she'd arrived at Psalm 34:19, her heart had skipped a beat as she read: "Many are the afflictions of the righteous: but the Lord delivereth him out of them all" (KJV). Sharon didn't feel righteous—she felt miserable. But she'd clung to the hope in that verse.

*God, forgive me,* she prayed repeatedly. *Give me another chance. And please, please don't let me be pregnant.*

But she was. Now she would have to reap the consequences of what she'd done.

Raul's face lit up with a smile. "We're going to have a baby? That's great!" He gave her an enormous hug. "Now we can get married!"

Sharon's jaw dropped. All she could do was stare at Raul. How could he be so happy? Her life was over! All her plans to finish college and be a missionary had vanished in the one evening she wanted to forget.

Still, she was in love with Raul. She looked at him, seeing that goofy grin on his face, and realized they were going to be a family. She felt a rush of determination. Yes, she'd made a mistake. But now she was going to make certain her children would be raised as Christians. *And I can still lead Raul to God,* she told herself fiercely. She knew it would be a challenge, and it scared her a little. But the thought of life without Raul frightened her even more.

So did the thought of telling her parents. She knew they wouldn't share her optimism about the future of such a marriage.

Her parents liked Raul, and as missionaries appreciated their daughter's efforts to lead him to God. But Sharon knew they didn't approve of the way her relationship with him had developed. If her parents silently frowned on her continued dates with Raul, they certainly wouldn't endorse her marrying him.

One evening several weeks later, she and Raul broached the subject with her father during dinner. Her mom and sister were gone on a missions trip to Colombia, but Sharon knew she couldn't wait for them to come back before bringing this up. Sharon and Raul needed to marry as soon as possible if they were to hide her premarital pregnancy.

She looked nervously at Raul, who took a deep, quavering breath. He grabbed her hand under the table.

"Mr. Farrel," Raul said politely, "I would like to marry your daughter."

Sharon's father set down his fork. He looked at the young couple, his expression grave. "No," he said. Then he turned to his 20-year-old daughter. "Honey, you can't get married right now. You need to finish college first. But more important, you need to wait until Raul develops a closer walk with the Lord."

Sharon's dad picked up his fork again, then quietly finished eating his vegetables. Pushing his chair away from the table, he got up and walked into the other room.

Sharon's face crumpled. *Great,* she thought tearfully. *What am I gonna do now? I'm pregnant, I need to get married, and Dad just said no.*

There was only one thing they *could* do, she thought—plan for the wedding anyway.

Without her father's consent, Sharon began doing just that. She bought material to make a dress. She sent a letter to her mother and sister before they returned, informing them that there would be a July wedding.

After Sharon had been preparing for several weeks, her parents realized she was serious.

"I told you we want to get married," she reminded them one day, cutting through the white silk that would become her bridal gown.

Her dad and mom said nothing. Then the two of them went into another room, where Sharon could hear them talking quietly.

Several minutes later, they returned. "A wedding is a once-in-a-lifetime event," Sharon's dad said. "So we're going to throw you a huge one and invite everyone we know. We want to give you the best wedding ever!" Later Sharon learned that her mother, sensing Sharon was pregnant, had concluded that her daughter still should not be deprived of her wedding day.

Sharon blinked in disbelief. She'd simply hoped they would bless her marriage to Raul; she hadn't expected them to finance a big celebration. They couldn't afford that; after all, they were missionaries!

"Thank you," she whispered to them, her green eyes shining with gratitude.

From that point on, Sharon's mom and dad supported the upcoming marriage. Raul's parents, ecstatic with their son's choice of a wife, did also.

But Raul and Sharon never told either family that she was pregnant. Sharon couldn't face shaming her family, though she suspected her parents knew. She planned to tell them after the wedding, when things had calmed down.

The night before their wedding, on July 5, 1968, Sharon had trouble sleeping. Tossing and turning in bed, she reviewed her plight. She was going to have a dream wedding, marrying the man she loved; but Raul wasn't a Christian, and she was four months pregnant!

*Lord,* she prayed, *I know I've disappointed You. I'm so sorry. I've disappointed myself, too. Please give me wisdom as a wife and mother. And please, Lord, can You fix the terrible mess I've made of my life?*

She stared at the ceiling for what felt like hours. Finally, she fell into a restless sleep.

Arriving for the ceremony the next day, Raul was blissfully happy. Sharon, on the other hand, could barely hold herself together. Anxious about what their future might hold and upset over the poor choices she'd made, she couldn't help realizing this was not the dream wedding she'd anticipated since she was a girl.

As the service began, Sharon masked her sadness with a forced smile. But her sorrow turned to frustration when she and Raul began reciting their vows. Instead of taking his vows seriously, Raul kept whispering compliments to her.

It was clear that Raul wasn't going to focus. So Sharon found herself saying her vows to the Lord.

As she did so, a warmth and tenderness she'd never experienced came over her. Standing next to Raul at the altar, she felt peaceful—as if the Lord were reminding her that He would always be her true Husband. No matter what happened in her wedded future, she believed He would protect, guide, and love her through it.

☙❧

The Rieses moved to an apartment in Anaheim, California; Raul was still posted nearby at Camp Pendleton. As Sharon prepared to give birth to their baby, she dreamed about their family's future. She still didn't understand Raul's schedule—he was often released past midnight—but didn't question him about it.

When Raul was home, he lavished attention on her. The two of them talked and talked; Sharon would try to communicate her thoughts about God, while Raul discussed his plans to open a kung fu studio someday—perhaps even in Mexico, his native land. Sharon was sure God was smiling on her.

Late one night in November, Raul came charging through the door of their apartment. He was waving a bundle of papers.

"You are looking at a free man!" he announced, a mischievous smile on his face. "Look at this! I got an *honorable* discharge! Can you believe it?" Raul hugged his very pregnant wife, shrieking with joy and disbelief.

Sharon wrinkled her brow in confusion. "You fought in Vietnam and were wounded twice! Why *shouldn't* you get an honorable discharge? And why are they releasing you almost two years early?"

"I'll tell you why," Raul replied, tossing his wallet and keys on the counter. "It's because the doctor on base doesn't like me. Read this!" He handed Sharon the therapist's analysis.

Her eyes scanned the paper. "Raul's outbursts of anger have caused him to be released from the Marines," she read. She laughed in disbelief. "You're right! That doctor has no idea what he's talking about! I don't think I've *ever* seen you angry, Raul. You don't have an angry bone in your body."

Raul looked down, and the smile suddenly disappeared from his face.

Sharon's stomach flip-flopped—but this time, she knew, it wasn't the baby. "So . . . did you get angry?" she found herself asking.

"Oh, you know," Raul said with a shrug. "When they asked me to do stupid stuff like polish my shoes, sometimes I got mad. Nothing big."

Sharon wasn't convinced. She thought back to their high school days, when Raul had been suspended from homecoming because of a fight. Back then she'd brushed it off. But now it worried her.

*How well do I really know this man?* she wondered.

It wouldn't take long for her to find out.

❧

Raul tiptoed through the front door, careful not to bump into anything in the dark. Quietly he passed Raul, Jr.'s, room, where their infant son was sleeping, then headed for the bedroom he shared with Sharon. Suddenly he froze. The light was on! She had been waiting up.

Sharon put down the book she had been trying to read. She stared through red-rimmed eyes at her husband of almost one year. Raul's shirt was torn, and his face bore traces of blood. Obviously, he'd done more than go on "a few errands."

"Raul," she asked, her voice quivering, "it's two o'clock in the morning! You've been gone for almost eight hours! Where have you been?"

"Out," was his curt answer. Without further explanation he ignored her pleading eyes, pulled off his shoes and shirt, and collapsed into bed.

Raul promptly fell asleep. But Sharon stayed awake worrying for most of the night.

There was plenty to worry about. Six months before, they'd moved back to Covina, near Baldwin Park, to be near family. Within days of their arrival, however, Raul had begun to change. Instead of seeing Sharon and Raul, Jr. between work and class, as he'd done in Anaheim, he showed a disdain for family life. He spent all his free time with his old friends, partying, cruising—and, of course, fighting.

These days Raul came home when he pleased. He'd stopped telling Sharon his whereabouts, often lying to her when he left in the evening. If Sharon asked him to change his plans, he became angry. It seemed everything about her annoyed him now—especially her desire for them to attend church as a family.

The sweet, loving, attentive demeanor with which Raul had won Sharon's heart was gone—replaced with a simmering, hardened attitude she had never seen.

Worse, Raul had begun to abuse her. During the past few months he had knocked her down, kicked her, and thrown things at her. The bruises weren't obvious, and shame had kept her from telling anyone about Raul's temper.

But it scared her. *How will this affect the kids?* she thought. "Raulie," as they'd nicknamed their son, was only six months old. Sharon recently had discovered she was pregnant again.

The morning after Raul's 2:00 A.M. arrival, Sharon confronted him. "Raul, why were you out half the night? Why didn't you call me? Who were you with?"

Raul grunted, ignoring her questions. He'd kept the details of his rough past to himself in high school, and he wasn't about to tell Sharon about them now. She'd never approve.

Besides, he felt exhilarated, adventuresome, and dangerous when cruising the streets with his buddies. He'd forgotten how much fun street life was, and he wasn't going to give it up again. He brushed past her, strutting into the kitchen to grab some breakfast before his Saturday kung fu classes.

Sharon followed him. "You can't live like this! You're a husband and a father! God's given us so much," she continued. "Let's just have fun and enjoy this time together."

"Don't tell me how to live my life!" Raul shouted. He whipped around and leaned in toward Sharon, his face only inches from hers. "Leave me alone!" Then he turned on his heel and flung open the refrigerator with such force that the bottles clanged together.

Sharon jumped back, trembling as she leaned against the doorframe for support. "Oh, please don't say that, honey," she pleaded. "I just worry about you, and when I don't know where you are at night, it scares me. I wish you'd spend more time with me and Raulie."

Her explanation only angered him more. "Are you telling me to forget about my friends?" he shouted, clenching his fists until his knuckles were white. "You'll never take their place, Sharon!"

Setting down his cup of orange juice, he stormed back toward his wife. He shoved her out of the doorway. Then he tore out of the house, slamming the door behind him.

Sharon bit her lip as her elbow hit the doorjamb. *Lord, help me,* she prayed, tears blurring her vision. *Please protect my family.*

Leaving the house, Raul could remember the pain in his wife's eyes. But he didn't feel too guilty about the abuse. *At least I'm not belting her like Dad does with Mom,* he told himself. He was simply acting out what he'd seen his parents do for years. Besides, didn't he always apologize later when his temper had cooled?

This time would be no different. That night, after he had returned from a long day of kung fu lessons, Raul placed a bouquet of yellow roses on the kitchen table. Tucked among the flowers was a note: "My beautiful redhead, I'm so sorry. I know that I have hurt you really, really bad, and I feel horrible. I love you. Will you forgive me?"

Sharon did. She wasn't ready to leave Raul. She desperately wanted her marriage to work, and her missionary roots gave her hope that Raul could change. Anyone could turn his or her life around; she had seen evidence of it over and over throughout her childhood.

After many of their clashes, Sharon tried to explain to Raul how God felt about anger and violence. She would quote Scripture, hoping the words would somehow reach him.

She also started spending more time attending church, reading the Bible—and praying. *Lord,* she would petition, *please be with Raul. Change his heart, God. Save him for me, please.*

Raul, however, wasn't impressed by Sharon's devotion. Often the first thing he saw when arriving home from his job at the supermarket or a kung fu class was his wife curled up in a chair with a Bible on her lap, reading or praying. Sharon always put the book down when her husband walked through the door, ready to give him her full attention. But instead of admiring her faith as he'd done in high school, Raul was irritated.

"You and your stupid religion!" he'd sneer, throwing her Bible across the room. "You think you're better than me because you're more religious, don't you?"

"No, Raul!" Sharon would answer, trying to push him away. "That's not true, and you know it!" She was doing the only thing she could think of—going to God for help.

Despite Sharon's prayers, however, the abuse continued—and intensified.

∾∾

*S*haron gave birth to their second son, Shane, in March 1970. The moment she was alone with her newborn, she lifted him into the air and whispered, "He's Yours, God."

She meant it. Apart from her involvement in church, Sharon spent all her time with her children. Raulie and Shane were the only bright spots in her life, and she relished being with them. She would do whatever it took to ensure they grew up to be godly men.

But as Raul's abuse became more frequent, Sharon found it harder to protect her children from the verbal and physical torment. Though she had promised in her wedding vows to stay with Raul forever, she knew she had a responsibility to her boys, too.

*Lord,* she prayed, *how long do I have to stay with him? What if he hurts Raulie and Shane? What if Raul's influence teaches our sons to abuse their own wives someday or keeps them from knowing You?*

Those thoughts frightened Sharon—but God kept reminding her of scriptures like Jeremiah 29:11: "'For I know the plans I have for you,' declares the Lord, 'plans to prosper you and not to harm you, plans to give you hope and a future.'"

She held on to that hope. But as the months passed, life became even harder. Two years after Shane was born, her greatest joy was stripped from her.

Raul finally had saved enough money from teaching kung fu lessons to open his own studio. Sharon was happy that her husband had fulfilled his dream—until he insisted that she had to find a job to help support the fledgling business while he also worked part-time.

Sharon was devastated. She couldn't imagine being separated all day from her boys, now two and three years old. She argued against the idea, but Raul was adamant. For the first time in several years, she would have to work outside the home.

Sharon found a job as a secretary. Two days a week, her mother watched the boys. But on the other three mornings Sharon would leave Raulie and Shane at their next-door neighbor's house. To save money, she came home at lunch. But she couldn't see her boys then; the neighbor maintained that since noon was the children's nap time, they would be tired and upset for the rest of the day if their mother visited.

It broke Sharon's heart to sit next door to her children at lunch, unable to see them. That's why, when Raul came home one day at lunchtime, he found his wife crying over her sandwich.

"What's wrong with you?" he demanded.

As she explained, Raul hovered over her in silence, staring at her with a frightening coldness.

His thoughts were angry. *Why can't she toughen up and sacrifice once in a while? She's so weak! What good is her religion if she can't deal with life?*

He didn't say those things, though. "Just take a minute to calm down," he muttered. "You can't go back to work like this."

"I know," whispered Sharon, the tears starting again.

"Well, I gotta go. I have a class in 10 minutes." Raul grabbed his wallet and keys.

Sharon's face twisted in grief. *He has no heart,* she thought. *He doesn't care about anyone but himself.*

Raul exited the kitchen, glimpsing his wife's eyes. They looked dark, hollow. Gradually, over their three years of marriage, his abuse had beaten the joy, the life—the very thing that had first drawn him to her—out of Sharon.

He pushed the image out of his mind.

✎

"Move it!" Raul screamed over a year later at his oldest son, who happened to be in the way. "Why don't you watch where you're going?"

Four-year-old Raul, Jr., looked defiantly up at his dad. "Why don't *you* watch where *you're* going?" he shot back.

Raul's frown turned to a scowl. Picking up his son, he threw Raulie into the corner of the hallway. "You little brat!" he yelled at the tiny heap on the floor. "That'll teach you not to talk back to your father!"

It was a Sunday morning, and Raul had a full schedule of kung fu lessons and demonstrations. He was in no mood to be disrespected by his son. Ignoring a twinge of guilt over hearing the boy cry, Raul swaggered toward the bedroom, where he came face to face with Sharon.

She didn't say anything to him. Walking over to Raul, Jr., she picked the boy up, then smoothed his hair and kissed his brow. Carrying her son, she stalked past her husband.

Sharon sighed. Even though she'd left her job and was able to be with her boys all day, their dad's influence had worsened.

*Lord,* she prayed, trying to calm her son, *please wipe this incident from Raulie's mind.*

It was something she had prayed several times over the last year as she'd contemplated separating from Raul. Sharon had warned her husband that she might leave if he didn't change. Each time he had threatened her—with death.

She didn't believe he would kill her, though. And she couldn't put up with his abuse anymore—especially now that Raul was hurting their sons, too.

This, Sharon decided, would be the last time Raul harmed any of them. *I'm taking the boys and going to my parents', then to live in Santa Cruz with my sister,* she vowed.

She would pack their suitcases and leave that night after church.

⁘

With the rifle still resting in his lap, Raul brushed aside his memories of Sharon and the seven years they'd shared.

It was 1972 now; they'd been married four years. He knew Sharon would leave him and he would never find peace. Killing her and the boys was his only way out.

It was quiet, too quiet. He went to the TV and switched it on.

*Click, click, click.* He cycled through the channels. None of the shows interested him.

One more click, and the face of a balding, gentle-looking man appeared. The man was talking about Jesus.

*Just what I need to hear,* Raul thought irritably. He wasn't the least bit interested in what the man had to say.

He stood up to peer out the window. No sign of Sharon yet. Scowling, he sat down on the couch again. He didn't bother to change the channel.

"Jesus died on the cross for your sins," the man was saying. "He took the guilt upon Himself. When He had the nails driven into His hands and feet, He was dying for all the wrong you've ever done in your life."

Raul stared at the TV, half listening. He had done a lot of terrible things—beating up people, abusing his wife and children. Did this preacher really mean guys like him could be forgiven?

It seemed impossible. He watched for several more minutes, wanting to know what the man said about people who'd *really* messed up.

"God is reaching out to you," the man continued calmly. "It doesn't matter who you are or what you've done; He still loves you. And once you ask Him into your heart, you'll never be the same."

By now the preacher had Raul's full attention. It felt as if the man were speaking directly to him!

His eyes burning and his heart pounding, Raul laid his gun down on the carpet.

*If you don't accept Me today,* he felt a voice inside telling him, *you never will.* Overwhelmed, Raul fell from the couch to the floor. For the first time since childhood, he began to weep.

He didn't want to be full of anger all the time, constantly miserable. He didn't want to hurt Sharon and the boys, the people he loved most in the world. Feeling helpless and weak, he lay his head on the couch.

"I want all of you who are watching to pray with me right now," said the man on television. Then he began leading viewers in a prayer.

With tears rolling down his face, Raul prayed along with the preacher—asking for God's forgiveness and pleading for Jesus Christ to come into his life and save him.

Afterward, Raul felt an emotional release greater than any fight, physical or verbal, had ever brought him. He no longer felt guilty. All thoughts of death and shooting were erased from his mind; he wanted life for himself and his family.

God was real, and Raul had a relationship with Him! He couldn't wait to tell Sharon. He jumped up from the floor and grabbed his keys, hoping to meet his wife at the church and pray with the pastor at the altar. He had seen people do that when he'd occasionally visited the church with Sharon.

*Man, is she going to be surprised!* Raul thought happily.

She was.

◈

"Sharon, let me in!" pleaded Raul, knocking on their front door an hour later. He had just returned from church—where, to his dismay, he'd just missed Sharon and their sons. Now, Raul remembered he'd left the rifle on the floor. What if Sharon had seen it?

The thought made him feel ill. "I promise I won't hurt you or the boys!" he persisted. "I just want to give you some good news!"

The door opened a few inches, as far as the safety chain allowed. Sharon peered out. Saying nothing, she stared warily at him.

"Sharon, I've been born again!" Raul said tenderly. "I'm a Christian! I heard a guy preaching about God on TV, and I asked Jesus into my life! Can you believe it?" Sharon's expression turned colder. "No, I can't," she told him, and closed the door in his face.

*I've heard this before,* she thought. She remembered how, in his letters from Vietnam, Raul had insisted he was a Christian. Now, after years of lies, Sharon would have to see it to believe it.

Raul knocked again, undaunted. "Honey," he said, his voice softer, "please let me in."

Sharon stood with her back against the door. There was a sweetness in his voice she hadn't heard before. It wasn't likely, but what if her husband *was* telling the truth? God did change lives, didn't He? With a sigh of resignation, she opened the door and waved him inside.

Raul raced past her into the living room, where he'd left the gun. Strangely, it was gone. He hurried back into the kitchen to find Sharon. Pulling her close, he kissed her.

"Sharon, I want us to start over!" he said. "I know I've hurt you so much, but we're going to have a new life together—I promise!"

Sharon pushed him away, ignoring a twinge of guilt. Hadn't Raul angrily thrown their son into a heap on the floor, just hours ago? How could she trust him?

She studied her husband's face. "It took me all these years to decide to leave you, and now you show up saying you're born again? I don't know, Raul."

"But I *am* born again!" he insisted.

Sharon shook her head. She had been looking forward to starting over, getting away from Raul. But now, if he was really a Christian, she'd have to stay with him.

Tears rose in her eyes. "I hope you're telling me the truth," she said quietly. "Raul, you can't expect me to trust you so quickly! It's going to take time."

A wave of sadness swept through Raul. He understood his wife's reaction; she had every reason not to trust him. "Don't worry," he assured her. "I'm going to show you how much I've changed!"

And he did. That night Raul called Sharon's sister, Shirley, and her mother to tell them the good news. Early the next morning, he found Sharon's Bible and spent time reading it and praying.

As he did, he thought of things he could do that day to show love for his wife. During a break from his kung fu classes he decided not to hang out with his friends. Instead, he drove home and vacuumed the house and cleaned up the dog messes in the back yard—something he'd rarely done in the past. That night he helped his wife put the boys to bed, too.

Watching the "new" Raul in action, Sharon felt numb. All day she wondered, *What if he's lying? What if this is just another ploy to get me back?*

That night, when Raul tried to be intimate with her, Sharon pushed him away. "You may be okay," she said, "but I'm struggling with this." Raul's hands, which so recently had been tools of violence, made Sharon shiver. She wasn't ready for him to touch her.

Folding her arms, she braced herself for a sarcastic response.

But this time his response was gentle. "Dear, I'll wait for as long as it takes! I love you, and I understand."

To Raul's own surprise, he really did understand. From the moment he had given his life to God, Raul had been touched with a new sensitivity.

Throughout the next week, Raul continued to show Sharon that he had indeed changed. He phoned all his buddies from high school and eagerly told them about Jesus Christ. Most of his friends thought Raul was crazy; only one expressed an interest in his new life.

But their scoffing didn't bother Raul. Learning more about God was his focus now. He bought a Bible and read it with an intensity he'd previously reserved for kung fu. He attended Christian concerts with Sharon on Saturday nights at Calvary Chapel, Costa Mesa. He went to church with her and the boys every Sunday morning, trying to absorb everything the minister said.

Raul's excitement about being a Christian reached into every corner of his life. At the kung fu studio he informed students that everyone was invited to hear about Jesus Christ after the lessons, if they chose to do so. Most of his students attended simply because they were too afraid of Raul *not* to go—but after hearing his testimony, many expressed an interest in God.

Elated by the response of his students, Raul began leading a Bible study at home. Within two months the house was bulging with friends and students whose lives had been changed by Raul's testimony.

But Sharon was battling mixed emotions. She couldn't ignore the fact that people had become Christians through Raul. She also knew he was trying to love her and regain her trust by being more sensitive to her feelings, helping her with household chores, and spending more time with her. He was reading his Bible, attending church, and praying—and had cut ties with his old friends, surrounding himself with Christians.

But anger was still a major part of Raul's life. A few weeks after her husband's conversion, just when Sharon began to think that maybe he *had* changed, bits of the old Raul resurfaced.

It had begun as a minor disagreement about where to take the boys to dinner. Sharon looked up from tying Shane's shoelaces and told Raul, "Raulie and Shane really want to eat at McDonald's. Why don't we go there?"

"I'm sick of McDonald's," Raul said impatiently.

"Come on, Honey," said Sharon, looking from her husband to their sons' disappointed faces. "It would mean a lot to the boys."

Suddenly, Raul erupted. "Don't try to tell me what to do!" he yelled.

Sharon gasped. "I was just—"

"Shut up, stupid!" Raul ordered. He grabbed a pillow from Shane's bed and hurled it at her with such force that Sharon almost fell over.

Struggling to regain her balance, she stared at Raul, feeling betrayed. "I knew it!" she shrieked. "I knew this wouldn't last!"

*Raul's just playing church,* she thought. *He's trying really hard to be a Christian, and now it's blowing up in his face.*

Raul froze when he saw her tears. "I'm sorry, Sharon," he mumbled after a long pause. Abruptly he left the room and went outside for a walk, shaken by his outburst.

Wandering through the neighborhood, Raul silently cried out to God. *Why did this happen, Lord? The old Raul would have hurt Sharon, but I never thought the new Raul would. Shouldn't I be a different person? Shouldn't I have changed? I'm so sorry I messed up.*

As he walked and prayed, he sensed God's forgiveness. Slowly he began to feel more peaceful. But when he returned home more than an hour later, he found Sharon still upset.

"I thought you were a Christian," she declared. "Why can't you control yourself? You know, Raul, when you explode like that, I feel like throwing something at *you*—and I'm not usually an angry person!"

"I know I blew it, Sharon," Raul said softly. "But I won't let it happen again." Sharon could only stare at him in frustration. Even if his intentions were good, she thought, he probably would continue to lose his temper and hurt her.

Sharon knew nothing short of God's grace could help Raul release his anger—but she doubted he would ever find freedom. She wondered again whether Raul had a sincere faith. As a daughter of missionaries, Sharon had seen a lot of hypocrisy in people who turned to God in desperate situations.

Raul's relationship with God *was* authentic, but he wasn't able to keep his promise to Sharon. He hurt his wife occasionally over the next few months—jabbing her with his finger, pushing her, grabbing her roughly, and calling her names. His abuse wasn't nearly as intense as it had been before he'd become a Christian, but it was still there.

"You can't be a Bible teacher and share the Gospel and then come home and treat me like this!" Sharon would tell him. "God will not honor your ministry."

Sometimes Raul received her criticism; sometimes it made him more angry. But he revered God's Word, and when Sharon used the Bible to show him that he was out of line, Raul eventually was overcome with contrition.

He didn't want to hurt his wife. In his heart, he knew he was wrong. He kept praying, *Lord, help me to control my temper.* It would take time to break his old, destructive habits, he told himself.

Then one day, several months after receiving Christ, Raul found a scripture during a break in his kung fu classes that cast his behavior in a new light. He read:

> Meanwhile, Saul was still breathing out murderous
> threats against the Lord's disciples. . . . As he neared
> Damascus on his journey, suddenly a light from heaven
> flashed around him. He fell to the ground and heard a
> voice say to him, "Saul, Saul, why do you persecute me?"

"Who are you, Lord?" Saul asked.

"I am Jesus, whom you are persecuting," he replied (Acts 9:1, 3-5).

As Raul meditated on those words, he was overcome with the realization that when he'd been persecuting Sharon, he had also been persecuting Jesus, who had died for his sins. He wasn't just hurting his wife with his outbursts of anger; he was hurting God, too.

Raul buried his face in his hands, dismayed. For months he'd wanted nothing more than to learn about the Lord and grow in his Christian faith. But now he knew that to have a right relationship with God, he needed to honor his wife as well. He needed to let go of his temper. If he didn't do it soon, his anger could permanently damage his family—and maybe his faith.

That was the motivation Raul needed to change. His pulse racing, he set down his Bible and called his wife from the studio. As soon as he heard her voice, tears started down his cheeks.

"Sharon," he said hoarsely, "I want you to know how sorry I am for hurting you." Then he explained what he'd just learned.

At home, Sharon listened, saying nothing. *How often am I going to hear this?* she wondered. She was tired of his empty promises.

"The thing I want most in life is to please God," Raul continued. He took a deep, shaky breath. "Now that I know it hurts Him when I hurt you, I don't think I could ever abuse you again."

Raul kept his word, though it was tough. From that day on, with God's help, he was able to stop physically hurting his wife and children.

As he prayed and studied the Bible, Raul began to see that when he became irate he needed to remove himself from the situation rather than immediately react in anger. Soon, whenever he got mad, he would leave the room and walk around the neighborhood, using the time to pray. Usually by the time he returned, he found that the anger had dissipated.

Raul also came to understand the roots of his rage. It had come from watching the abuse caused by his father. Raul learned that the only way to forgive his father was the way God had forgiven Raul—unconditionally. Several years later Raul's dad, too, found forgiveness in Christ through one of Raul's Bible studies.

God had worked some miraculous changes in Raul's life, but the Rieses' marriage was still far from healthy. Sharon had some things to let go of as well.

◇✕◇

*S*haron stood in the den of her in-laws' house, staring at the pictures hanging on the wall. She sighed, depressed. It had been almost six months since her husband had given his life to God. While she appreciated Raul's efforts to be gentler with her and the boys, she was still having trouble trusting him.

The emotional wounds remained. Though Raul no longer physically abused her, he still had an aggressive and forceful personality that reminded her of the violent past.

*I'm not sure if I even like this man anymore,* she thought.

It had actually been easier for her to cope with Raul when he was a non-Christian. She'd been able to justify his temper; she'd been the one sacrificing her happiness by staying with him.

But now she had no choice but to remain married to Raul. She knew God had designed marriage to last a lifetime.

She gazed at a framed photo of Raul as a young Little League player. Poised as if ready to swing the bat, wearing a blue baseball cap, he was smiling a toothless grin. *How ironic that he looks so cute here,* thought Sharon. *It's hard to believe that there's an angry man hiding behind that sweet smile.*

Raul had recently shaved his head and grown a goatee in hopes of being profiled in a martial arts movie. To Sharon he looked more evil than ever. Some days, when she caught Raul giving her a harsh look or muttering angrily under his breath, she couldn't help but wonder if she was married to some kind of converted devil.

Now, standing in the Rieses' den, Sharon felt a twinge of guilt. She knew she needed to let go of her bitterness toward Raul, yet sometimes it seemed impossible. He had hurt her and the boys so badly.

Then suddenly, it was as if God's voice cut through her thoughts. *Sharon,* the Lord seemed to tell her, *nobody could put up with Raul—not his parents, teachers, or military leaders. But I know you can. Will you love him for Me? He's My child.*

Sharon sank into a swivel-backed chair, allowing the words to register for several minutes. She did *want* to love Raul. But she was tired of trying. Yet she didn't like what her own hostility was doing to her heart, and didn't want to disobey the Lord.

She stared at the picture again from across the room. As she did, she realized she was failing to see Raul the way God did—as a child of His, just as the Little League photo portrayed. She needed to look beyond the macho, sometimes rough man she'd married to see that in Raul's heart, there had been rebirth. She couldn't expect changes to happen all at once; it would take time for the Holy Spirit to modify Raul's behavior—maybe even a lifetime.

*Will you love him for Me?* God seemed to persist.

Sharon paused. Then she nodded and whispered, "Yes." As she did, the love of God seemed to flood her being.

⟡

*S*haron soon had to follow through on her decision to love Raul. Their physical relationship still existed, but Sharon was generally cold and unresponsive toward her husband. Many nights, when Raul tried to be intimate, she would push him away.

"Don't touch me," she'd tell him. "Not tonight."

Raul was hurt. But instead of fighting with her about it, he would simply say, "Okay, I'll wait." He knew that all he could do was pray for his wife, love her, and continue to grow in his relationship with God.

Yet the lack of intimacy was making it harder for their marriage to heal, and Sharon knew it. One night, soon after the experience in her in-laws' den, she faced the problem once more.

Raul dropped onto the bed next to Sharon, who was reading. He ruffled her hair. "You are so beautiful," he whispered.

Sharon smiled awkwardly and mumbled, "Thanks." Scooting out of his reach, she picked up the book again. This time, though, she glimpsed the expression on Raul's face. He was obviously wounded by her not-so-subtle rejection.

For several minutes Sharon tried to read her book, but couldn't concentrate. *This has to stop,* she finally decided. *I'm hurting our marriage by constantly rejecting Raul like this.* She set down her reading on the nightstand and turned toward him.

"I'm sorry," she whispered, squeezing his hand. "I don't want to push you away."

So that night, for the first time in six months, she didn't.

It was difficult. Raul didn't realize it, but Sharon had to tearfully pray the entire time, asking God to allow her to be intimate with her husband and to help her surrender her wounds from the past. She knew it was the only way she would be healed.

Her obedience brought God's healing. After that night, Sharon felt free. Her bitterness, which for so long had constrained her, was replaced with love and affection. Slowly, their marriage was getting healthier.

❧

*A*s the Rieses' relationship grew stronger, so did Raul's home Bible study. The group soon numbered 30 members; he had to move it to the kung fu studio, where there was more room.

Every week Sharon and the boys would rush to the studio after Raul's last class, hurrying to help him scrub the bathroom, clean the floors, and straighten up before everyone arrived. Many people became Christians through the Rieses' Bible study; sometimes the group would stay up all night praying. By 1975 it had grown to 300 members, and they started meeting in a movie theater.

Meanwhile, flocks of people from the Bible study had begun coming to church with the Rieses. Soon the group wanted to meet at the theater on Sunday mornings, too. But Raul didn't want to start a church. He had no formal biblical training. And since English was his second language, communicating effectively was sometimes hard. He dismissed the idea—even though he was spending more time doing ministry work than running his kung fu studio.

Business had begun to suffer as a result. Raul had stopped doing kung fu demonstrations, and some students had left the studio since he'd become a Christian. Sharon privately worried whether Raul was making a mistake by cutting back so much on the business. She was pregnant again, and couldn't help but wonder how he would provide for their growing family.

God was about to work that out, too.

Ever since Raul had become a Christian, he and Sharon had driven from West Covina to Calvary Chapel in Costa Mesa on Saturday nights to attend Christian concerts. There Raul realized that Chuck Smith, pastor of Calvary Chapel, had been the man on television who had led him to God on that life-changing night. Excited, he and Sharon bought copies of Chuck's tapes to use in their weekly Bible study. In time Raul developed a relationship with the pastor, and told Chuck how the pastor had helped save the Rieses' lives.

Soon after Raul's Bible study expressed interest in starting a church, Chuck invited him to attend "Shepherd's School"—one week of intensive Bible classes hosted by Calvary Chapel. The experience made Raul realize that, more than anything else, he wanted to preach the Gospel. He stepped up his study of the Bible and worked more intently on his English. If God ever wanted him to preach full-time, Raul wanted to be ready.

The opportunity came more quickly than he anticipated.

Just weeks after Raul went through "Shepherd's School," Chuck Smith approached him. "For a long time, I've talked about the need for a Calvary Chapel in your area," he said. "But last week, I realized we already have one—your group!" He grinned. Raul had been called and ordained by God, the pastor said, and the church wanted to affirm that.

Raul's eyes were wide with delight and disbelief. "So I can call our Bible study Calvary Chapel West Covina?"

Chuck nodded.

Raul jumped up from his seat. "Oh, that's so cool!"

Now he could finally concentrate on ministry! To Raul, it was an answer to prayer. Eventually he closed the kung fu studio, devoting his time to study.

To ease Sharon's fears about finances, he took a part-time job stocking shelves at a grocery store. The five dollars an hour he made there wouldn't cover all expenses, but it would help. Raul didn't feel right about asking the church for money right away; he wanted to be more established first. Even in his short time as a Christian, he'd seen some leaders mishandle money, and Raul didn't want to be one of them. Besides, he wasn't concerned. He knew that if God called him to ministry, He would provide financially.

God did supply the right amount of money to pay the hospital bills—$800—when their son Ryan was born in November 1975. An envelope containing $400 from an anonymous donor appeared one day in the mail; the next week, people from their church threw a shower for Sharon and gave her a check for $400. As God provided day by day, Sharon grew more confident about Raul's call to become a pastor.

Raul breathed a sigh of relief. He was thankful she'd seen him change over the past three-and-a-half years since he'd become a Christian. Having Sharon's support made him feel more confident than ever about his decision.

Sharon's affirmation of Raul's faith and his desire to go into ministry further strengthened their marriage. With his gifts of teaching and evangelism and her unending desire to work in missions, the Rieses sensed God had prepared them to be a dynamic team. There was nothing Raul wanted more than to pastor full-time, and Sharon longed to work alongside him.

He couldn't wait to get started.

❧

aul stood on a hill overlooking the rugged, majestic coast of Long Beach, California, conducting a wedding for a young couple in his church. Nearly 13 years had passed since Raul's entrance into full-time ministry, and Calvary Chapel West Covina had grown by the thousands.

Raul breathed in the fresh, salty air and silently offered a quick prayer for the bride and groom. Marriage wasn't easy—he and Sharon had learned that firsthand—and he took seriously his role of performing wedding ceremonies.

Clearing his throat, Raul looked into the eager face of the groom. "One day, Gary," he said, "you're gonna have to present your bride, Debbie, to the Lord. So listen closely to what Paul says about it in the Book of Ephesians."

Raul began to read: "Husbands, love your wives, just as Christ loved the church and gave himself up for her to make her holy—"

Suddenly Raul's voice trembled. He paused, blinking tears from his eyes, then continued. "Cleansing her by the washing with water through the word, and to present her to himself as a radiant church, without stain or wrinkle or any other blemish, but holy and blameless" (5:25-27).

His face wet with tears, Raul struggled to get out the rest of his remarks. Many of the wedding guests dabbed at their eyes with handkerchiefs, touched by the pastor's apparent feelings for the bride and groom.

Sharon, however, knew better. Sitting in the front row, her own eyes shining with emotion, she watched her husband weep as the soloist performed a familiar wedding song. Then she gazed at the white, wooden cross that rose on the hill behind Raul. *God's showing Raul something about me,* she thought.

And He was.

In Raul's mind's eye, he saw Sharon approaching the throne of God. There, she looked radiant as he presented her to the Lord—but Raul knew it was only because of God's grace. If it weren't for the way Jesus Christ had miraculously forgiven and changed him, his wife would have appeared bruised and battered before God's throne, having endured years of his emotional and physical abuse.

Raul shuddered, staring at the white-capped Pacific as the wedding song filled the air. *Lord,* he prayed, *help me to always be tender toward my wife, to love her and take care of her.*

He caught Sharon's eye in the crowd. More than anything else, he wanted to honor her. Sharon's prayers and tireless efforts to love and speak God's truth to him had changed his life.

But Raul knew his wife wasn't at the root of it—Jesus Christ was. Defying all odds, He had restored their hope, saved them from anger and bitterness, and healed their marriage.

Raul wiped his eyes. Now he had faith that God could restore anyone's marriage. There was nothing the Lord couldn't do—and the Rieses' lives gave living proof.

꩜

*Raul and Sharon Ries served at Calvary Chapel West Covina for 21 years—then moved in 1993 to Calvary Chapel Golden Springs in Diamond Bar, east of Los Angeles. There, with Raul as senior pastor, the church has grown to 14,000 members.*

*Raul also can be heard daily on his 30-minute syndicated radio program,* Somebody Loves You—*and is the evangelist for* Somebody Loves You *crusades, popular youth-oriented festivals in Southern California and overseas. In addition, Raul travels internationally, speaking at conferences and crusades. He has written several books, and the Rieses' story has been told in the movie,* From Fury to Freedom.

*Besides leading the women's ministry at Calvary Chapel, Sharon speaks at women's conferences and seminars. Through her work in the church she has fulfilled her lifelong dream of becoming a missionary, participating in church-sponsored missions trips to South America. Along with others, she has helped to plant fourteen churches and a Bible school in Chile and eight churches and two Bible schools in Colombia.*

*The testimonies of Raul and Sharon have affected those close to them, too. Raul's parents and siblings have all become Christians. So have many of his high school buddies, with two even serving with Raul as pastors in Calvary Chapel churches.*

*Raul and Sharon live in LaVerne, California, near their three adult sons. The Rieses feel awed and thankful when they consider how God has blessed their ministry and marriage.*

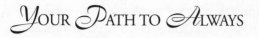

# YOUR PATH TO ALWAYS

What an inspirational story this is! I was gripped as I read it by the reality that Jesus Christ can change anyone and any situation.

For me, the essence of the story is that Raul and Sharon Ries's problems came about because they chose to dishonor God, and that turning that around was the key to the saving and healing of their marriage. Let's look at Sharon first.

Raised in a Christian home by missionary parents, she became a Christian herself at an early age and felt the call of God to one day pursue a missionary career of her own. Yet when she chose to dishonor Him by giving higher value to Raul and dating him, knowing that dating a non-Christian was contrary to God's will, her troubles began. They compounded when she got pregnant out of wedlock and then married a man she didn't really know at all.

By God's grace, however, Sharon learned from her mistakes and was willing to humble herself and take steps to repair the damage to her relationship with God. Claiming the promise of 1 John 1:9 ("If we confess our sins, he is faithful and just and will forgive us our sins and purify us from all unrighteousness"), she turned back to Him and confessed her disobedience, her self-centeredness, and her poor choices. She began honoring Him again, restoring Him to His rightful place of preeminence in her life. Then she trusted Him to take care of her.

Raul had spent his entire life dishonoring God, not valuing Him at all. Instead, he valued his carousing, his pleasure-seeking lifestyle, and the thrill of fighting. Those were his gods. And they led him to the point of being ready to kill his wife and children and then take his own life.

Once again, though, God's grace broke through, convicting Raul of his sin and his need of a Savior. When Raul accepted Jesus into his life, he also gave God the place of highest honor. Then he couldn't wait to tell his wife and his friends and even his kung-fu students what God had done for him.

As Raul now sought to honor God with his life, God's Spirit led him to realize that the way he treated his wife and children was dishonoring both to them and to their heavenly Father. So he said to them, "I'm sorry for the way I've treated you, because that's not honoring to God. Will you forgive me and let me start over in a way that pleases Him?"

We can all learn from the Rieses' experience. Spiritually and in our relationships, we get into trouble when we choose to dishonor God. But when we become willing to turn to Him and put Him in His rightful place of honor in our lives, He heals our relationship with Himself and begins to rebuild our other relationships as well.

I also have to commend and recommend to all of us Sharon's persistence in prayer. Once she was back in fellowship with God, she started praying for Raul to find his way to the Lord and never stopped, even through some extremely difficult circumstances. I'm reminded of Luke 18:1-8, a passage that has been the foundation of my prayer life for the past 25 years. Humanly speaking, the widow lady in that parable had no reason to expect justice from the judge, who had no respect for God or man. Yet she never gave up, reappearing before him day after day until she wore him out and he gave her a fair ruling after all.

God is nothing like that unjust judge; He delights in answering the prayers of those who love Him. Jesus said in Luke 11:13, for instance, "If you then, though you are evil, know how to give good gifts to your children, how much more will your Father in heaven give the Holy Spirit to those who ask him!" But He doesn't always answer right away or in the timing we think is best. In Sharon's case, she had come pretty much to the end of the line, believing she had to leave with her children to keep Raul from hurting them. And God, as is so often the case, chose that moment to say, "Okay, I'll answer all those prayers you've brought to Me about your husband."

Finally, the Ries story shows us the necessity and the power of forgiveness. Both of them needed to be forgiven for the sins they'd committed. Raul also had to go to Sharon and say, "I'm sorry for the things I've said and the way I've treated you. Will you forgive me?" And she said yes. This is *the* key step in restoring a damaged relationship.

Forgiveness has two aspects to it. First, it means "releasing people from the consequences of their actions toward me," wiping the slate clean. It *doesn't* mean the offenses didn't occur, but it means we no longer hold those offenses against those who hurt us. And second, forgiveness means we pray for the offender's release from whatever is holding him or her back from God's best.

If we won't forgive, 1 John 2 tells us, our hearts are filled with darkness. But if we will, as Sharon did, then God is honored and the most incredible healing of broken relationships is suddenly possible.

—Gary Smalley

# IN THE EYE

# OF THE

# STORM

*Dave and Jan Dravecky*

MARRIED IN 1978

"**D**ad, Mommy's crying!" Jonathan and Tiffany Dravecky exclaimed in unison as they bounded, breathless, into their father's office that day in September 1989.

Startled, Dave sat up straight. Just minutes before, he and his wife, Jan, had been interviewing a prospective writer for Dave's book, *Comeback.* Jan had left the room to answer the phone. Now, except for the sounds of muffled weeping coming from upstairs, the house was silent.

"I'll be right back," Dave murmured to the man seated across the desk. Shadowed by dread, Dave pushed himself out of his chair and headed upstairs to the bedroom.

He found her holding the telephone receiver, her shoulders shaking. "What's wrong, Honey?" he asked as he sank onto the bed next to her.

Jan could hardly choke out the words: "Pastor called . . . Dad . . . he's gone. . . ."

Her healthy 64-year-old father, a pharmicist who had never suffered any health problems, had died suddenly of a heart attack while filling a prescription. Jan couldn't believe it. Seven years before, her mom also had died without warning.

As the pain from her mother's death resurfaced, Jan felt overwhelmed with loss and loneliness. She hadn't been able to say good-bye to either of her parents, the two people she had depended on most.

She buried her face in her hands, sobbing. Then she felt Dave put his hand on her shoulder.

"I'm so sorry," he whispered.

Jan shook her head in disbelief. The past year had already been filled with crises. *God, how could You allow this to happen now in the midst of everything?* she asked silently. *I don't have time for this!*

Bleary-eyed, she looked at her husband of 10 years. Dave's left arm was in a brace, the result of a painful break he'd suffered just two weeks earlier. The weakened bone was an ever-present reminder of his battle with cancer, a fight that had begun a year before.

It had been a nightmare, discovering a tumor in Dave's arm and having it removed. It had been a career crisis, too. Dave was a pitcher for the San Francisco Giants—a left-handed pitcher.

During the past year, Dave had endured intense rehabilitation in hopes of making a professional comeback. With an emotional crowd watching, he'd pitched against and beaten the Cincinnati Reds. But just six innings into his second game, as Dave had hurled the ball toward home plate, a sickening *crack* had echoed throughout the stadium. The overstressed bone had snapped in two; Dave had fallen to the turf, grimacing in pain.

He had made national headlines that day, August 15, 1989. Thousands of letters had poured in as people told Dave and Jan their own stories of suffering. Mail was stacked knee-high in their garage, waiting for someone to respond.

The media had gone crazy, too; it seemed every major news reporter and magazine journalist was at the Draveckys' doorstep, pressing for an interview. Movie producers wanted to film a Dave Dravecky "Movie of the Week." Every publisher in America, it appeared, wanted to do a book telling Dave's story—and get it out immediately.

Jan remembered the prospective writer, still waiting downstairs. Motioning for Dave to rejoin the man, she dried her eyes. She would have to push this pain away, just as she'd been pushing away the pain of the last few years. Taking a deep, determined breath, she steeled herself for what lay ahead. She had a sick husband to care for; the United States of America was at their doorstep, with Dave in too much pain to handle the details of the interviews; their two children needed her as well.

Her grief would have to wait.

❧

The following days grew even more hectic. Jan logged 20-hour days, waking up at 6:00 A.M. and crashing at 2:00 A.M. Between coordinating media interviews, answering letters, working with the writer for Dave's book, and taking care of her husband and children, she flew to Ohio to oversee the details of her father's funeral. There friends and relatives kept asking how she was.

"I'm fine," she'd reply, pushing her feelings aside.

"But with everything you've had to deal with lately, are you sure?" they would persist.

"Of course." Jan stared at them, almost puzzled by their concern. She'd always been capable and energetic; nothing kept her down for long. Besides, she didn't have time to be upset. None of her obligations seemed negotiable.

That was especially true of the media commitments. In every interview, Dave and Jan had been able to steer the conversation toward their Christian faith, explaining that God was the One who allowed Dave's miraculous comeback. The Draveckys believed the Lord was putting them in the spotlight for a reason—to tell people about Him—and they took the responsibility seriously.

*How can I drop this chance to be a witness and an encouragement to others simply because I'm tired and stressed?* Jan asked herself. So she pressed on, believing the pressure would eventually ease.

But it was about to get worse.

Just two months after Dave broke his arm on the pitcher's mound, the Giants were one win away from the World Series. Dave, his arm still in a sling, put on his uniform and sat with his teammates in the dugout.

Jan knew the players would go berserk if they beat the Chicago Cubs. It would be a mob scene—dangerous for someone who was already injured. "Please," she begged her husband before he left home for the ballpark, looking pointedly at his fragile arm, "don't run out on the field if they win!"

But Dave did. As Jan watched the game from the stands, she saw— much to her chagrin—that her ebullient husband was the first to storm the field when the Giants won. Less than a minute later, she watched in horror as an eager player bumped Dave's arm. Even from the stands she could see her husband's face twist in pain.

His bone had snapped again, this time in a new place.

The second break was even worse than the first. Dave was in constant, excruciating pain. For six weeks he would spend each night trying to sleep in a reclining chair; the doctors felt lying down risked jostling his arm too much.

Lack of sleep left him exhausted. Soon the pain—and his unspoken worries over whether he'd be able to return to baseball—made him moody and depressed.

*He's such a bear now!* Jan often thought, watching him. In the public eye, Dave could smile and praise God in the midst of his suffering. But at home, the effects of his emotional and physical pain emerged. Even little things, such as coming home to a messy house, made him impatient as never before.

"Why are Tiffany's and Jonathan's toys all over the place?" he yelled one day, his voice booming through the house. "Kids, come here and clean up your stinkin' mess! *Now!*" Kicking a doll and a pile of Legos® out of his way, he waited for the children to scurry downstairs.

Jan's throat tightened at the sound of her husband's voice. Hurrying from the kitchen where she was making dinner, she went into the living room. There, with Tiffany and Jonathan, she began gathering the toys.

"Don't worry, Honey," she reassured Dave, who towered over them and scowled in disapproval. "We'll get it cleaned up."

Dave grunted and stormed into his home office—the only room that, in his opinion, wasn't a pigsty.

Jan hated seeing Dave in such a foul mood. She didn't like having Jonathan and Tiffany, ages 4 and 7, witness their father's explosions, either. The angrier Dave became, the more Jan tried to keep his moodiness at bay by making sure the house was in perfect order.

Having to keep everything spotless made it almost impossible for Jan to relax. But it seemed better than having to face an irate husband. Many nights she stayed up into the early morning—scrubbing the bathroom, folding clothes, ironing. *This won't go on forever,* she assured herself as she fell into bed. *I'm sure things will lighten up soon, and then I'll get my rest.*

Until then, Jan was determined to hold the family together. If she didn't, who would?

❦

*A*t the end of October, just a few weeks after Dave broke his arm for the second time, the Draveckys moved back to their home state of Ohio. Dave's parents and many family friends still lived there—and right now, Dave and Jan knew they needed all the support they could get. There was no immediate need to stay in San Francisco, either; the Draveckys weren't sure what would happen with Dave's career, not knowing whether his arm would heal properly or if the cancer would return.

Since Dave couldn't help with the move, Jan handled all the details herself—packing and unpacking boxes and getting the kids situated in their new elementary school. Then, instead of resting, the Draveckys took on a new responsibility. Less than a week after moving in, they invited Kristen, a young family friend in crisis, to live with them for two months.

Helping Kristen was no small task. The girl needed to talk, and Jan listened to her late into the night. She and Dave decided to try counseling Kristen and her boyfriend, Paul, together. One day Paul came to their home to talk.

The next day, Paul committed suicide.

The Draveckys were devastated—Jan especially. Though she didn't know Paul well, she was deeply affected by his death. The incident darkened the black cloud that had seemed to settle over her. She felt as if she were in a spiritual boxing match; as soon as she pulled herself together after one crisis, she was knocked down by another. She didn't know how much longer she could cope.

And only too soon, trouble struck again.

Just a few weeks after the move, Dave went to Cleveland for a routine checkup on his arm. The doctors discovered a lump—and hoped it was scar tissue. But when he and Jan sought a second opinion in New York, the worst was confirmed: The lump was a cancerous tumor. Dave would have to undergo more surgery. He and Jan scheduled the operation for five weeks later, after Christmas.

The news that his cancer had returned threw Dave into a tailspin. Until moving to Ohio he'd kept going to the ballpark, secretly hoping that once his arm healed he'd be back out there with his teammates, pitching for the Giants. Now he had to face the truth: His baseball career was over.

Jan encouraged him to retire immediately, but Dave resisted until he could put it off no longer. In his heart he knew he couldn't try for another comeback; his health was far too precarious. But the decision was still painful. He'd always been a ballplayer, and the future looked bleak without baseball in it.

Worse, he might not *have* a future—thanks to the recurrence of his cancer. The thought of impending death scared him. Instead of expressing his fears, though, he grew more irritable and moody.

As he did, the gulf between him and Jan grew wider.

Jan, meanwhile, continued living on adrenaline. She still worked 18-hour days to keep the family going. But as she faced the holidays, her energy began to fade. This year she couldn't get excited about Thanksgiving and Christmas, usually her favorite holidays. For one thing, it would be the first such season without her father present.

For another, Dave's upcoming surgery cast a shadow on the festivities. His new diagnosis had frightened her. After his first surgery she had thought the cancer was gone. Now it looked as though it might be an ongoing battle. *What if I lose Dave and my father in the same year?* she thought.

But as quickly as the disturbing thoughts came, Jan pushed them aside. If she dwelled on her fears, she reasoned, she'd worry herself crazy.

Some days, however, she wondered whether she might already be losing her mind.

During the last few weeks she had become increasingly forgetful, and it scared her. She'd always had an accountant's mind, easily remembering details—but now she would often stop talking midsentence, forgetting where she was going with a thought. Even the names of people she'd known for years were sometimes slipping her mind.

Cringing, she thought of a recent Dravecky family gathering. She had stood in the kitchen of Dave's parents' house, chatting with her sister-in-law—when suddenly she couldn't remember the woman's name.

Jan had been horrified. *I can't believe this!* she thought, her heart pounding wildly. *I forgot my own sister-in-law's name!* This wasn't some distant, long-forgotten relative; she was a close family member and friend. Jan continued talking and listening, never letting on what was happening in her mind. Finally, after several minutes, the name came to her. *It's Missy,* Jan thought, relieved. *Thank goodness I remembered.*

On the way home, she had relayed the incident to Dave.

"I forgot Missy's name tonight, David," she told him, shaking her head. "And that wasn't the first time I've been forgetful. I'm starting to wonder if I have a brain tumor or something."

At her mention of the word *tumor*, Dave felt his stomach turn. The last thing he wanted to hear from his wife was that she had cancer as well! *What an insensitive thing to say!* he thought. *And right after I've been diagnosed . . .*

"That's ridiculous!" he said a little too loudly. "You don't have a brain tumor! You're just working too hard. You need to slow down, that's all."

Jan stared helplessly out the window. She didn't have the luxury to stop and breathe! *How can I rest when I'm not the one who's sick anyway?*

And didn't the packed-full days serve their purpose? When she was busy, there wasn't time to think about her sadness and anxiety. It was easier to keep up the frantic pace, holding her fears at bay, hoping that soon life would return to normal—whatever normal was.

But before long, more signs of Jan's stress began to surface. As the date of Dave's surgery drew nearer, she began to suffer from insomnia. Often she'd wake up two hours after falling asleep—and couldn't doze off again. She also lost her appetite. Though it was the holiday season, she was almost never hungry. When she did eat, she felt pain in her stomach, like severe heartburn.

Jan tried not to dwell on her growing list of symptoms. Instead, she propped up her happy, capable, confident facade. She coped with Dave's moodiness while helping him finish writing his book *Comeback*. She played hostess to her brother and his family, who came to visit for Christmas one day after their houseguest, Kristen, moved out.

Before they knew it, the Draveckys were flying to New York on January 1 for Dave's surgery.

His 14 days in the hospital were grueling. The rest of his deltoid muscle was removed; intense radiation was beamed at his arm in the hope of killing any remaining cancer cells. Weakened by blood loss during surgery, as well as the side effects of radiation, Dave felt wiped out—and needed more help than ever from Jan. Jan, meanwhile, needed help of her own. She maintained her frantic schedule, pushing herself to meet everyone else's needs, never getting more than four or five hours of sleep a night. She credited her seemingly superhuman stamina, a trait of which she'd always been proud.

But as the stress mounted, her body began to break down. As she was about to discover, her emotions—which she'd pushed away all these months—could not be so easily ignored.

∿✕∿

The Dravecky family stepped through the grand double doors of the J.W. Marriott Hotel in Washington, D.C., staring in awe at the lobby's elaborate decor.

It was now the beginning of March 1990, just two months after Dave's surgery. He, Jan, and their children had been invited to the White House by President Bush, who was to present Dave with an Award of Courage from the American Cancer Society.

Jan guided Tiffany and Jonathan toward the front desk, where Dave was meeting the top officers of the American Cancer Society. She approached the huddle of suit jackets, and the president of the Society stuck out his hand in greeting.

"Nice to finally meet you, Jan," he said warmly, shaking her hand. "How was your flight?"

Jan smiled back. "Good—uneventful," she said. "You know, we're honored to be—"

Suddenly her voice trailed off. The blood drained from her face. Jan tightened her grip on her children's shoulders. The room seemed to spin, and she couldn't breathe. All she wanted was to run from the hotel lobby into the cool March air.

Heart hammering, she looked at Dave, who was chatting with the Cancer Society officers. She tugged at her husband's jacket.

"Dave!" she gasped, hoping the other men wouldn't notice. "I . . . can't . . . breathe! I need air."

Dave's eyes widened. "What are you talking about?" he whispered. But Jan was already rushing out of the lobby.

"Excuse me," Dave said to the men. In a few strides he was outside, catching up with his wife and grabbing her by the elbow. "Jan!" he exclaimed, irritated. "Come back inside! Just calm down until we can get into our room. You'll feel better when you can lie down."

They reentered the lobby. Dave explained to the Cancer Society officers that his wife needed to rest. But once the Draveckys were in their room, Jan's panic intensified.

Still gasping for air, she insisted, "Something's . . . wrong . . . with . . . me, Dave. I s-still . . . can't breathe." She fell onto the bed, hyperventilating. "Please—I need . . . you to p-pray . . . for me!" *Am I going to die?* she thought. *Why is this happening?*

The kids watched from the corner of the room, trembling. Dave prayed, but not because he wanted to. For some reason he always got frustrated when his wife asked him to pray for her, even though he knew it was the right thing to do.

Frowning, he looked down at her. She was still taking shallow breaths, as if practicing Lamaze exercises. *I can't believe this,* he thought. *This is one of the most important days of my life, and Jan decides to fall apart!*

"You know, this is stupid," Dave said, his jaw clenched. "All you've gotta do is take a breath."

Tears rose in Jan's eyes. Dave wasn't even trying to understand. She wasn't making this up; she felt like she was going to die!

Staring up at the ceiling, she tried to steady her breathing. *I'm ruining our trip. What's wrong with me?* She'd never had anything like this happen before. For the first time ever, Jan—always the capable one—couldn't handle everything.

It was just a glimpse of things to come.

☙❧

The Draveckys' two days in Washington, D.C. went by in a blur. They were given a private tour of the White House and met President Bush. Jan held herself together, barely managing to smile and nod at all the right times. As she stood in the Oval Office she was gripped with fear, wondering if or when she would experience another episode like that of the previous day. When their appointment with the President was over, Jan was secretly relieved.

Yet the stress had only begun. Several weeks later, the Draveckys flew from Ohio to San Francisco, where they kicked off the release of Dave's book *Comeback*. As she watched her husband go from press conference to book signing to media interview, Jan's symptoms returned. She knew Dave wasn't well, and the intensity of his schedule frightened her. What if his body couldn't take the constant pressure? Just thinking about his demanding agenda made her heart race; the whole time she was in San Francisco, Jan experienced dizzy spells, weakness, insomnia, and periods of breathlessness.

As her symptoms worsened, she grew more worried. As soon as her schedule lightened up, she told herself, she would see a doctor. She felt certain that something was wrong with her body; both her parents had died of unexpected heart attacks, and Jan's palpitations made her fear that she had a heart problem, too. *I don't want to die yet, Lord,* she prayed repeatedly. *Please take care of me.*

Dave paid little attention to his wife's weakened state. He was too busy and stressed to empathize—and was suffering physically, too. Surgery and radiation had chipped away at his energy and patience. When Jan panicked, he told her to "suck it up," to be tough. That had always been his approach in the ballpark, and it had worked. *Jan just needs to be stronger,* he thought. *She's letting too many things get to her.*

Dave's solution, however, only frustrated Jan. She knew it wasn't as easy as that. She couldn't make her symptoms go away.

Worse, the episodes were coming in droves now. One had even struck while she was driving the kids on the freeway in San Francisco. The experience left her petrified, afraid of driving at all—but she didn't tell Dave about it. She knew he would respond in anger, and she didn't want to add to his already heavy load. *I should be able to take care of myself anyway,* she thought.

Jan was able to keep her episodes of panic to herself until April 6, 1990, when she flew with Dave to New York to tape an interview for *Good Morning, America*. While she was getting her makeup done on the set, Jan's heart began thudding so hard that she could see it palpitating beneath her blouse. *Lord,* she prayed as she pasted on a smile for the camera, *please don't let them ask me any questions. I won't get through this if I have to talk.*

Her heart continued to pound as the camera pointed in her direction. *"The Lord is my shepherd; I shall not want. . . ."* she recited silently, working her way through Psalm 23 in an effort to stay calm. When questions came her way, she uttered short answers.

No one seemed to notice her discomfort. She sighed in relief when at last the interview was over. But then the camera crew returned with bad news: Due to a technical glitch, the whole interview would have to be retaped.

When Jan heard that, her knees began to buckle. She grabbed Dave's right hand. "I can't do this, Dave!" she said, gasping. "Take me to the hospital."

Dave froze. "What?"

"Take me to the hospital!" Jan said more urgently. Then she put his hand on her chest. "Feel my heart."

Dave's mouth dropped open in surprise when he felt her heartbeat. Immediately he called out, "Something's wrong with Jan! She needs help, *now!*"

A technician rushed the Draveckys to the nurse's station. After a quick examination, the nurse insisted that Jan fly home immediately and see a doctor. Her heart rate had shot up, and she had a slight fever. Canceling the interview, Dave took her to the airport and put her on a plane for Ohio.

Dave was concerned, but stayed on for the book tour. *All she needs is a little rest,* he told himself. He knew she hadn't been sleeping well lately.

But Jan needed more than rest. Back in Ohio that night, she felt no better. Besides her physical symptoms, there was the loneliness; Dave was away, and the parents upon whose support she'd relied were both gone. Late that night, sleepless, she called her close friend Patty, pleading for prayer. Jan felt her life was slipping away. She needed help—and fast.

The next day, Patty took Jan to the doctor's office. After conducting a thorough checkup, the doctor sat on his stool and faced Jan. "Tell me what's been going on in the last year," he said, taking off his glasses and leaning forward.

Jan complied, and her list seemed to go on and on. There had been her father's death; countless media interviews; moving to Ohio; taking care of Dave, the kids, and their houseguest, Kristen; the suicide of Kristen's boyfriend; Dave's surgery; the book tour.

The doctor stared, incredulous, and shook his head. "Well, it's no wonder you're feeling this way!" But instead of suggesting a physical cause, he began to ask Jan more personal questions—about her emotional state.

Impatient, Jan tried to steer the conversation back toward her physical symptoms. "You need to check my heart," she insisted. "I'm worried about having heart problems." She was desperate for the doctor to find something; maybe he could figure out what her problem was before it was too late.

But the doctor kept asking questions. What were Jan's sleeping and eating habits? Did she cry often? Had she lost interest in hobbies? Did she ever feel worthless? Did she have trouble concentrating?

Jan sighed and gave reluctant answers. Yes, her sleeping was often disrupted. Yes, she hadn't had much of an appetite lately. She cried a lot. She wasn't volunteering in the church like she used to. Her mind often wandered from one subject to the next.

The doctor jotted a few notes. Then, setting down Jan's chart, he told her, "You're depressed! All the signs point to it."

"I don't think so," she said. She wasn't some sad person who wandered around crying all the time! Besides, Christians weren't supposed to be depressed, were they? Weren't they supposed to have the joy of the Lord?

"Well, it's not just about feeling down," explained the doctor. "Depression is a physical illness as well. Your state of mind can affect how you feel; that's why you're having so many physical problems."

Jan wasn't convinced. *Is this all you doctors know how to diagnose?* she thought. Sure, there was a lot of stress in her life, but she wasn't suffering emotional problems! There was something physically wrong with her. *Why can't the doctor see that?* she wondered. She folded her arms and glanced over at her friend Patty, whose eyebrows also arched in suspicion.

They left the office that day with a prescription for an antidepressant—and a referral to a psychiatrist, whom the doctor said could better treat Jan for depression. Jan didn't want to see a psychiatrist, though. She'd always agreed with their pastor, who preached that Christians only needed to take their problems to God. Going to a psychiatrist or counselor—especially a non-Christian—was sinful, the pastor said. It was taking one's problems to "the world" instead of to the Lord.

A self-reliant person, Jan had found it easy to accept that theory. But as the week went on, she became more desperate. Even as she asked for God's help, she seemed to be getting worse. She grew weaker with each passing day; finally, she could barely hold up her head.

She fought insomnia, too. Each night her symptoms grew more frightening and extreme, and she worked herself into a frenzy worrying about them. Something had to be done, she knew. So, despite her own convictions, she asked Patty to take her to the psychiatrist.

Walking into the psychiatrist's office, Jan felt an immediate coldness from both the surroundings and the people. The doctor asked her a few questions, took her off the medication, and then dismissed her.

There was no explanation, no follow-up appointment. Jan decided not to return.

The next morning, after Jan had suffered through another night of heart palpitations, dizziness, and chills, she called her husband. Only a week had passed since she'd seen him, but it felt much longer.

"Dave," she whispered into the receiver, still lying in bed. "I'm not doing well. I need you here." Her voice trembled, and she fought back sobs.

For a moment Dave was quiet on the other end. Then he promised, "I'll be home tonight." He could tell from the urgency in her voice that this was serious.

Jan leaned over and hung up the phone, flooded with guilt. Dave's early return home would cause major problems for his book tour; he would be forced to cancel signings and interviews. Everyone involved was sure to be angry with her. She closed her eyes, wishing she could shut out the world.

Late that night, Dave arrived home to find Jan weak and pale, almost unable to function. Trying not to reveal his shock, he fired off a list of questions.

"How long have you been this sick? What doctors have you seen? And what did they do to you?"

Jan cringed. Dave seemed angry, not concerned. She tried to answer his questions, but the answers didn't seem to make him any happier.

Finally he left the room, then returned to issue an edict: "You will not go back to that psychiatrist!" *I can't believe she went to see a secular psychiatrist,* he thought. *Who knows what kind of nonsense they were trying to put in her head?*

The next day Dave got on the phone to friends, explaining the situation and asking advice. One friend, a pastor who had endured depression himself, directed Dave to his own counselor in San Francisco. When Dave called the counselor and described Jan's symptoms, the man said, "She's burned out!"

It was a term Dave found easier to accept than "depression." But as he hung up the phone, he still wasn't sure what to do.

He glanced over at Jan. She lay in bed, staring at him with big, brown, hollow eyes. Dave turned from her and fumbled with his suitcase, trying to unpack with his good arm. He was tired, weak. His left arm was a mess; even four months after surgery and radiation, the skin had not grown back to cover the bone.

*If anyone should be flat on his back, it's me,* he thought. After all, his problems were *real:* cancer, constant pain, the disintegration of his pitching arm—and his career.

What did Jan have to complain about? She didn't have to jet all over the country to promote the book. She didn't have to do countless interviews and book signings. All that pressure was on *him,* not her! *Just when I need her to be strongest for me, she loses it,* he thought.

God was sustaining *him* though it all. Jan just needed to trust God to do the same for her, didn't she?

On the other hand, maybe their pastor friend in San Francisco—the one Dave had talked to on the phone—had been right. The man had advised postponing the book tour and concentrating on getting Jan to a good Christian psychologist. Despite his misgivings about counselors, Dave decided to give it a try.

ᢙ×ᢚ

The Christian counselor's voice was soothing, but as they entered his office the Draveckys felt anything but peaceful. Dave sat stiffly in his chair, wondering what was about to happen; Jan slumped in hers, so listless she couldn't lift her head. When the counselor asked how he could help, Dave jumped in—describing his wife as "practically bedridden."

Gently the counselor asked Jan what had been going on in her life. Breaking into tears, she recounted the seemingly endless barrage of crises that had pounded them during the last few years. As Dave listened, his impatient frown softened. He began to realize that Jan wasn't—and couldn't be—the invincible Superwoman she'd tried to be for so long.

After hearing Jan's story, the counselor rendered his verdict quietly but firmly: Jan was depressed, filled with backed-up pain. She needed to let herself grieve her losses, especially the loss of her parents.

When they left the counselor's office, Dave and Jan didn't want to go back. Wasn't counseling supposed to help? They felt worse than ever—Jan especially. She didn't want to revisit losing her parents. She didn't want to feel the pain; she wanted it to stop!

When their pastor heard about the counseling session, he warned the Draveckys not to take the man's advice. There was no need to dredge up the past, the minister claimed, quoting Philippians 3:13-14: "Brothers, I do not consider myself yet to have taken hold of it. But one thing I do: Forgetting what is behind and straining toward what is ahead, I press on toward the goal to win the prize for which God has called me heavenward in Christ Jesus."

Jan, however, was desperate enough to try the counselor again. When she did, she found herself having to confront her pain once more.

"Jan, you're just so alone," the counselor said. "You've been looking for someone to lean on since your mother died, haven't you?"

At the mention of her mom, Jan broke down. "Yes," she sobbed, "I need someone."

"God didn't intend for you to do this alone," the counselor said. "Why are you insisting upon doing it alone?"

Jan wept, thinking about Dave. Why didn't she lean on him? *Because I'm afraid of losing him,* she thought. She was determined not to be dependent on anyone—not even her husband.

She was also determined not to be dragged through the pain of the past again. After one more unproductive session, she stopped seeing the counselor—a decision Dave supported. After all, they reasoned, counseling wasn't relieving Jan's stress; it seemed to be making it worse.

Instead, Jan saw a Christian physician. Dr. McGowen could tell right away that Jan was depressed, and told her so. But he also ordered a test that revealed Jan had mitral valve prolapse—a condition in which a heart valve fails to close properly. Stress made the condition worse, Dr. McGowen said, and medication could help block the effects of stress on her heart. Soon Jan was taking the medicine, and her heart was no longer racing.

Things seemed to be looking up. When Dr. McGowen urged her to be treated for depression, Jan didn't see the need. The Christian counselor had told her that six weeks of complete bed rest might cure her depression; she'd take that route.

It was a route that led nowhere. As she lay in bed, her outlook grew darker. The stack of Christian books on her nightstand and the Bible in her lap provided little comfort. *I'm a horrible mother,* she thought, hearing the sounds of her in-laws entertaining Tiffany and Jonathan downstairs. *I can't even take care of my family.* Before long, Jan felt so drained that getting up for a shower seemed an impossible task. She continued to lose weight, too—having already lost 20 pounds during the last two months.

Dave, meanwhile, was spending most of his time on the road promoting his book. Since Jan no longer organized his office, his desk was covered with mounds of paperwork and mail. When he was home, he tried to answer some of the letters—but that was getting harder. There was more pain and numbness in his arm, and his shoulder contained a hole that seemed to deepen every week.

Just a few days into Jan's bed rest, Dave went to New York for a checkup. Once again, the news was bad: More tumor, requiring another operation.

Hearing the report over the phone, Jan was in shock. This time the doctors were saying surgery was necessary to save Dave's life, not just his arm.

*They've never said that before,* she thought. The threat of losing her husband pulled her out of bed; Dave's parents agreed to stay with the kids, and somehow Jan made it to her husband's side at Memorial Sloan-Kettering Hospital in New York.

Jan wasn't much help, though. Still feeling exhausted, she lay on her husband's hospital bed—while he sat in the bedside chair, awaiting surgery.

The operation was long, more complex than the doctors had hoped. When it was over, a weakened, weary Dave looked down at his arm in despair. *It looks gross,* he thought. The thing that used to give him incredible joy as it threw a baseball now made his stomach turn. *Here goes another round. When is this gonna stop? I'm sick and tired of it.*

Even more discouraging was the fact that the operation might be in vain. The biopsy report showed that not all of the cancer had been removed. It probably was just a matter of time, the doctors said, before Dave would lose his arm completely.

༼ༀ༽

*P*raise the name of Jesus . . . Praise the name of Jesus . . . He's my Rock . . .

Jan sang the praise song silently, forcing herself to move her legs off the mattress and to place her bare feet on the floor. She was back in Ohio, spending most of her time in bed. There was no joy in her singing; it was simply the only way she'd found to get herself up to take a shower.

Her mood had grown even darker, her limbs more leaden. Trudging to the bathroom, she could hear Dave's folks loading the dishwasher and vacuuming the floor. Things had gotten so bad that her in-laws had moved into the house to help out.

Jan closed the bathroom door behind her, the sounds of housework fading. She appreciated her in-laws' generosity. But she hated herself for making it necessary. *This is all my fault,* she thought. *I should be taking care of the kids. I should be helping Dave, especially now.*

She thought of her husband, having to drive himself to and from intensive radiation treatments for eight weeks. It was a three-hour drive each way. And where was she? Trapped in her own house, moving in slow motion like a zombie. Sighing, she turned on the water in the shower.

*Praise the name of Jesus . . . Praise the name of Jesus . . .*

The song was without sound, and without feeling.

Dave, meanwhile, was singing a tune of his own—a heartfelt praise number, along with a tape he'd popped into the car stereo. Barreling down the highway, on his way back from the latest radiation treatment, he thought about the last few weeks. *These drives have turned out to be like mini-services,* he thought. To pass the time, he'd played Chuck Swindoll tapes and Christian music. He'd found himself praying, even worshiping.

These quiet times were helping him bounce back from the latest surgery, he thought. Not that he felt great. But focusing on God had taken his mind off the pain and tiredness, even given him a kind of spiritual high.

Glancing at his watch, he realized he'd be home soon. The thought brought a frown, and the spiritual high began to evaporate. He knew what he'd find when he reached his destination: an emaciated Jan lying on the bed, unable to cope with life. The anger would rise up in him, and he'd say something like, "Okay, you've lost a little weight, but you look fine. Get yourself out! You can't tell me you can't get out of bed. If anybody's got a reason to not get out of bed, it would be me. Why in the world can't *you* get out of bed?"

Maybe he wouldn't say it this time; maybe he'd just think it. Either way, the encounter would leave them both mad and frustrated. It always did.

Watching the road, he narrowed his eyes. *Sure, she's been under stress. But she ought to be there for me, and she isn't. And I can't fix her.*

These days, it seemed no one could.

Back at the Dravecky residence, Jan finished her shower and shuffled back to the bedroom. Dave would be home soon, she knew, and another confrontation probably would begin.

With a groan she lowered herself into the bed. *Why can't he be more understanding? Why is he so insensitive?*

It wasn't enough that he dismissed her symptoms. Sometimes he even made fun of them—in front of friends. Tears stung her eyes as she recalled the time they'd been with a few other couples and Jan had begun to hyperventilate. Her hand had flown to her chest; she'd started panting, trying to calm herself. Suddenly Dave's hand had gone to his own chest in mockery, and he'd started panting, too.

The others had laughed. But inside Jan, something had died.

Now the rest of her seemed to be dying, too. She dropped her head to the pillow and pulled up the sheet, hoping in vain that it might hide her from the world forever.

❧

*A*fter a month in bed, Jan was no better. Unable to stand the guilt of being a burden anymore, she forced herself to get up. Her world expanded slightly, but the gray cloud of gloom and anxiety dogged her wherever she went.

Dave's parents moved out, but life didn't get back to normal. The truth was that the Draveckys weren't sure what normal was anymore.

They were so tired of the struggle, in fact, that they began to consider advice they'd rejected. Jan, for one, was ready to admit she was depressed. She did so in a conversation with their pastor, asking him to gather the elders to pray about her depression.

The pastor refused, saying the church leaders would never get anything done "if we prayed every time women had an emotional problem." Stunned, Jan began to think another unthinkable thought: *Maybe we should find another church.*

As for Dave, even he didn't resist when Dr. McGowen suggested starting Jan on Prozac, a powerful antidepressant. Dave didn't like the idea—but nothing else had worked.

Prozac did. Despite the opposition of their pastor and members of their church, the warnings of friends and relatives, and Dave's misgivings, Jan found herself improving. Within a few weeks she could drive again, and sleep through the night.

Still, there was a wall between Jan and Dave—and, she felt, between her and God. She found herself confronting the latter just a week after she started the Prozac.

It was a sweltering August day, and the kids came to Jan with a request: "Mom, would you take us swimming?"

Jan sighed. She wanted to go, but fear wouldn't let her. *What if I have a panic attack?* she thought. When Dave offered to take the kids, she stayed behind—for what seemed like the millionth time.

Standing alone in the family room, Jan wanted to scream. She didn't just want to let off steam, though; she wanted to vent her anger at God.

"I can't believe that a year ago I could be on such a spiritual high!" she yelled. "That I could feel Your presence, and know You were there. And now I don't feel You, I don't sense You, I don't see You anywhere. I don't see any evidence!

"God, You know what I ought to do?" she continued. "I ought to walk away from You. I ought to just turn to the world because You don't make any sense. Maybe I believed a lie my whole life!"

She paused, her words hanging in the air of the empty house. *I know,* she thought. *I'll go shopping. I'll go to the mall. I'm just gonna forget about God.*

Trying to work up enough nerve to leave the house, she envisioned the clothes she'd buy at the mall. Then a more exotic goal occurred to her: a new car. *That's it,* she thought. *I'll buy a new car.*

No, that didn't sound right, either. She'd aim for something else. *Maybe I'll take up tennis and get my life busy and quit thinking about God.*

Suddenly, as she listened to her own thoughts, the truth struck her. *The clothes wear out, the thrill's over with. The car eventually rusts. The body gets old.*

She swallowed. *Everything I want to turn to is temporary. Everything I want to run to wears out. The only thing I can hold onto is Your Word. It's the only thing that's eternal, the only thing that offers hope. It's the only thing.*

Her anger draining away, she recalled a verse she'd memorized: "I have hidden your word in my heart that I might not sin against you" (Psalm 119:11).

She shook her head. God's Word was so embedded in her soul that she couldn't run from Him. *Okay,* she thought, finally feeling a glimmer of hope. *I can't run from You because I know You're the truth. So I'll hold on to Your promises.*

For Jan, it was a major turning point. In the days to come, however, she would need to cling more tightly than ever to those promises—for the sake of her sanity as well as her marriage.

∽❀∽

*I*t was a breath of fresh air—literally and figuratively.

Standing at the crest of a rocky hill in Montana, Dave and Jan held hands as they gazed at the azure sky. The world was so vast here, so open. Maybe that was one reason why the Draveckys, closed off from each other by their own struggles during the past year, were inspired to open up.

"It's nice to have you back again, Babe," Dave said, smiling.

Jan smiled, too. It really was as if she'd been gone, wasn't it? Deep down she knew the love between them had never disappeared, but they'd lost their connection. Being battered by constant crisis had driven them apart.

Maybe things would be all right now, she thought. She felt better than she had in months. Was it the Prozac, which she'd been taking for several weeks? Or was it just being here in "big sky country," invited to join some of the staff of Focus on the Family for a weekend retreat?

Either way, it felt so good to be here, holding Dave's hand and breathing the clean, warm September air. Jan looked into Dave's eyes, feeling the urge to make things right between them. "I'm so sorry that I let you down when you needed me," she murmured.

Dave shook his head. "I'm not concerned so much about your being there for me. I just want to make sure you are okay. I don't understand what happened to you. I'm just glad you're getting over it."

Jan looked down at the grass. She hoped that was true. Sometimes she wasn't sure she'd ever be her old self again; she wasn't even sure she wanted to. But she was trying.

They talked for a few more minutes, and Dave put his arms—both of them— around her. They kissed, and he continued to hold her. She couldn't believe how wonderful it felt.

"I think the medicine is helping me," she said finally. "I'm starting to feel alive again. Maybe soon I'll be strong enough to get off it."

Dave relaxed. That sounded good to him. He'd never liked the idea of Jan being on Prozac. Neither did their pastor; he seemed to take every opportunity to tell them so. It had been hard for Dave, an elder in the church, to face the other leaders when he knew they disapproved.

When the Draveckys returned from Montana, they felt refreshed and primed for better times.

Unfortunately, that's not what they got.

First, Dave discovered that a life-threatening staph infection was raging not only in his arm, but throughout his body. Grounding him from a planned speaking tour, Dr. McGowen sent Dave to the hospital for five days to receive antibiotics.

It wasn't enough. For months the infection persisted, and for months Dave kept taking the medicine. His arm continued to deteriorate; soon a trio of holes perforated it, each of them weeping fluids. Jan cleaned and dressed the wounds daily, but nothing seemed to help. The arm was nearly useless, dying.

Jan, meanwhile, had gradually stopped taking Prozac. After all, she reasoned, she was doing better now. Perhaps her pastor was right; she didn't need medication or counseling.

But as fall turned to winter, Jan felt herself slipping. Before long the feelings of hopelessness returned.

*I'm going down,* she thought. *Down, down, down.*

There seemed to be no way out. Jan didn't want to go back on Prozac; Dave and their church didn't want her to see a counselor. Dave, who'd been reading a book about how suffering can lead to victory, tried to convince her that God had great things in store for them on the other side of this dark valley.

*It's nice that he has hope,* she thought. *But I don't.*

One day, though, Jan bought some reading material of her own at a Christian bookstore. *When Your World Makes No Sense* by Dr. Henry Cloud seemed aimed directly at Jan. By the time she finished it, Jan knew two things—that she was indeed depressed, and that Dave and their church couldn't help because they didn't understand.

*It's like I'm up against a brick wall,* she thought. How could she change Dave? He was stubborn. *But he has a heart for God,* she realized. *I know that about him. He may not listen to me, but he'll listen to God.*

Jan began to pray—that God would change her husband's attitude toward her depression, and toward getting the help she needed.

༚

*D*uring the weeks that followed, Dave's resistance to counseling didn't soften. But when their pastor preached still another sermon condemning those who used counseling or medication to combat depression, Dave finally agreed with Jan on one issue: It was time to find another church.

Leaving friends behind was painful, but in Spring 1991 the Draveckys found a new fellowship. To her surprise, Jan discovered that one of the pastors had worked at a Christian counseling clinic; another had been treated for depression as an inpatient at such a facility.

Sensing that Jan might be struggling with a similar problem, the wives of both pastors phoned her. After hearing her story, they suggested she enter the clinic for treatment. They could make the arrangements—if Dave would agree.

Jan gulped. *How can I get Dave to do that?* she wondered. Broaching the subject would be like tiptoeing on eggshells. But she knew she had to try.

That afternoon Dave came home and sat at the kitchen table. As usual, he felt lousy. For six months he'd been taking antibiotic pills—ineffective against the staph infection, but they made his stomach feel as if it were on fire. His left arm, wrapped in bandages that were wet with blood and fluid, was little more than dead weight. His energy was at a low ebb.

He looked across the table at Jan. What was she saying? The associate pastor went through depression? *Oh, great. Here we go again.*

He frowned. *Now she's saying some clinic helped him get better. I know where she's going with this.*

Sure enough, Jan asked whether she could go to the clinic, too. *As an inpatient! Isn't counseling bad enough? Does she have to check herself in, too, like some basket case?*

"No!" Dave growled. *Why does she have to look for someone other than me to help her? Why doesn't she just go to God? God is safe, but some other man . . .*

He could feel his whole body tensing, coiling up. When Jan revealed that the two pastors' wives had set everything up, that all it would take was a phone call, he exploded. "Where was I when they were setting everything up?" he shouted.

She started to explain, but there was too much pressure inside him, too much rage, too much pain. Springing to his feet, he grabbed the portable phone and flung it with all his might against the wall.

The *crack* as the phone shattered mixed with the sound of Jan's gasp. Bits of plastic flew everywhere, and the broken receiver fell to the floor.

His face red, Dave stalked out of the room.

Picking up the pieces, Jan sobbed. She'd asked God to change her husband's attitude, hadn't she? Help had seemed so close, and now it seemed so far away.

*I'm going down,* she thought. *Down, down, down.*

❧

*J*ust a week later, the Draveckys sat across from a Christian psychologist—Dr. James Dobson. They weren't there for counseling, though. The setting was a recording studio; the Draveckys were featured guests on the *Focus on the Family* radio broadcast.

The irony wasn't lost on Jan. She was too tired to think about it, though. She hadn't wanted to come here to California at all, and had tried to talk Dave out of it. But he'd insisted, saying Dr. Dobson wanted to interview them both about how they were doing.

*What can I say?* Jan thought, waiting for the taping to begin. She didn't feel like a role model; she felt like a patient. *Maybe Dr. Dobson can help me,* she thought absently. *After all, he's a psychologist.*

The interview went well enough—though some listeners may have been surprised at Jan's candor. She admitted that she was depressed, that the battle wasn't over, that she and Dave didn't know what might happen next.

When the interview ended, Dr. Dobson invited the Draveckys into his office. The three of them sat down. Dr. Dobson asked Jan how she was doing, and before she knew it she'd told him everything.

A few minutes later, the psychologist turned his attention to Dave. The former ballplayer fidgeted. *What's he going to say?* Dave wondered. *This is Dr. Dobson, man! Whatever he says, you'll have to take it seriously!*

"Look at her, Dave," Dr. Dobson said. "She's exhausted."

Dave swallowed, then admitted he didn't know what to do. He wasn't sure counseling was right. What was Dr. Dobson's opinion?

"Dave, you've got to let your wife get help. She's depressed and she's struggling, and she needs counseling." The psychologist assured him that the clinic in which Jan was interested was overseen by a godly man. "Dave, it's not ungodly to get counseling. It's godly to get godly counsel."

Jan watched Dave's face. Before her eyes a barrier inside Dave was broken down; she could tell that he would no longer stand in the way of getting therapy.

Her prayer had been answered! *And to think that I didn't even want to come on this trip . . .*

There was another surprise to come, however. Leaving Dr. Dobson's office, Jan was taken aside by the Draveckys' literary agent, Sealy Yates. "I have a book for you to read," he said. "It's called, *When Your World Makes No Sense* by Henry Cloud."

Jan's eyes widened. It was the very book she'd been reading! It turned out that Dr. Henry Cloud—and his partner, Dr. John Townsend—were clients of Sealy Yates. And their counseling practice was here in California.

*This is my chance*, Jan thought excitedly. God had arranged it—affirmation from Dr. Dobson, and opportunity from Sealy Yates. "Do you think you could make an appointment with Henry Cloud?"

The agent went to work. Henry Cloud wasn't available, but John Townsend was able to make a last-minute appointment.

Hearing the news, Jan felt her pulse quicken. This time, though, it was no panic attack. It was anticipation of a new beginning—and she hoped Dave felt it, too.

ave liked John Townsend right away. *He's not stuffy*, Dave thought. *And he speaks my language. No Christianese, no hyperspiritual talk.*

Casually dressed, sitting in his office with the Draveckys that Sunday afternoon, the therapist listened as Jan told her story. Then he came right to the point: Jan had a mountain of stress and loss in her life. It was amazing, in fact, that she and Dave were still married!

Turning to Dave, Dr. Townsend pulled no punches. Jan was sick, he said—emotionally and physically. Dave wasn't the one to help her, though; she needed professional aid, even if Dave felt threatened by that.

Dave listened intently. *No surprises so far.* But then the therapist dropped a bomb. "You need help, too," he told Dave. According to Dr. Townsend, Jan wasn't the only one who was depressed. Dave had lost so much, too—a high-profile career, the use of his arm, the assurance that disasters like cancer couldn't touch him—and he was reeling.

A bell seemed to ring in Dave's head. He wasn't convinced yet that he needed help, but all at once he saw the path he and Jan needed to travel—together. *This is serious stuff,* he thought. *We're not playing around here. We need to seek counseling, and we need to seek godly counseling.*

When they left the therapist's office that day, both Draveckys were ready for the next step. On John Townsend's recommendation they began seeing Dr. Loren Sommers back in Ohio—twice a week, two hours at a time, together. Each visit required two-and-a-half hours of travel, which Dave and Jan made the most of—talking, helping their relationship to mend.

"I'll see Dr. Sommers on one condition," Dave had said at first. "Jan's got the problem, not me. I'm only there to support her." Within six weeks, though, Dave had begun to open up, to assess the damage the last two years had wreaked on him. He wouldn't use the word *depressed* to describe himself, but had to concede that he wasn't the Man of Steel after all.

It was a good beginning, and one he would need to face the monumental challenge that lay ahead.

⟡

*S*itting in the spotless examining room at New York's Memorial Sloan-Kettering Cancer Center, Dave felt his heart thudding against his ribs. This could be it, the moment he would hear the words.

He wasn't afraid of the words, exactly. He wasn't eager for them, either. It was just the uncertainty, not knowing whether he would hear them, and knowing they could change his life so completely.

Dr. Brennan had just finished peering at a set of X-rays taken after Dave's last surgery. Now he turned to look Dave in the eye.

"Dave," he said quietly, "I think it's time for your arm to come off."

Dave exhaled. *Oh, man, finally.* "You know," he said, "I just want to get this thing off and get on with my life. Let's get this over with."

He had good reason to want the arm to disappear. It was an albatross, nearly immobile, wracked with infection, aching, fragile. It kept him from wrestling with his kids, from hugging his wife. It was dangerous, too—harboring cancer that could take his life.

After listening to Dr. Brennan explain how the amputation would be done, Dave called Jan. She was on her way to an appointment with Dr. Sommers, the counselor they'd been seeing for just two weeks, and picked up the car phone.

The conversation was subdued, but without tears. Dave and Jan had known for a year that he might lose his arm; they hadn't talked much about it, but the possibility had become a fixture in their lives. Now it was reality, and they would have to deal with it a step at a time.

Ten days later—June 17, 1991—Jan and Dave and several members of his family gathered in New York. That evening, in Dave's hospital room, his father approached Dave's bed and started to cry. "I'm so tired of seeing you walking around, dragging your arm, and just looking the way you look," he finally said, choking out the words. "Just cut it off." It was his way of affirming what they all knew had to be done.

Dave couldn't have agreed more. "This is the best thing that could happen to me," he assured his father gently. "Don't feel bad, Dad. Everything's okay."

In fact, Dave felt more than okay. He was fired up, even excited. This was a great opportunity to share his faith. *Where will I find the opportunity to pray for the doctors?* he kept thinking. *I want to pray for the doctors. I want to pray for the nurses. I want to ask God to guide their hands, their minds, their hearts in dealing with me and my whole family.*

The next day, around noon, it was time for surgery. Dave and Jan felt at peace; God was in control, they knew. Dave was wheeled into the operating room, received anesthesia, and lost consciousness. There seemed to be no time for the prayer he'd planned.

When he awoke, his arm was gone. His shoulder was gone. So were his shoulder blade and the left side of his collar bone. When he saw himself in the bathroom mirror the following day, he was stunned at how much had been subtracted.

Still, he felt at peace. *Okay, God,* he prayed. *This is what I've got to live with. Put this behind me; let me go forward.*

That calm confidence stayed with Dave as he began his recovery—and even turned to elation when he found out what had happened in the operating room before his surgery. He heard the story from the anesthesiologist, who stopped by his room the day after his operation.

"I just want you to know," the woman said, "how much I appreciated the prayer you prayed before surgery."

Dave's eyebrows rose. "What?"

"Yeah, you not only prayed once, but you prayed twice."

"I don't recall that," Dave said.

"I have never seen a team of doctors react the way they did when you prayed for them," the woman declared.

*Well, that's cool,* Dave thought, grinning.

The account was confirmed later, when one of the doctors visited Dave's room. Standing at the foot of the bed, the man said, "I want you to know, my parents are missionaries in Mexico. It was incredible, that moment when you prayed for the doctors before they went into surgery. I just wanted you to know the impact that had."

Dave chuckled. "Doc, you've gotta be kidding me. I don't remember that at all."

"Well, you did," the physician said, and left.

Dave shook his head, smiling. This was great! Ministry was happening, even when he didn't know it! God was not only getting him through this— God was using him. Even after amputation, the future looked bright.

Jan was feeling good, too. She and Dave had started serving people as a team, right at the hospital. So many floral arrangements had poured in from all over the country that Dave's room had started to look like a greenhouse; the Draveckys decided to share their bounty, taking flowers and fruit baskets to other patients.

Just six days after surgery, Dave was released from the hospital. He and Jan felt better than they had in a long time. Jan could recall the doctors' warning that many amputees were full of hope after surgery, only to fall into depression about two weeks later as their loss hit home. But would that happen with Dave? Looking at him now, it didn't seem possible. Still, she had to wonder . . .

❧

Four months later, Dave hit bottom.

It had taken him longer than most, but the frustration of learning to live a one-handed life finally had gotten to him. He missed his arm; he missed being able to clap his hands, to open a jar, to write with his dominant hand. Even though Jan assured him she'd love him even if he had *no* arms, he sometimes hated looking in the mirror. And there was the phantom pain, the illusory throbbing of his missing limb. At times it felt as if his left hand were cramping—even though his left hand no longer existed.

He was, in a word, depressed.

The realization that he was depressed almost took his breath away. Now he was suffering as Jan had suffered, lying on the bed, unable to get up, surrounded by an ominous cloud.

*This was what she was trying to tell me about,* he thought. *And I just abused her by not listening, not paying attention. I mocked her for what she was going through.*

He swallowed. *I have to tell her,* he thought. *I have to tell her I'm sorry.*

The words were hard to say. But he said them one day, lying in bed, feeling as if he might never be able to get up. Looking over at Jan, he whispered, "I . . . I'm depressed. I'm so sorry. I am so sorry for everything I put you through."

Jan looked down at Dave, tears springing to her eyes. She could feel his helplessness, his sorrow over having hurt her. *He needs to cry,* she thought, *but he can't. That's always been hard for him.*

Reaching down, she put her arms around her husband and held him. The tears streaming down her cheeks were on his behalf, and there was no need for words.

❧

Admitting his depression to Jan and asking her forgiveness was hard enough. But for Dave to tell *others* that he was depressed seemed impossible. One week later he would have the chance—if he was willing to take it.

Dave had been taking speaking engagements since August, despite his doctors' misgivings about his readiness. Having received 1,500 requests to speak since his amputation, he felt bound to say yes to some. He'd been giving inspirational talks; the only problem was that he didn't feel inspired anymore.

On this particular day he was in West Palm Beach, Florida, scheduled to address a gathering of men at the PGA National Golf Course. All he could do was lie on the bed in his room, staring at the ceiling.

Suddenly the phone rang. Reluctantly he reached over to pick it up. Jan was on the line, trying to encourage him.

It didn't work. "I'm just feeling terrible," Dave muttered into the phone. "I don't feel like talking. I don't have anything to say. I don't want to tell them about Jesus. I don't want to do anything. I just want to come home."

Seeing that her pep talk hadn't worked, Jan asked a few friends to call Dave. But their efforts were in vain. When Dave hung up after talking to the last of them, he flopped back on the bed and sighed. *I'm not feeling any better,* he thought.

Just then Jan called again. When she found he was still miserable, she confronted him. "Well, you have two choices," she said. "You can either go out there and be honest and tell them you're depressed, or you can fake it."

Dave sat up, his grip on the phone tightening. "You mean that's what I've been doing all along?" he asked angrily. "Just faking it?"

He slammed the phone down. *Who does she think she is?* he thought.

He sat there for a long time. *What should I do?* he wondered. Finally he decided. Getting up from the bed, he got dressed and headed for his speaking engagement.

When the time came for him to address the group, he listened to the glowing introduction. He stepped up to the microphone, then stood there for several seconds, looking at the crowd. At length he said, "You know what? I don't want to be here. I don't feel like telling you about Jesus, and I'm . . . depressed."

*Ouch,* he thought. It was painful, finally admitting it in public. And in front of *men!*

But it was true. And maybe, just maybe, it was the first step toward a comeback of the heart.

❧

*F*ollowing his admission that he was depressed, Dave came to realize that he'd never really learned how to communicate what was going on inside. He knew how to yell at Jan and the kids; he knew how to throw phones against the wall. But when it came to expressing his feelings in words, without hurting anyone, he was a rookie.

So, for the next 18 months, he and Jan learned the art of communicating.

They started by talking. They talked for two hours every time they met with Dr. Sommer, who often acted as referee. They talked in the car, driving to and from those appointments. Dave hadn't talked to Jan that much in their whole marriage. Together they made up for lost time.

Through the counseling and talking, they discovered some uncomfortable truths about themselves. Jan saw that she was a people pleaser, trying to placate everyone; she had to start drawing boundaries, setting priorities, telling people what she really thought. Dave found that he had to grow up—taking responsibility for his own anger and its results.

Soon things were changing in the Dravecky house. Dave found it harder and harder to use his anger as a weapon against his wife. One day, during a disagreement with Jan, Dave tried to halt discussion with his usual threat: "Do you want me to get angry?"

Refusing to be manipulated, Jan stood her ground. "Knock yourself out," she said. "But I'm not gonna stick around and listen to it." Turning, she marched out of the room.

Dave chased her. "Don't you dare do that to me, Jan!" he called.

When Jan ignored his tantrum, Dave sighed. *Throwing a fit doesn't work anymore*, he thought. *I may as well give it up.*

Gradually, Dave and Jan came to see the truth of Proverbs 19:19: "A hot-tempered man must pay the penalty; if you rescue him, you will have to do it again." Jan had always tried to rescue Dave from the consequences of his anger; now she wouldn't, and they both grew as a result.

The Draveckys learned to grieve, too—Dave over the loss of his arm and career, Jan over Dave's illness and the deaths of her parents. Slowly the cloud of depression lifted; they became less self-absorbed, better able to see each other's needs.

They also saw the needs of strangers. Ever since Dave's battle with cancer had made him a public figure, cancer victims and their families had shared their stories with him and sought his help. As he and Jan spent more and more time comforting and encouraging those people, it became clear that God was giving them a new direction.

In July 1993, the Draveckys moved to Colorado Springs, where they founded Dave Dravecky's Outreach of Hope. The ministry began publishing *The Encourager,* a magazine for cancer patients and their families; sent books to patients; and made calls to cancer sufferers, especially unbelievers who were at crisis points. Dave continued his speaking schedule; Jan began to address women's groups on the subject of overcoming depression. They were awed to see how, as God had lifted them up, they could lift up others.

Things weren't perfect, of course. Soon after moving to Colorado, Dave felt burned out and again sought the help of a counselor. In the process he gained new tools for dealing with stress and anger, and he and Jan grew closer still.

The Draveckys had come a long way. They could see their progress one night in 1999.

It was an ordinary trip to the hardware store. Dave and Jan were alone in the car. A thunderstorm had rolled in; sheets of rain washed across the windshield and glinted in the headlights.

Inside the car, however, there was peace. As the wiper blades worked back and forth, Jan began to talk about how happy she felt, how content. Dave smiled. They both felt it, a joy that disregarded the storm outside. They talked about Tiffany and Jonathan, safe at home and doing well.

*It's just fun to be together,* Dave realized. It hadn't always been this way, but it was now.

*Pinch me, God,* Jan thought. *Because I can't believe I could feel this good. I'm just going to enjoy this while I can, because you never know what's going to come around.*

If the Draveckys had learned anything, it was that life would bring them storms, even hurricanes. But just as they could find peace despite the wind and pelting rain, God had enabled them to experience joy in the midst of turmoil—even as a result of it.

They knew that when trouble came again, they could choose not to react with their old patterns of anger, fear, and doubt. They could face it hand in hand, knowing that God would ultimately knit everything together—including their marriage—for good.

*Dave and Jan continue the ministry of Dave Dravecky's Outreach of Hope. Dave also speaks to corporations and other groups about his personal story, the value of suffering, and what gives a person worth after he or she has "lost it all." Jan addresses conferences and organizations on the reality of God's love in the midst of pain.*

*Reflecting on their marriage, Dave says, "Our relationship has been taken to a much deeper level of trust than I think either one of us could have ever imagined. And I think it's been through the struggles that we've come to understand and appreciate that word,* trust. *There is a fiber that knits us together that can't be broken, no matter what. A lot of that has to do with what we've been through."*

*For more information on the Draveckys' ministry of encouragement to cancer patients, write: Dave Dravecky's Outreach of Hope, 13840 Gleneagle Drive, Colorado Springs, CO 80921.*

# *Your Path to Always*

The Draveckys learned a valuable lesson about independence. I believe the story of Moses echoes what they discovered.

The Israelites went to war with the Amalekites (Exodus 17). As long as Moses held up his hands, the Israelites were winning; if his hands went down, the Amalekites had the advantage. Moses couldn't keep his hands up alone. He needed Aaron on one side, lifting his arm up—and Hur on the other side, doing the same. The Israelites won that battle because Moses was willing to let others help.

God works through our brothers and sisters in Christ to help us through the hard times. He uses doctors, pastors, friends—and, as the Draveckys found, even Christian counselors!

The Draveckys also discovered that healing doesn't happen unless we admit our hurts. Jan and Dave tried ignoring their problems, shoving them aside and putting on happy faces. This never works, as their story shows. Pain doesn't leave us when we ignore it. It just takes a vacation—until one day it returns with a vengeance.

The road we must travel to deal with pain is not easy. But it's the road described in the following Scripture:

"Consider it pure joy, my brothers, whenever you face trials of many kinds, because you know that the testing of your faith develops perseverance. Perseverance must finish its work so that you may be mature and complete, not lacking anything" (James 1:2-4).

This is the answer: We must face our trials, not ignore them. When we confront our trials, we will grow stronger and more mature in our faith.

But we often need help to do that. When Jan finally realized she needed help and sought it, her pastor condemned her. Even Dave initially ridiculed her for being "weak." Later, though, Dave realized that it took courage to ask for assistance; it was something he had to learn to do as well.

True, feeling "down" for a short time doesn't always require counseling. Most of us have days here and there when we feel depressed.

Many times we *can* pray, asking for God's strength to pull us through; we cope and move on. But clinical depression should never be trivialized. To tell a person suffering from debilitating depression that he or she should just "shape up" only compounds the problem. It adds a load of guilt over being unable to "just deal with it!"

To handle depression, we need the support of others. Not everyone understands that. When Jan asked her pastor to pray for her, his answer stunned her; he implied that it was a waste of time to pray for women with emotional problems, because that would interfere with the work of the church.

Consider the story in Matthew 26 at a place called Gethsemane.

Jesus knew He was about to face death. It would be a death so horrible and painful that we cannot even begin to comprehend Christ's sorrow. Perhaps the worst part was knowing that His Father would look away from Him when the weight of the world's sins was placed on His shoulders. Jesus didn't want to suffer the overwhelming physical and emotional pain.

He asked that the assignment be taken from Him. In His grief and with anguish in His soul, He asked His closest friends to pray with Him. He needed the support of their presence and their prayers.

Three times He checked on them, hoping they were praying—only to find them sleeping. It broke His heart. When He needed them most, they weren't there for Him.

If Jesus needed the loving support of the people closest to Him, how much more do we need that kind of support?

The Lord is always there for us, and wants us to come to Him (Matthew 11:28). But He also understands that we are like the little boy who was scared by a thunderstorm. That boy ran to his mommy, who cuddled him and prayed for his fear to subside. After thanking Mom for the prayer, the boy admitted that he just needed someone "with skin on."

We all need that, though it's often hard to request. On any given Sunday morning, many couples in church might look happy, as the Draveckys did—but they may be wrestling with depression or other problems. Just as sufferers need to ask for help, the rest of us need to be sensitive, looking beyond the "I'm fine" masks and giving encouragement.

If you suffer from depression, be assured that Jesus understands your heart and your pain. He stands ready to comfort you, not only through the Holy Spirit and the Bible, but also through people—including those trained to offer godly counsel. As the Draveckys learned, seeking that counsel can make all the difference in a life, and in a marriage.

—Gary Smalley

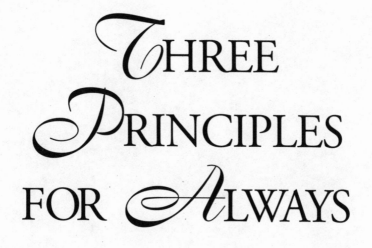

# THREE PRINCIPLES FOR ALWAYS

BY GARY SMALLEY

*A*ll of the couples whose stories you've just read have something in common. They discovered three truths—three basic principles that govern our lives.

My wife and I, in the process of overcoming difficulties in our marriage, discovered these principles, too. We've isolated them and analyzed them and written them out. They are so powerful and effective that I regularly see them at work in the lives of my three children and *their* marriages.

I believe that if you understand and apply these three principles, you can discover that power. You can have a quiet, peaceful assurance deep in your heart that when you face your share of marital difficulties, you'll get through. Even though it's going to be painful, it will work out for you.

All three principles center around *honor*.

∽✺∾

*T*he first principle is to *honor the Lord.* All the couples in this book did that—sooner or later. The sooner they did it, the sooner they found peace amid chaos and conflict.

What does it mean to honor the Lord? To me, it means making sure there is nothing more valuable to me in heaven or on earth than my relationship with Jesus Christ. I need to honor the Lord above everyone else.

"Bless the Lord, O my soul: and all that is within me, bless his holy name" (Psalm 103:1, KJV). The word *blessing* means to bend your knees in the presence of someone very valuable. My relationship with Christ is the most valuable I can experience as a human. I have experienced, as these couples did, that Jesus Christ is faithful and true to His promises.

Honoring the Lord is obeying His Word: "Love the Lord your God with all your heart and with all your soul and with all your strength" (Deuteronomy 6:5). This means to exchange or substitute your will for His will, your heart for His heart, your goals for His goals. You decide to do His will, not your own. You tell the Lord that you want Him to be everything to you—that He is your life, and you are going to take His values and His direction.

What does He direct us to do?

> One of the teachers of the law came and heard them debating. Noticing that Jesus had given a good answer, he asked him, "Of all the commandments, which is the most important?"
>
> "The most important one," answered Jesus, "is this: 'Hear, O Israel, the Lord our God, the Lord is one. Love the Lord your God with

all your heart and with all your soul and with all your mind and with all your strength.' The second is this: 'Love your neighbor as yourself.' There is no commandment greater than these" (Mark 12:28-31).

Basically, God's Word tells us to do two things: Love Him and love others. Value Him and value others. Honor Him and honor others.

It's not complicated. Loving the Lord your God with all your heart is the basis of all the other commandments. If you obey this rule, you're obeying all the others.

When I love God above everyone else, another vital thing happens. He keeps His promise to fill me up to the fullness of Himself (Ephesians 3:19-20). To explain what that means, let's use an analogy.

Imagine that we humans have batteries in our hearts and would like to have them fully charged. We think that if we could just know the right people, get the right job, make the right amount of money, and have the right home, our batteries would be charged up.

So we plug our batteries into these people, jobs, money, and possessions. We do it with a 110-volt extension cord. This cord is like our expectations; we expect to be fulfilled through the things God created.

Unfortunately, that expectation makes humans miserable.

It made the couples in each of our stories miserable. They expected that certain things would happen—a compliant spouse, good health, a chosen career. When those things didn't happen and tragedy struck them in some form, they became miserable—a natural consequence of expecting to be satisfied by temporal things.

When I was 35 years old, I finally realized I was plugged into the wrong things, with the wrong power cord. I saw that God had wired my "battery" to be charged by Him alone. In a sense, Jesus Christ is the transformer that funnels all the power of God down to a 220-volt electrical current that is designed to fully charge my battery—and yours.

When we finally unplug from the inadequate 110-volt source and confess our weakness and humanness, our vulnerability, and acknowledge that we can't do things on our own, we can relax. We can ask God to fulfill us by His Spirit. We can plug into the 220-volt Source and wait for Him to fill our lives—whether it takes a day, a month, or ten years. Whatever it takes, He is faithful. He will fill our lives when we stop struggling and wait for Him to do it through His Spirit.

That's how my battery has been filled since I was 35 years of age, when

I finally allowed Jesus Christ to be the Source of my life. What I've done since—and what my wife and I have done as a couple—is to seek the Lord first, knowing that all the things we need will be added to us (Matthew 6:33). I know that my wife is not going to be my source of joy; I'm not my wife's source of joy. The true Source of love, joy, and peace—and everything else we need—is the Lord.

That's the same message we heard from each of these couples.

Remember the story of Sue and Larry Wright? For years Sue was frustrated by Larry's alcoholism. If only he'd change, she thought, she would be happy. But when Sue received Christ as Savior, she plugged into God's power and found a new peace. Suddenly it didn't scare her so much that she had an alcoholic husband and her marriage was crumbling. She knew God loved her, and would get her through it.

All these couples learned what my wife and I have learned—to seek the Lord first and above all. This principle completely changes the dynamics in a marriage as husband and wife look to the Lord, not each other, for ultimate fulfillment. This relaxes us so we can enjoy each other.

Hard times may drain our batteries. But I can guarantee you, based on God's Word, that if you wait upon Him He eventually will bring that charge back up to full. We will go through periods of grief, hurt, frustration, and fear, but Jesus is able to restore us in time.

❧

The second principle is the second half of Christ's commandment—to *love, or honor, people.*

Let's imagine your mate is made up of various metals—tin, brass, iron, steel, copper, aluminum. He or she even contains a little bit of silver and gold. As your marriage begins, you decide to add value to your mate over the years—by adding gold. The more gold you add, the more valuable your mate becomes—to himself or herself, to you, and to others.

Let's say you know how to extract tin and aluminum and copper from your mate and replace it with gold. You can put in 14 karat, 18 karat, or 24 karat gold. The higher the gold's purity, the more valuable your mate would be.

As the years pass, through the things you say and do, you can exchange the tin for gold and add value to your mate. Or you can *extract* value from your mate and replace the gold with tin—thereby *devaluing* your mate.

One of the world's leading marriage experts, Dr. John Gottman of the

University of Washington, says that the number one killer of marriages is belittling your mate. He calls this contempt; other experts call this invalidation. Either way, it means drawing value away from your mate. This pulls out some of the gold and replaces it with tin.

How can you add value to your spouse? Here are some things you can say that add gold rather than extracting it:
- "I love you, which means I value you."
- "I care about you because you are valuable to me."
- "You are someone I want to treasure."
- "I have chosen to add value to you."
- "I have decided to spend my life with you."
- "I have decided to have children with you."
- "I want to take you to a social event, because I've chosen you out of all the other males or females in the world."
- "I've chosen you and place the highest value on you out of all the other men or women in this world."

These are just a few things we can say on a regular basis. We can ask our mate how often he or she needs to hear them. We can put them in cards, letters, e-mail messages, or phone calls.

The verbal expression of "I value you" is so important for humans; *everyone* needs to hear it! If you don't hear it from your spouse, you may come to assume that he or she doesn't love you anymore. You may think your value has lessened in your mate's heart and he or she just doesn't want to admit it.

In Scripture, God's love letter to us, we can read as often as we want to that nothing will ever separate us from His love (Romans 8:35-39). Thus we know that God loves us and cares for us. We need to hear a similar commitment from each other in our marriages. You may want to put yours in writing, giving your mate a letter that says something like, "I love you and will love you forever."

In addition to words, actions demonstrate that you value your mate. Having fun—weekly, monthly, as often as you can—says, "I want to spend time with you and enjoy our life together." Planning and saving money for a major trip says, "I plan to be with you the rest of my life."

Reminiscing about past fun—even all the way back to the days when you dated—is another way to honor each other. Remembering has a way of renewing your feelings of love for your mate. It helps you see how much value you placed on him or her, and that you can do so now.

The couples in this book certainly learned the importance of honoring each other. When Helen Tucker nervously revealed to her husband the scars of her breast cancer surgery, he took the opportunity to value her with a prayer of thanks. Years after Julia Flannery's affair nearly shattered her marriage to Pete, she still needed to affirm that she valued him: "Nothing is as wonderful as living a life of integrity. Because I'm living it with *you*, I'm so thankful you stuck by me through this."

Even the pranks of Steve and Donna Thurman were a way for them to say to each other, "I like having fun with you. Even after all we've been through, playing tricks on each other is one of the traditions we share. Let's not give that up."

~⚬~

The third principle is to *repair the damage to honoring the Lord or honoring people*.

Let's look at our relationship with the Lord first. What can we do when we dishonor God? To answer that question, we need to understand a few things about sin and grace.

When I sin, I devalue my relationship with Jesus Christ. His Word prescribes a specific remedy in 1 John 1:9: If I sin, I need to admit it, confess it, and acknowledge that I am weak—that I'm incapable on my own of living a life that pleases God.

Left to our own devices, we're addicted to behavior that dishonors God. One of my favorite books is *Addiction and Grace* by Gerald G. May (Harper San Francisco, 1991). The author says an addiction is an attachment to something temporal, one of God's creations. Thus attached, you think you must have this thing—food, shopping, alcohol, sex, drugs, tobacco, whatever—to be fulfilled. The more you have it, the more you need to have it—or think you do.

Only Jesus Christ, His grace, and His Spirit can free us from these addictions. This can happen only *after* we confess that we are humanly incapable of breaking this habit on our own. That's when His grace is sufficient. He gives grace to the humble (James 4:6).

Some of the stories in this book provide dramatic examples of people who humbled themselves and received God's grace. Larry Wright had to concede that he couldn't overcome alcoholism on his own; his wife Sue had to admit that her habit of verbally attacking Larry was destructive. Steve and Donna Thurman both acknowledged to God the ways in which they'd contributed to their marital conflict, and asked Him to change their hearts. Raul Ries, tough and swaggering, had to go to his knees and ask God's forgiveness before his addiction to violence could be broken and his marriage salvaged.

They learned that the only way to repair a damaged relationship with God is by God's grace. That doesn't mean we should sin like crazy in order to get a life of love and joy, of course. Sin is missing the mark, missing God's best. Sin takes my life, devalues me, takes gold away from me. I don't want that! I want to let God's Spirit turn me into 24 karat gold.

When I dishonor God through sin, I want to confess it. I don't want the gold in my life to be replaced with worthless metals and dirt and rocks. I want to exchange those for the gold of the Holy Spirit. I get that as a gift from God as I confess my sin.

But what about the second part of this principle? How do I repair the damage when I've dishonored my spouse?

Sometimes I injure my relationship with my mate. I damage the honor that I want to give her. I want to give her value, but I do and say things that take value away. Sometimes I'm harsh; I forget a promise; I say degrading words.

Perhaps you know the kinds of words I mean. Here are some examples from the stories in this book:

- "Now, Sweetie, did you really think it was necessary to tell the Vanderbilts your father never went to high school?"
- "You don't take care of your responsibilities around here! And look at the example you're giving your girls! What kind of father are you?"
- "Oh, I get it. Now you're going to start with your 'holier than thou' act."
- "Are you telling me to forget about my friends? You'll never take their place!"
- "You know, this is stupid. All you've gotta do is take a breath."

When I say something devaluing to my wife, I know it by the expression I get back—hurt, frustration, or fear. Those are the main emotions that indicate I've offended her by doing something critical or demeaning or belittling. It means I've pulled value away from her, as if I've grabbed a hunk of gold off and slapped some aluminum or tin in its place. She is less valuable than she was a few seconds ago because of my behavior.

That's why Scripture says in Ephesians 4:26-27, "Do not let the sun go down while you are still angry, and do not give the devil a foothold." Anger darkens our hearts and minds so that we can't walk in the light of

God (1 John 2:9-11). If I provoke my mate to anger, producing fear, frustration, and hurt feelings, I'm opening her heart to temptation.

I don't want that. I want my mate to be as close to 24 karat gold as possible. Anytime I do something that damages who she is, that takes value away from her, I want to repair that immediately. I want to put value back on her and go on with our relationship in harmony and love and joy.

How do I do that?

As soon as I am capable of it—which is not always immediately—I remember how much I value my wife and want to honor her. That eventually gives me the energy to go to her and say I'm sorry for what I did or said, and ask her to forgive me. Asking forgiveness adds the gold I just took off.

There are times when words aren't enough, and you have to do restitution. Let's say I make a date with my wife, but get busy and forget it and get home late. I was involved with some big project and the date slipped my mind; it wasn't something I did on purpose. When I finally get home, she's got her arms crossed and her facial expression tells me I've done something wrong.

I ask, "What in the world is the matter?"

And she says, "Where were you? I couldn't find you. We missed our date!"

I have offended her. My oversight communicated to her that something else was more important to me than she was.

Now if she attacks me, I might be defensive or quiet. I might get angry; I might want to escalate the argument. But honor has a way of convicting me and her. It has a way of saying, "Wait a minute! This conversation is not honoring! This conversation is not gold. This conversation is dirt. It is of low value! This is not our life goal. This is not what we have purposed to do."

It isn't long before we see the truth. Having previously set up boundaries, we don't escalate the hostilities. We don't let ourselves get out of control by saying hurtful things to each other—at least not for more than a few seconds. By now we know how to stop and walk away and take a time-out. We say, "Let's discuss this later when we've calmed down."

When I've calmed down, my heart has softened before the Lord. I think, *What I said was really demeaning to my wife. Lord, I want to clear this up.*

As soon as I get the chance and the strength—which I get from honor and the Lord, who gives me power through His Holy Spirit to do these things—I go to my wife. "Hon," I say, "I was really wrong in what I said. I know that hurt you. I know that offended you. I know that demeaned you.

You know that's not my goal. My goal is to love you and honor you. That is what I'm doing now. I do love and honor you. I'm sorry for what I said. I confess that it was wrong. Will you forgive me?"

If I'm holding her real gently—because gentleness turns anger away, as Proverbs 15:1 says—anger drains out. I'm gentle, not as an act, but because honor is gentle. Honor expresses itself. If I just put on an act, she's going to know it's phony. But honor has a way of revealing your heart.

So I've sought forgiveness. Now comes restitution. If I forgot the date, we might go right then. If she says, "No, I don't want to go now," I have a couple of choices. I may say, "Let's go ahead and go! We're not that late. We could still have a great time. Let's do something different." Or I could make a date for the future—and promise that if I ever forget a date again, I'll work part-time somehow and give her a thousand dollars.

Why? Because she's valuable.

She does the same thing with me—though I tend to be the more offensive one in our family. She doesn't devalue me as often, though sometimes she uses cute, little words that can be demeaning. When I point those out to her, however, she's open to doing something about it. She repairs the damage.

Honor the Lord.

Honor your spouse.

Repair the damage when you've dishonored either.

Following these three principles may not be easy. But as the couples in this book discovered, the effort is worth it—always.

# FOR FURTHER READING

*For Better or for Best* by Gary Smalley and Steve Scott (Harper Prism, 1991)

*Forever My Love* by Neil Clark Warren (Tyndale, 1998)

*Forever Love: 119 Ways to Keep Your Love Alive* by Gary Smalley (Word, 1997)

*Hidden Keys of a Loving, Lasting Marriage* by Gary Smalley (Zondervan, 1993)

*It Takes Two to Tango: More Than 250 Secrets to Communication, Romance, and Intimacy in Marriage* by Gary and Norma Smalley (Tyndale, 1997)

*Joy That Lasts* by Gary Smalley with Al Janssen (Zondervan, 1984)

*The Language of Love* by Gary Smalley and John Trent (Tyndale, 1999)

*Learning to Live with the Love of Your Life* by Neil Clark Warren (Tyndale, 1998)

*Love for a Lifetime* by Dr. James Dobson (Multnomah, 1993)

*Making Love Last Forever* by Gary Smalley (Word, 1996)

# Other Faith and Family Strengtheners
## *From Focus on the Family* ®

### It Takes Two to Tango
Couples *can* stay married happily ever after, and *It Takes Two to Tango* reveals how! For the very first time, Gary and Norma Smalley have teamed together to share their unique perspectives on accepting, pleasing and truly honoring a mate. It's the ideal gift book for the newly engaged, the just married or those celebrating their silver anniversary! Hardcover.

### Learning to Live With the Love of Your Life
Is there a secret to experiencing a meaningful marriage? Actually, there are 10 of them, and Dr. Neil Clark Warren's *Learning to Live With the Love of Your Life* reveals them all! This paperback is filled with the distinct characteristics shared by more than 100 couples with outstanding relationships. It's a valuable resource for newlyweds *and* longtime lovers. Previously titled *The Triumphant Marriage.* Also available on audiocassette.

### Dr. Rosberg's Do-It-Yourself Relationship Mender
*Dr. Rosberg's Do-It-Yourself Relationship Mender* draws from the ultimate health handbook, God's Word, to deliver a proven plan for mending fractured relationships and strengthening healthy ones. This paperback is just what the doctor ordered for increasing intimacy and reducing resentment in your marriage or any relationship. Study guide included.

● ● ●

Look for these special books in your Christian bookstore or request a copy by calling 1-800-A-FAMILY (1-800-232-6459). Friends in Canada may write Focus on the Family, P.O. Box 9800, Stn. Terminal, Vancouver, B.C. V6B 4G3 or call 1-800-661-9800.

Visit our Web site (www.family.org) to learn more about the ministry or find out if there is a Focus on the Family office in your country.

9BPXMP

# FOCUS ON THE FAMILY®

## $\mathcal{W}$elcome to the $\mathcal{F}$amily!

Whether you received this book as a gift, borrowed it from a friend, or purchased it yourself, we're glad you read it! It's just one of the many helpful, insightful and encouraging resources produced by Focus on the Family.

In fact, that's what Focus on the Family is all about—providing inspiration, information and biblically based advice to people in all stages of life.

It began in 1977 with the vision of one man, Dr. James Dobson, a licensed psychologist and author of 16 best-selling books on marriage, parenting, and family. Alarmed by the societal, political, and economic pressures that were threatening the existence of the American family, Dr. Dobson founded Focus on the Family with one employee—an assistant—and a once-a-week radio broadcast, aired on only 36 stations.

Now an international organization, Focus on the Family is dedicated to preserving Judeo-Christian values and strengthening the family through more than 70 different ministries, including eight separate daily radio broadcasts; television public service announcements; 11 publications; and a steady series of books and award-winning films and videos for people of all ages and interests.

Recognizing the needs of, as well as the sacrifices and important contribution made by, such diverse groups as educators, physicians, attorneys, crisis pregnancy center staff and single parents, Focus on the Family offers specific outreaches to uphold and minister to these individuals, too. And it's all done for one purpose, and one purpose only: to encourage and strengthen individuals and families through the life-changing message of Jesus Christ.

• • •

For more information about the ministry, or if we can be of help to your family, simply write to Focus on the Family, Colorado Springs, CO 80995 or call 1-800-A-FAMILY (1-800-232-6459). Friends in Canada may write Focus on the Family, P.O. Box 9800, Stn. Terminal, Vancouver, B.C. V6B 4G3 or call 1-800-661-9800. Visit our Web site—www.family.org—to learn more about the ministry or to find out if there is a Focus on the Family office in your country.

We'd love to hear from you!